TRAVELS OF A CONSULAR OFFICER IN EASTERN TIBET

TRAVELS OF A CONSULAR OFFICER IN EASTERN TIBET

TOGETHER WITH
A HISTORY OF THE RELATIONS BETWEEN CHINA, TIBET AND INDIA

BY

ERIC TEICHMAN, C.I.E., B.A. (CANTAB.)

OF HIS BRITANNIC MAJESTY'S CONSULAR SERVICE IN CHINA
AUTHOR OF TRAVELS OF A CONSULAR OFFICER IN N.W. CHINA

WITH ORIGINAL MAPS OF EASTERN TIBET AND PHOTOGRAPHS TAKEN BY THE AUTHOR

GYAN

Published by

Gyan Publishing House
5, Ansari Road
Daryaganj, New Delhi-110002
Phone: 011-47034999, 9811692060
E-mail: books@gyanbooks.com

Distribution Network
gyanbooks.com
India, USA, Canada, UK, Australia, France

ISBN : 978-81-212-2909-8 (PB)
First Published, 1922

2nd Impression 2021

Printed at: Gyan Press, Delhi.

Travels of a Consular Officer in Eastern Tibet
Author: Eric Teichman

TRAVELS OF A CONSULAR OFFICER IN EASTERN TIBET

TOGETHER WITH
A HISTORY OF THE RELATIONS BETWEEN CHINA, TIBET AND INDIA

BY

ERIC TEICHMAN, C.I.E., B.A. (CANTAB.)
OF HIS BRITANNIC MAJESTY'S CONSULAR SERVICE IN CHINA
AUTHOR OF *TRAVELS OF A CONSULAR OFFICER IN N.W. CHINA*

WITH ORIGINAL MAPS OF EASTERN TIBET AND PHOTOGRAPHS TAKEN BY THE AUTHOR

CAMBRIDGE
AT THE UNIVERSITY PRESS
1922

PREFACE

THE writer has followed the history of Sino-Tibetan relations from the Chinese side with close attention for many years, and also chanced to find himself stationed in Western China when hostilities broke out between Chinese and Tibetans on the border in 1918. The affairs of China being at that time in great disorder, and the authority of the Peking Government not extending as far as the Western frontier province of Szechuan, it devolved upon him, in accordance with Great Britain's policy of promoting peace between China and Tibet, to offer his services as mediator between the local frontier leaders on both sides, with a view to the restoration of peace on the border pending a final settlement of the boundary question by negotiation with the Central Government of China when the latter should once more be in a position to deal with Tibetan frontier affairs.

The long and arduous journeys through remote and largely unknown regions of Eastern Tibet necessitated by these frontier peace negotiations appeared to be of sufficient interest to warrant their being recorded in this book. For some people, including the writer, there are few pleasures, sports, or pastimes to compare with the interest and excitement of travelling through and surveying, however inadequately, remote regions hitherto unmapped and unexplored. Every untrodden trail invites the traveller into the unknown, every mountain range demands to be crossed to see what lies on the other side, and every unmapped river asks to be followed up to its unknown source.

To the account of these journeys is prefixed an historical introduction, recording briefly the history of the Tibetan question, in other words, the story of the relations of Tibet with India and China, her neighbours on the south and north, from early days down to the end of the year 1918[1]. The

[1] In case this historical introduction should appear somewhat patchy and disjointed, it should be explained that its various parts were largely compiled on the spot at the time of the events narrated. Thus Part II, dealing with events of 1906–10, including the Dalai Lama's visit to Peking, was originally compiled while the writer was in Peking during those years. The greater

questions at issue are comparatively simple to state, if they are not easy of solution.

Tibet seeks, if not complete independence, autonomy and freedom from interference in her internal affairs on the part of China, India, or any other Power, and would extend her boundaries to embrace all those parts of High Asia inhabited by peoples of Tibetan race. The Tibetans base their claim to manage their own affairs without Chinese interference on the history of their country as an autonomous State from the earliest days, and further argue that on the disappearance of their nominal overlords, the Manchu Emperors, at the time of the Chinese revolution in 1911, they became, either entirely independent, or equal partners in the new Commonwealth with the Chinese themselves and other constituent elements of the former Manchu Empire.

India, having learned by experience that satisfactory relations and friendly intercourse can only be maintained with her northern neighbour by direct dealings with a responsible Tibetan Government, without the intervention of any Chinese Authority, supports the Tibetan demand for internal autonomy, while fully recognising the status of Tibet as an integral, though self-governing, portion of the Chinese Commonwealth of Nations; and, while indifferent to the exact location of the Sino-Tibetan frontier, she seeks to promote a friendly settlement of the boundary dispute, on terms acceptable to both parties, in the interests of her trans-frontier trade and the peace of her long north-eastern border. For hostilities between China and Tibet must inevitably result in turmoil and unrest on the Indian border and in the Native States of Nepal and Bhutan. India has not, and never has had, any designs against the territorial or administrative integrity of Tibet, and the Tibetans have for many years past shown their appreciation of this fact by their openly expressed desire for closer and more friendly relations with their southern neighbour.

portion of Parts III and IV, including the story of Chao Erh-feng's campaigns in Eastern Tibet and the collapse of Chinese power in Kam at the time of the Chinese revolution of 1911, was written from first hand information when the writer (who was in Chengtu at the time of Chao Erh-feng's murder) was stationed in Western China during the years 1911–12. Part V, including the account of the resumption of hostilities between China and Tibet in 1918, was written on the spot immediately after the events narrated.

China, suspicious of India's motives, and ever mindful of the fate of Korea, while recognising in principle the justice of the Tibetan demand for autonomy, seeks as far as possible to assert herself in Tibet, and to restrict the boundaries of the Dalai Lama's dominions by incorporating in China Proper many frontier districts inhabited by peoples of Tibetan race. As a result China is to-day disliked and mistrusted in Tibet.

The Chinese at times profess to resent the interference of India in Tibetan affairs; but perhaps they overlook the fact that Indian territory marches with Tibet in the south and west as Chinese territory does in the north and east; and that India cannot therefore be entirely indifferent to the fate of Tibet and to disorders in that country, and must concern herself with the maintenance of satisfactory relations with her northern neighbour.

It having been found impossible to reconcile the conflicting boundary claims of China and Tibet at the tripartite conference held in India in 1914, the Tibetan question dragged on unsettled through the years of the Great War, when no one had the leisure to attend to Tibetan affairs. Then, shortly before the termination of the Great War, came the resumption of active hostilities on the Sino-Tibetan frontier, and the restoration of peace on the border at the end of 1918. During these years, however, new obstacles to a definite settlement had arisen, namely, the disunited state of China and the lack of control exercised by the Peking Government over the Western Provinces and the Tibetan frontier.

Since this book and its historical introduction were compiled at the end of the year 1918 down to the time of writing, there have been no material developments in the situation; that is to say, peace has reigned on the border, but, while Tibet has continued to maintain her complete *de facto* independence from all Chinese control, a definite settlement of the Tibetan boundary question and of the status of Tibet as an autonomous portion of the Chinese Commonwealth awaits the cessation of internal strife in China. In the meantime, however, while a definite settlement restoring normal relations between China and Tibet continues to be delayed, Tibet drifts further and further from the orbit of her nominal suzerain.

China having recognised the principle of Tibetan autonomy under Chinese suzerainty, it is mainly the question of the boundary between China and autonomous Tibet which has proved so difficult of solution. In the summer of 1919 the Chinese Government did, indeed, offer to settle the boundary question on apparently equitable terms, which amounted to a reversion to the old historical frontier between China and Tibet as delimited by the Manchu Emperors nearly two centuries ago. Before, however, Great Britain, in her character as middleman, could press the Tibetan Government to accept this settlement, the Chinese withdrew their offer on the ground that, with their country still torn by internal dissensions and civil wars, the time was inopportune for finally determining the Tibetan question, which particularly concerned the western frontier provinces of Szechuan and Yunnan, then, as now, independent of Central Government control.

For some reason or other, whenever the settlement of the Tibetan question comes up for discussion, individuals of a certain class who have presumably their own reasons for desiring to abuse Great Britain, seize the opportunity to accuse her in the most fantastic terms of aggressive designs in Tibet and of so-called "demands" made on the Chinese Government in connection with a settlement of the Tibetan question. It was a press campaign of this nature which was largely responsible for the eleventh hour refusal of the Chinese Government to proceed with their offer of a settlement in 1919. What actually passed in the negotiations of that year is recounted in the following statement issued by Reuter's Agency in the press of China on December 2nd, 1919:

> As the result of the invitation by the British Government to the Chinese Government to settle this long outstanding question, which has remained in a state of suspense during the War, the Chinese Government on May 30 last submitted certain formal proposals for a settlement. These proposals were based on the unsigned draft convention prepared during the tripartite negotiations in India in 1913 and 1914, which arrangement was at the time accepted in principle by the Chinese Government with the exception of the clause laying down the boundary between China and Tibet.
>
> The Chinese offer of May 30 suggested a boundary line which amounted to a reversion to the old historical Sino-Tibetan frontier as laid down by the Manchus in 1727 and which continued for nearly two centuries afterwards.
>
> This Chinese offer was duly submitted to the British Government, who

replied after mature examination that it was acceptable in principle as far as they were concerned. At that moment a settlement of this old question, the only outstanding issue of importance between Great Britain and China, appeared imminent.

A few days later, however, in August last, the Chinese Government suddenly expressed the desire to postpone the conclusion of the negotiations on the ground that, the proposed settlement having met with popular opposition in the country, it was necessary to enlighten public opinion on the subject before proceeding with a settlement. The British Government has since been waiting for the Chinese Government to resume negotiations on the basis of China's own offer.

Since the Chinese left Lhasa as the result of the revolution in China seven or eight years ago Tibet has in fact been independent of her suzerain. The settlement now proposed entails the return of Tibet to the fold of the Five Races of the Republic on the basis of a self-governing Dominion, together with the re-admission of a Chinese Resident and his staff to Lhasa in return for a guarantee of internal autonomy.

The British Minister has made no demands on the subject of Tibet as has so repeatedly been alleged in the press. There has been no secret diplomacy regarding the Tibetan question, nor is there anything in the whole long history of the negotiations which could not be published for the information of China's millions. Great Britain's only interest in the matter is to secure a stable settlement of the question in the interests of the peace of her Indian frontier, and the maintenance of good relations between India, China and Tibet. She never had and has not now any intention of interfering in the internal affairs of Tibet, nor in the relations between Chinese and Tibetans beyond endeavouring to make peace between the two parties on equitable terms acceptable to both. She is willing and anxious to meet China's wishes in every way, provided that the resulting arrangement is one which the Tibetans can be induced to accept.

This book has no official imprimatur of any kind. No secrets are made public, nor, so far as the writer is aware, are there any to divulge. Most of the information contained in the historical introduction has been published at one time or another, in the works of Mr Rockhill, Mr Sandberg, and Sir Francis Younghusband (to whom every acknowledgment is made), in Blue Books, and in the press. All that has been done is to piece the various items of information together to make a consecutive story, which will, it is hoped, do something towards dispelling the fog of suspicion and misunderstanding which is apt to enshroud the Tibetan question.

The writer has lived too long in China not to be imbued with regard for the Chinese and admiration of their many outstanding qualities. At the same time he cannot avoid strong feelings of sympathy with the Tibetans in their gallant struggle for autonomy and regret that the Chinese should in this case have placed themselves so much in the wrong.

In accordance with the traditional Chinese, or perhaps rather Manchu, attitude towards the peoples of the Dependencies of the Manchu Throne, the Chinese are somewhat apt to regard the Tibetans as disobedient children requiring to be chastised into good behaviour. But if the Tibetans were formerly children, it must be realised that they have now grown up, and that, while they desire nothing better than to live on good terms with the Chinese and enjoy the benefits of Chinese trade, they insist on managing their own internal affairs without Chinese interference. The history of the past ten years has shown that they are fully capable of doing so; and it seems indeed paradoxical that the Chinese, who have so signally failed to maintain law and order in their own country, should put forward any claim to have a hand in the administration of peaceful and orderly Tibet. As stated above, however, the Chinese have now recognised the principle of Tibetan autonomy, and it is at present the question of the boundary between China and Tibet which stands in the way of a settlement, the difficulty being the nominal incorporation in China Proper of certain frontier districts which contain a purely Tibetan population, are claimed by the Tibetans as part of Tibet, and are actually being administered by Tibetan officials. It is indeed largely a question of "face," calling for mutual concessions. Once these are made, and the boundary dispute settled within a reasonable space of time, the Tibetans will yet, the writer believes, willingly enter the Chinese Commonwealth of the "Five Races[1]."

Since this book was written three well-known figures in Eastern Tibet have passed from the scene. The Kalon Lama and the ex-Rajah of Chala died in the early summer of the present year, and Dr Shelton was murdered by brigands in February last. The majestic presence of the Kalon Lama, Governor and Commander-in-Chief in Eastern Tibet, overshadowed all other figures in the drama of the Sino-Tibetan borderland, and will not readily be forgotten by the three or

[1] The Chinese Republican Flag is composed of five colours, representing the "Five Races"—Chinese, Manchus, Mongols, Tibetans, and Mahomedans of Turkestan—who are in theory equal partners in the Chinese Commonwealth.

four foreigners who were privileged to make his acquaintance. The Chief of Chala, to whom many European and American visitors to the border town of Tachienlu have been indebted for assistance and small favours, was the first of the semi-independent Rajahs of Kam to be deposed by the Chinese when they began their forward movement on the frontier in 1905, and had since passed a somewhat precarious existence at Tachienlu, hankering vainly after his lost Kingdom, sometimes in and sometimes out of favour with the Chinese Authorities. Dr Shelton, of the American Mission at Batang, was ambushed and shot by brigands in Chinese territory a few miles from Batang when returning to the latter place from a tour (in circumstances very similar to those attending the attack on the author's caravan as related in Chapter IX). He had earned to a remarkable degree the affection and regard of the Chinese and Tibetan communities of Batang and of the native inhabitants of the wild border region in which he worked, and will long be remembered by foreigners who knew him as a broad-minded, courageous and devoted worker in the cause of Christianity and humanity in these remote back-blocks of China's hinterland.

In conclusion the writer desires to express his acknowledgments to his forerunners on the Chinese-Tibetan frontier, Messrs Louis King and Oliver Coales of H.B.M. Consular Service, to whom is due the credit of doing much to open up the way for succeeding travellers in Eastern Tibet.

E. T.

PEKING, *August* 1922.

CONTENTS

HISTORICAL INTRODUCTION

A BRIEF HISTORY OF THE RELATIONS BETWEEN CHINA, TIBET AND INDIA FROM EARLY TIMES UP TO THE END OF THE YEAR 1918

PART I

RELATIONS BETWEEN CHINA AND TIBET UP TO THE TIME OF THE BRITISH EXPEDITION TO LHASA IN 1904

PART II

THE BRITISH EXPEDITION TO LHASA, THE TREATIES OF 1904 AND 1906 AND THEIR RESULTS, AND THE WANDERINGS OF HIS HOLINESS THE THIRTEENTH DALAI LAMA

PART V

THE TRUCE BETWEEN CHINA AND TIBET FROM 1914 TO 1917, THE RESUMPTION OF HOSTILITIES AND THE TIBETAN ADVANCE IN 1918, AND THE SUBSEQUENT RESTORATION OF PEACE THROUGH BRITISH MEDIATION BY LOCAL NEGOTIATIONS ON THE FRONTIER

TRAVELS IN EASTERN TIBET

CHAPTER I

FROM TACHIENLU TO KANZE BY THE MAIN NORTH ROAD

CHAPTER II

FROM KANZE THROUGH THE TZACHUKA GRASS COUNTRY TO JYEKUNDO IN THE KOKONOR

CHAPTER III

FROM JYEKUNDO, ACROSS THE GRASS-LANDS OF THE UPPER MEKONG BASIN, TO NANGCHEN AND CHAMDO

CHAPTER IV

FROM CHAMDO TO BATANG BY THE MAIN ROAD *VIA* DRAYA AND MARKAM GARTOK

CHAPTER V

FROM BATANG TO CHAMDO BY THE SHORT ROAD *VIA* JYASE GOMBA AND THE ONG CHU VALLEY

CHAPTER VI

FROM CHAMDO TO DE-GE GÖNCHEN, AND THENCE THROUGH CENTRAL DE-GE TO RONGBATSA ON THE YALUNG

CHAPTER VII

FROM RONGBATSA ON THE YALUNG THROUGH GONJO TO DRAYA, AND THENCE *VIA* YEMDO TO CHAMDO

CHAPTER VIII

FROM CHAMDO, THROUGH TSAWARONG, TO YENCHING ON THE YUNNAN BORDER, AND THENCE BACK TO BATANG

CHAPTER IX

THE RETURN JOURNEY FROM BATANG TO TACHIENLU

LIST OF ILLUSTRATIONS

LIST OF MAPS

MAP I

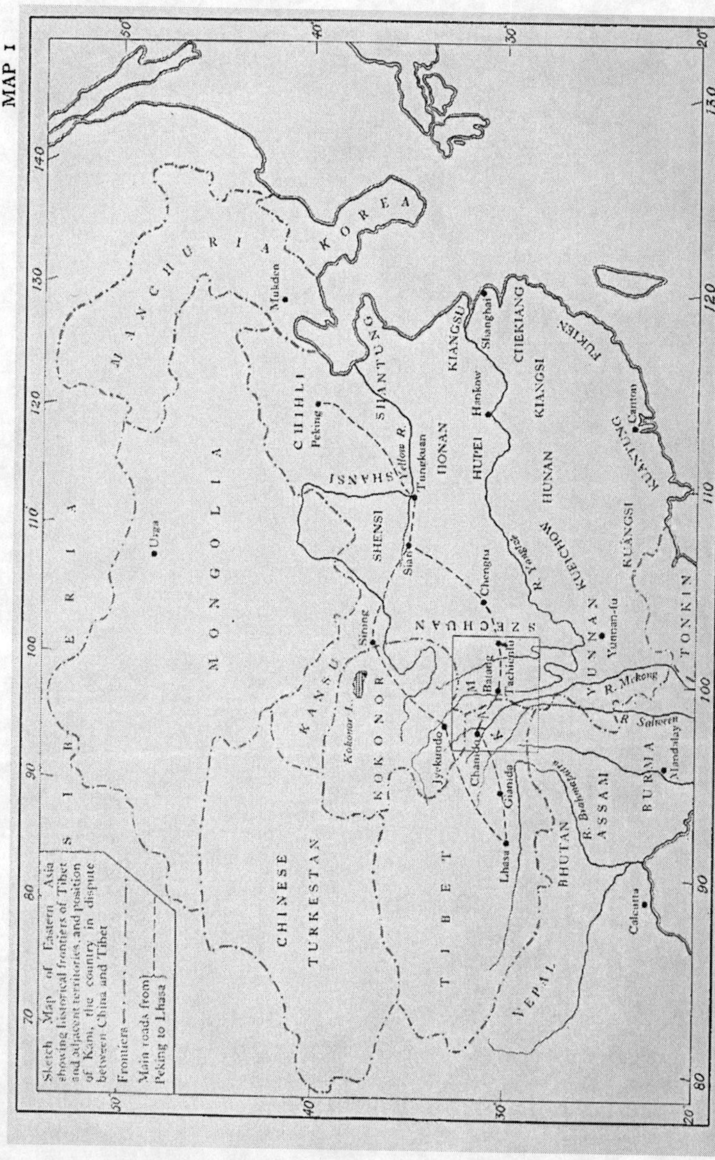
Sketch Map of Eastern Asia showing historical frontiers of Tibet and adjacent territories, and position of Kam, the country in dispute between China and Tibet
Frontiers
Main roads from Peking to Lhasa
SIBERIA
MANCHURIA
KOREA
MONGOLIA
CHINESE TURKESTAN
KANSU
KOKONOR
Kokonor L.
TIBET
CHIHLI
SHANTUNG
SHANSI
SHENSI
HONAN
KIANGSU
HUPEI
SZECHUAN
HUNAN
KIANGSI
CHEKIANG
FUKIEN
KUEICHOW
YUNNAN
KUANGSI
KUANTUNG
TONKIN
BURMA
ASSAM
BHUTAN
NEPAL
Urga
Mukden
Peking
Tungkuan
Yellow R.
Hankow
Shanghai
Canton
Sian
Chengtu
Sining
Jyekundo
Chamdo
Batang
Tachienlu
Giamda
Lhasa
Yunnan-fu
R. Yangtse
R. Mekong
R. Salween
R. Brahmaputra
Mandalay
Calcutta

HISTORICAL INTRODUCTION

A BRIEF HISTORY OF THE RELATIONS BETWEEN CHINA, TIBET AND INDIA FROM EARLY TIMES UP TO THE END OF THE YEAR 1918

PART I

RELATIONS BETWEEN CHINA AND TIBET UP TO THE TIME OF THE BRITISH EXPEDITION TO LHASA IN 1904

Early relations between China and Tibet—Manchu suzerainty over Tibet—Invasion of Tibet by the Dzungarian Mongols, their expulsion by the armies of the Manchu Emperor, and the resulting settlement of Tibetan affairs early in the eighteenth century—List of the Native States of Eastern Tibet—Invasion of Tibet by the Nepalese, their expulsion in turn by the troops of the Manchu Emperor, and further settlement of Tibetan affairs and consolidation of Manchu power in Tibet at the end of the eighteenth century—Decline of Chinese power in Tibet on the death of the Manchu Emperor Ch'ien Lung—Disturbances in Eastern Tibet and pacification and annexation of Nyarong by the Lhasa Government in 1865—Death of the Dalai Lama and accession of the present Pontiff in 1875—Conclusion of the Sikkim Convention in 1890 between China and Great Britain on the subject of Tibet—Further disturbances in Nyarong in 1894, its pacification by Chinese troops, and restoration to Tibetan control in 1898—Chinese intervention in De-ge—The political status of Tibet and adjacent territories at the beginning of the twentieth century.

In very early times the fertile lowlands of Western China were frequently invaded by raiding Tibetans, in the same way that the Marches of North China were harried by the Mongols, the Tibetan invaders penetrating on one occasion as far east as Sianfu in Shensi. In the middle of the ninth century a treaty of peace is said to have been concluded between China and Tibet on a footing of equality.

China's position as Suzerain of Tibet appears to date from the early days of the Manchu Dynasty in the latter half of the seventeenth century. Lamaism (Tibetan Buddhism) had by that time already spread over vast areas of High Asia from Ladak to Manchuria, and the early Manchu Emperors, by adopting Lamaism as their State religion and recognising the Dalai Lama of Tibet as its head, secured a hold over

T.T.T.

Tibet, Mongolia, and the other lamaistic countries of Asia, which lasted until the fall of their Dynasty two and a half centuries later in 1911. It was the Manchu Emperor, rather than the Chinese Government, who was for more than two centuries recognised by the Tibetans as their Suzerain; and up to the last days of the Dynasty the Emperor was represented at Lhasa by a Manchu and not a Chinese.

Early in the eighteenth century Tibet was invaded by the Dzungarian Mongols. The Manchu Emperor thereupon despatched two armies to the assistance of the Tibetans. Advancing by the Tachienlu road from Szechuan and the Sining road from Kansu, the Chinese succeeded in reaching and occupying Lhasa and expelled the Mongols. This was the first of three successful Chinese advances into Tibet, each of which assured the dominion of the Manchu Emperors over the country for a short time afterwards. On this occasion a Manchu Resident and a garrison of Chinese soldiers were left in Lhasa, while communications with China were assured by stationing small detachments of troops along the Lhasa-Chamdo-Batang-Tachienlu road. The boundary between China and Tibet was demarcated by a pillar, said to have been erected in the year 1727 (4th year of the reign of the Emperor Yung Cheng), on the Bum La (in Chinese Ning-ching Shan), a small pass two and a half days south-west of Batang. The country to the west of this point was handed over to the rule of the Dalai Lama under the suzerainty of the Manchu Emperor, while the Tibetan Chiefs of the States and tribes to the east of it were given seals as semi-independent feudatories of China. This arrangement lasted for nearly two centuries, until the Chinese forward movement initiated in 1905 as the result of the British advance on Lhasa in the preceding year. On the following pages is a list of the principal semi-independent Native States and Lama Principalities of Eastern Tibet, under the protection partly of Peking and partly of Lhasa, which were established by the Manchu settlement of 1727, and still existed at the beginning of the present century.

During the latter part of the eighteenth century Chinese power in Tibet was on the wane until, about 1790, the Nepalese invaded the country and sacked Shigatse. Roused to action the Manchu Emperor Ch'ien Lung despatched an

States under Chinese protection

Tibetan Name	Chinese Name	Rank of Chief (in Tibetan)
Chala	Mingcheng	Jyelbo (King)
(The most easterly of the States, with its capital at Tachienlu.)		
De-ge	Teko	Jyelbo
(The largest of the States, in the basin of the Upper Yangtze.)		
Nangchen	Lungch'in	Jyelbo
(Embraces the headwaters of the Upper Mekong in the Kokonor Territory.)		
Hlato	Nat'o	Jyelbo
(A small State between Nangchen and De-ge.)		
Lintsung	Lintsung	Jyelbo
(A small State on the Upper Yalung.)		
Ba	Batang	Deba (Hereditary Official)
Letang	Litang	Deba
Hor Kangsar	Huoerh K'ung-sa	Bonbo (Hereditary Official)
Hor Beri	Huoerh Paili	Bonbo
Hor Drango	Huoerh Changku	Bonbo
Hor Driwo	Huoerh Chuwo	Bonbo
Hor Mazur	Huoerh Mashu	Bonbo
(The above are the Five Hor States, in Tibetan Horsekanga, situated on the Upper Yalung; together with De-ge they were placed under the protection of Lhasa in 1865.)		
Ge-she	Keshih	Bonbo
Tongkor	Tungk'o	Bonbo
Tzako	Tsak'o	Bonbo
Yuko	Yuk'o	Bonbo
Seta	Set'a	Bonbo
(Small nomad States in the basin of the Upper Yalung.)		
Nyarong	Chantui	Bonbo
(Comprises the valley of the Yalung below Kanze; ceded to Lhasa in 1865.)		
Sangen	Sangai	Bonbo
(Comprises the valley of the Yangtze above Batang.)		
Mili or Muli	Mili	Lama
(A lama State on the borders of Yunnan.)		

Also: The Gyarong States, a number of petty principalities lying just west of the Chengtu plain in Szechuan.

STATES UNDER THE PROTECTION OF LHASA

TIBETAN NAME	CHINESE NAME	RANK OF CHIEF (IN TIBETAN)
Chamdo	Chamuto	Lama
Draya	Chaya	Lama
Riwoche	Leiwuch'i	Lama
(Lama Principalities in the Mekong basin.)		
Markam	Mangk'ang	Te-ji (Governor)
(A Lhasa province in the Mekong basin below Draya.)		
Gonjo	Kungchueh	Deba
(A dependency of Markam.)		
Jyade	San-shih-chiu-tsu	Bonbo
(The Country of the Thirty-nine Tribes, lying in the basin of the Upper Salween, south of the Kokonor border.)		

Also: Bashü, Tsawarong, Zayül, Bomed, and Gongbo, all Lhasa provinces, in South-eastern Tibet[1].

army into Tibet, which defeated and expelled the Nepalese and even pursued them into their own country. At this period the power of the Manchus was at its height, and Chinese armies, under Manchu leadership, were able to march thousands of miles from Peking across the plains and mountains of China and the deserts of Tibet to appear on the frontiers of Hindustan.

This was the second of the three Chinese advances into Tibet, and again the Manchus decided to consolidate their position and strengthen their hold over the country. By Imperial Decrees of 1793 two Ambans were appointed, given equal rank with the Dalai and Panshen Lamas, and made responsible for the superintendence of the administration of the country. The Dalai Lama was placed to some extent in the hands of the Ambans by a law providing that he could only communicate with the Throne by means of memorials forwarded through the Ambans.

After the death of the great Ch'ien Lung there followed the weak reigns of the Emperors Chia Ch'ing, Tao Kuang, Hsien Feng, T'ung Chih, and Kuang Hsü, and again Chinese power in Tibet waned to the point of extinction.

[1] The whole of Eastern Tibet covered by these States is known to the Tibetans as *Domed*, or *Kam*, a vague geographical term without definite political significance (cf. *Amdo*, the Tibetan name for the north-eastern portion of the Tibetan plateau on the Kansu border). The word *Menya* is another name vaguely applied by the local Tibetans to the country south-west of Tachienlu; it means "the lower Yalung valley" (cf. *Nyarong*, the valley of the Nya, or Yalung).

MAP 2

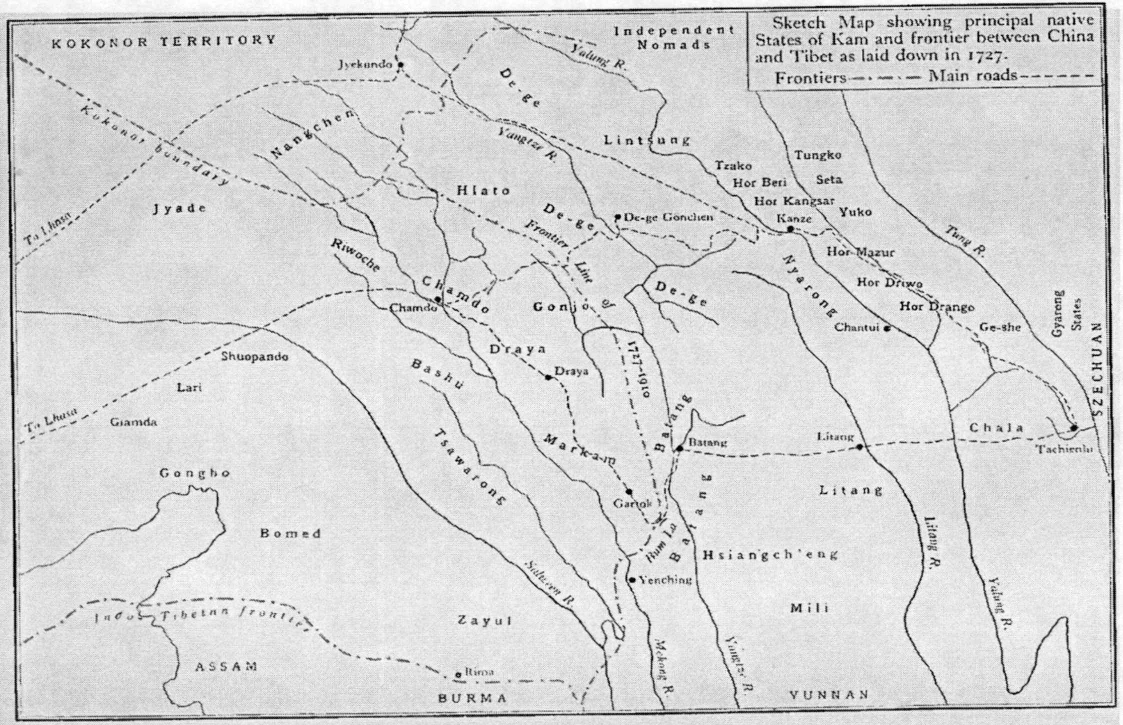

Sketch Map showing principal native States of Kam and frontier between China and Tibet as laid down in 1727.
Frontiers —·—·— Main roads - - - - -

In 1860 the Tibetans of Nyarong[1], under the leadership of an ambitious and warlike Chief named Gombu Nyamjyel, invaded and conquered the neighbouring States, including De-ge, and the Five Principalities of Hor. The whole of Eastern Tibet was upset by these disturbances, and all traffic between China and Tibet along the main South Road ceased for some years.

The Chiefs and peoples of De-ge and of the Hor States appealed to both the Chinese and Tibetan Governments for assistance against the Nyarong invaders. The former, preoccupied with the T'aip'ing rebellion and their troubles with foreign countries, were unable to take any action towards restoring order in the Tibetan States under their nominal protection; but the Dalai Lama responded to the appeals of the Chiefs by sending a Tibetan army into Kam in 1863 under the Kalon Pulung, by whom the disturbances were suppressed, Gombu Nyamjyel and his family being burned alive in their castle in Nyarong resisting to the last. The administration of Nyarong was then formally taken over by the Lhasa Government, by whom a High Commissioner named Punrab (known in Tibetan as the *Nyarong Chichyab*) was appointed to govern the country, and also to superintend the affairs of De-ge and the Five Hor States, which had been freed from the Nyarong invaders and restored to independence under the rule of their own native Rajahs.

The Tibetan claim to Nyarong, and to a lesser extent to De-ge and the Hor States, dated from this time (1865). Nyarong appears to have been annexed by the Dalai Lama with the approval of the Manchu Throne. It is said that the Tibetan Government offered at the time to give up the country to the Chinese in return for a sum of money as indemnity for the cost of their military operations. But the Peking Government were apparently unwilling to accept the responsibility of administering the State and formally handed it over to the rule of the Dalai Lama, in whose hands it remained until forcibly annexed by the Chinese under Chao Erh-feng in 1911.

In 1875 the twelfth Dalai Lama died, and was reincarnated

[1] Nyarong (the valley of the Nya, or Yalung river below Kanze) was originally divided up into five independent clans, which were unified in the middle of the nineteenth century under the chieftainship of Gombu Nyamjyel.

in the present Pontiff, the thirteenth of the long line of Priest Rulers of Tibet.

In 1886, the Tibetans raided the Sikkim frontier, and were expelled a year or two later by a small British expedition. As a result of these events the Sikkim Convention was concluded in 1890 between Great Britain and China, and a set of Trade Regulations for the control of commercial relations between India and Tibet was signed three years later. No Tibetan representative took part in the negotiations for the Sikkim Convention, Great Britain dealing with China as the master of Tibet. These events brought Great Britain for the first time on the scene of Sino-Tibetan relations.

In 1894 the Tibetans of Nyarong rose again and invaded the State of Chala. China being then internally at peace, the Viceroy of Szechuan, Lu Ch'uan-lin, despatched a Chinese force which occupied Nyarong and suppressed the disorders. Viceroy Lu thereupon proposed, in a Memorial to the Throne, to take over the administration of Nyarong with Chinese officials. In this he was, however, opposed by the Manchu Amban at Lhasa and the Manchu Commander-in-Chief at Chengtu, while the Dalai Lama also sent representatives to Peking *via* India and the sea route protesting against any Chinese annexation of Tibetan territory. As a result of these representations Viceroy Lu's Memorial proposing the change was rejected by the Throne, and the Tibetan Governor was reinstated in Nyarong.

From Nyarong Viceroy Lu's Chinese force penetrated into De-ge, where domestic trouble had broken out in connection with the family affairs of the native Rajah, whose second son, popularly supposed to be the offspring of an influential headman and the Chief's wife, had been placed at the head of a faction opposed to the Chief and his elder son. The Chinese commander played a trick on the De-ge Rajah and secured control of the State by a ruse similar to that employed by Chao Erh-feng some fourteen years later. He promised the Chief his assistance in expelling the faction of the younger son, and then, having been permitted to march his troops into the country and occupy De-ge Gönchen, the capital, he seized the Chief and his family and despatched them to Chengtu in Szechuan, where the lowland climate soon proved fatal to the old Tibetan Chief and his wife. Viceroy Lu then

PLATE I

Chinese photo

BATANG, LYING IN AN IRRIGATED PLAIN SURROUNDED BY MOUNTAINS: FOR TWO CENTURIES THE PRINCIPAL CENTRE OF CHINESE TIBET

PLATE II

THE CHINESE BORDER TOWN OF TACHIENLU, LYING AT THE JUNCTION OF THREE STREAMS, HEMMED IN BY PRECIPITOUS MOUNTAINS: THE ADMINISTRATIVE CENTRE OF THE SZECHUAN FRONTIER TERRITORY, AND FORMERLY THE CAPITAL OF THE NATIVE STATE OF CHALA

VIEW IN THE VALLEY OF THE TACHIENLU RIVER, SHOWING MAIN ROAD TO TIBET

memorialised the Throne with a proposal to take over the administration of De-ge as in the case of Nyarong. Owing to the objections of the Amban and the Dalai Lama as above related, the Emperor refused to agree, and the two sons were sent back from Chengtu to De-ge Gönchen, where the elder was installed as Rajah.

In 1900, or thereabouts, the elder brother of De-ge, named Dorje Senge, went to Lhasa and was confirmed in his rank as Rajah, or King, by the Dalai Lama. During his absence, however, the faction of the younger brother, named Ngawang Champe Rincha, which consisted mostly of powerful lamas, made an attempt to install the latter as Chief. The dispute was eventually settled by the intervention of the Tibetan Governor of Nyarong, acting in his capacity of representative of the Dalai Lama and superintendent of De-ge affairs.

In spite of this settlement the younger brother and his lama supporters raised another rebellion a few years later, and the elder was forced to withdraw for a time to Lhasa. In 1906 he returned with troops provided by the Lhasa Government, recovered his throne, and captured and imprisoned the Pretender. The latter, however, escaped, and with the assistance of the northern nomads, who throughout espoused his cause, started yet another rebellion. It was at this juncture (in 1908) that Chao Erh-feng appeared upon the scene, and expelled both the Chief and his brother, as related in a subsequent chapter[1].

At the beginning of the present century, before the British expedition to Lhasa in 1904 and the subsequent Chinese forward movement in Kam, that portion of High Asia inhabited by Tibetan-speaking peoples, and labelled *Tibet* on European maps, consisted of three separate entities, firstly, the Lama Kingdom of Tibet with its provinces and dependencies, secondly, the semi-independent Native States of Kam under Chinese protection, and thirdly, the Kokonor Territory under the control of the Chinese Amban residing at Sining in Kansu.

The Kingdom of Tibet, ruled by the Dalai Lama from Lhasa with the nominal assistance of the Chinese Amban, and commonly known as the *Deba Shung*, extended north to the Dang La range separating it from the Kokonor, and east

[1] See p. 24.

to the Bum La, the frontier pass near Batang. It included the frontier provinces of Markam and Gonjo, and the lama-ruled dependencies of Draya, Chamdo, and Riwoche, and also the outlying province of Nyarong (Chinese Chantui), situated amongst the Native States under Chinese protection. This was the Dalai Lama's realm, in which that Pontiff's temporal power, as apart from his spiritual authority, reigned supreme. The powers of the two Ambans had waned until their positions were little more than nominal.

The Native States on the Szechuan border east of the old Sino-Tibetan frontier on the Bum La (Chinese Ningching Shan) sent periodical tribute missions to, and were under the nominal protection of, Chengtu and Peking. Some, such as the great Kingdom of De-ge and the Five Hor States, had fallen under the influence of Lhasa, as related above; while others, such as the State of Chala (Tachienlu), and the territories of Batang and Litang, remained, owing to their situation on the main road, more under Chinese influence. The powers of the small Chinese military officials and commissariat officers stationed at Tachienlu, Litang, Batang, and other centres on the main South Road, had, however, dwindled to vanishing point, while the soldiers of the frontier garrisons were often unarmed or existed only in the official imagination for pay roll purposes.

The Kokonor Territory (in Chinese Ch'ing Hai) comprised the whole of the upper basins of the Yangtze and Yellow rivers and part of the Mekong headwater country. Where it was not an uninhabitable desert waste it was thinly peopled by Mongolian and Tibetan tribes, the former under the Princes of their Banners, and the latter under their own small Chiefs and Headmen, the whole area being nominally under the control of the Sining Amban on the Kansu border. It does not appear that the Lhasa Government ever exercised temporal authority over this vast region of mountain and desert, the inclusion of which in Tibet on European maps has given rise to some confusion in the past.

[9]

PART II

THE BRITISH EXPEDITION TO LHASA, THE TREATIES OF 1904 AND 1906 AND THEIR RESULTS, AND THE WANDERINGS OF HIS HOLINESS THE THIRTEENTH DALAI LAMA

Failure of the Tibetan Government to carry out the provisions of the Sikkim Convention and apparent inability of the Chinese Government to induce them to do so—British Mission sent to Lhasa in 1904 to open direct relations between India and Tibet—Conclusion of Anglo-Tibetan Convention of 1904 and withdrawal of British Mission from Lhasa—Negotiation of Adhesion Agreement between Great Britain and China in 1906—Conclusion of Anglo-Russian Agreement about Tibet in 1907—China re-establishes her position in Tibet during the years 1907 to 1910, and reasserts her claim to be the sole medium of communication between India and Tibet—Wanderings of the Dalai Lama—Flight from Lhasa to Mongolia on arrival of British Mission in 1904—Visit to, and reception at, Peking in 1908—Grant of Chinese titles and honours by Imperial Decree—Return to Tibet and flight from Lhasa to India on arrival of Chinese troops in 1910—Deposition and deprivation of Chinese titles and honours by Imperial Decree—Return to Lhasa on withdrawal of Chinese troops in 1912—Restoration of Chinese titles and honours by Presidential Mandate.

THE Sikkim Convention concluded between Great Britain and China in 1890 defined the boundary between Sikkim and Tibet, and contained a reciprocal engagement on the part of both contracting parties to prevent acts of aggression across the border. During the years following its conclusion, however, it became more and more apparent that no progress had been made in opening friendly relations between India and Tibet and that little satisfaction was to be expected from this instrument concluded with China over the heads of the Tibetans; for the latter appeared to consider that as they were not directly a party to the Convention there was no need for them to carry out its provisions. All attempts by the Authorities in India to open friendly relations with the Tibetan Government were frustrated, peaceful messengers were maltreated, and letters returned unopened. The Sikkim Convention had been concluded with the Chinese Government on behalf of the Tibetan Government at the request of the former. But when the Tibetans failed to observe its provisions and recourse was had to diplomatic representations at Peking, the Chinese Government were found to be apparently unable to influence the Tibetans in any way. At length in 1903 the British Government, realising the hopelessness of continuing to attempt to deal with the Tibetans through the Chinese Government and the absolute necessity of establishing direct relations with the Lhasa Government if trade was ever to be opened between India and Tibet and the peace of the frontier secured by proper treaty relations with the neighbouring State, despatched a Mission to negotiate a commercial agreement with the Tibetan Authorities direct. Whatever the advice tendered to the Tibetans by the Chinese Amban may have been, they refused to receive any communication from the Mission, which met with repulse after repulse, until, having started as a peaceful embassy, it eventually reached Lhasa in August, 1904, as a military expedition[1].

The Dalai Lama fled for the north shortly before the British force reached Lhasa. A Convention was, however, concluded with the remainder of the Tibetan Government in the summer of 1904. Under this Agreement Tibet undertook to recognise the Sikkim Convention (which she has faithfully observed ever since), while provision was also made for the

[1] It is questionable whether the Tibetans themselves were entirely responsible for the policy of seclusiveness which led to a British Mission proceeding to Lhasa. In his *India and Tibet* (Chapter XXIV) Sir Francis Younghusband wrote in 1910:

"It (the British expedition to Lhasa) has proved in the result that the Tibetans are not really the seclusive people we had believed. By nature they are sociable and hospitable and given to trade. They are jealous about their religion, but as long as that is not touched they are ready enough for political relationship, for social intercourse, and for commercial transactions. The present obstacle to neighbourly intercourse (between India and Tibet) is the suspicion of the Chinese. There is some reason to think that from the first they have instilled into the Tibetans the idea of keeping themselves secluded."

It is perhaps but natural that the Tibetan policy of the Chinese in those days should have aimed at the exclusion of all foreign interests from Tibet (as Chinese policy had formerly aimed at their exclusion from China) in order that the commerce of the country, and more especially the valuable trade in tea, might remain a monopoly in Chinese hands. It was indeed easy for the Chinese to foster Tibetan seclusiveness and retain their monopoly in the country as long as they were able to insist on their right to be the sole medium of communication between Tibet and the rest of the world. As Sir Francis Younghusband points out, they forfeited this right by their inability to induce the Tibetans to observe the Sikkim Convention which they had asked the British Government to make with them on behalf of Tibet; they attempted to reassert it for a short time after the conclusion of the Adhesion Agreement of 1906; but lost it again on the collapse of Chinese power in Tibet in 1912 after the revolution in China; since when the behaviour of the Tibetans, freed from Chinese interference, has fully endorsed Sir Francis Younghusband's estimate of their character quoted above.

opening of commercial relations between India and Tibet and for the establishment of Trade Marts at Gyantse and Gartok as well as at Yatung (the latter already opened under the Sikkim Convention). The British troops withdrew from Lhasa immediately after the conclusion of this Agreement, leaving the territorial integrity of Tibet and the independence of the Tibetan Government unimpaired[1].

Negotiations were soon after opened to secure the adhesion of China, the nominal suzerain of Tibet, to the Anglo-Tibetan Convention of 1904. The Chinese Government at first endeavoured to revive their claim to be the sole medium of communication between the Government of India and the Tibetans and to replace the Anglo-Tibetan Treaty by a new Agreement. Eventually, however, the Lhasa Convention was duly confirmed by an Agreement between Great Britain and China signed at Peking in April, 1906. Under this instrument China adhered to and confirmed the Anglo-Tibetan Convention of 1904, while Great Britain undertook not to annex Tibetan territory or to interfere in any way in the internal Tibetan administration of the country.

In August, 1907, an Agreement was arrived at between Great Britain and Russia under which both parties undertook to respect the territorial integrity of Tibet and to refrain from interfering in the internal affairs of the Tibetan Government.

In 1908 a set of Trade Regulations governing Indo-Tibetan trade was signed at Calcutta between British, Chinese, and Tibetan representatives.

The object of Great Britain in concluding these various agreements was to assure the territorial integrity of Tibet and to safeguard her existence as a peaceful autonomous buffer State between the three great Asiatic Empires, Russia, India and China, as well as to provide for the opening of friendly relations between the British and Tibetan Authorities in the interests of the peace of the Indian border and of trans-frontier trade. The fact, however, had been overlooked

[1] The British expedition to Tibet in 1904 was criticised in England at the time as an act of uncalled for aggression against a peaceful race of hermits who only desired to be left alone. But the result of sending the Mission to Lhasa was to dispel the misunderstandings which had up to that time existed between the Authorities in India and the people and Government of Tibet who have ever since been desirous of increased intercourse and closer relations with their southern neighbours.

that China had through these very agreements obtained a free hand in re-establishing and consolidating her position in Tibet without the possibility of foreign interference, and was thus enabled to keep the Tibetans for a few more years in a state of political and economic vassalage.

The Chinese were not slow to take advantage of the situation, and turned their attention in the first place to annulling the advantages of direct intercourse between the Authorities of India and Tibet obtained under the Anglo-Tibetan Agreement of 1904. Great Britain having intentionally denied herself the right of keeping in close touch with the Tibetan Government by stationing a British representative at Lhasa, the Chinese were able to carry out their plans without any opposition. The Tibetans were gradually led to believe that, though the Peking Government had not had time to send an army to expel the British from Tibet at the time of the 1904 expedition, yet it was fear of Chinese displeasure which had caused the British to withdraw their troops immediately after signing the Treaty; and that China had since compelled Great Britain to sign another Agreement cancelling the Lhasa Convention, acknowledging the right of the Chinese to control Tibet, and prohibiting all intercourse between British and Tibetans except through the medium of the Chinese Authorities. As a result the Chinese were successful in again insinuating themselves between the British and Tibetan officials at the Trade Marts in local affairs and between the British and Tibetan Governments in questions of greater importance. Thus within a few years of the signature of the Lhasa Convention of 1904 most of the advantages of direct intercourse with a responsible Tibetan Government had been lost, and the Authorities in India found themselves once more faced with procrastination and obstruction in all their dealings with Tibet. How all this happened is related in detail in the Tibet Blue Book of 1910, and in Sir Francis Younghusband's account of the British expedition to Lhasa and subsequent events[1].

* * * * *

[1] See *India and Tibet* by Sir Francis Younghusband, 1910; summing up the situation at the time the book was published, Sir Francis wrote (Ch. XXIII):

"And so the story ends much as it began except that, while formerly it was the Tibetans who were supposed to be the most impenetrable and unsociable, it is now the Chinese who are presenting the real obstacle to any reasonable intercourse between India and Tibet."

PLATE III

MOUNTAIN AND FOREST SCENERY IN EASTERN TIBET

MOUNTAIN AND FOREST SCENERY IN EASTERN TIBET. MEKONG-SALWEEN DIVIDE IN THE BACKGROUND

PLATE IV

DEEPLY-ERODED RIVER GORGE IN SOUTHERN KAM
(MEKONG BELOW CHAMDO)

TENTS OF A TIBETAN CHIEF IN KAM

Before recounting the history of the Chinese forward movement in Eastern Tibet, which began in 1905 immediately after the conclusion of the Anglo-Tibetan Agreement, culminated in the raid on Lhasa and the overthrow of the Tibetan Government by Chinese troops in 1910, and collapsed a year or two later after the revolution in China, it will be convenient at this point to record briefly the travels and adventures of the Dalai Lama during this period, namely the years 1904 to 1912.

Having left Lhasa for Mongolia at the time the British expedition was approaching the Tibetan capital in the summer of 1904, the Dalai Lama arrived in due course at Urga, where he resided for a year. His presence there was somewhat embarrassing to the Bogdo Khan, the Lama Pontiff of Mongolia[1], and as Tibetan affairs were by this time beginning to settle down after the withdrawal of the British troops, he started on his journey back towards Tibet in the autumn of 1905. In the early part of 1906 he arrived at the great monastery of Kumbum (in Chinese T'a-erh Ssu), on the Kansu Kokonor border near Sining, where he remained for two years. In the spring of the year 1908 he visited the famous Lama monastery of Wut'ai Shan in Shansi Province, whence he moved on shortly afterwards at the invitation of the Chinese Government to Peking.

The Dalai Lama arrived in Peking by train from Honan on September 28, 1908. Like his predecessor, who visited the Manchu Court in the seventeenth century, he was lodged in the Yellow Temple outside one of the Northern Gates. Elaborate arrangements were made for his audience with the Emperor and Empress Dowager; and, though after some argument he was permitted to kneel instead of prostrating himself in the Imperial Presence, care was taken to stress his position as a vassal of the Manchu Throne[2].

[1] The present Bogdo Khan (a Mongolian title meaning "Holy Prince") is the eighth Pope of Mongolia. During the Manchu Dynasty these Popes were Tibetan Priests, appointed by the Dalai Lama with the approval of Peking. One of the earliest pitched his camp on the banks of the river Tola near the Siberian border. A large monastery and town subsequently sprang up in the neighbourhood, known as Urga to the Russians, Bogdo Kuren to the Mongols, and Ta Kulun to the Chinese, which became second only to Lhasa in importance as the Holy City for all the lamaists of High Asia.

[2] Rule No. 14 of the *Regulations for the Reception of the Dalai Lama* read as follows (translated from the *Government Gazette*):

"The Board of Dependencies will memorialise the Throne asking that a date may

The question of the manner of the reception of the foreign Ministers at Peking and their Legation Staffs by the Dalai Lama gave rise to much discussion and conjecture in foreign diplomatic circles in Peking. The Chinese Authorities, however, who desired to belittle as much as possible the Lama Pontiff's political importance, settled the question by issuing, through the *Wai Wu Pu* (Foreign Office), the following notification in English (worded as though it referred to a public exhibition rather than to the reception of the Representatives of the Great Powers of Europe and America by the Ruler of Tibet and Pope of Lamaism, whose religious authority extended over half Asia):

If any members of the Staffs of the Foreign Legations desire to visit the Dalai Lama, they should proceed to the Yellow Temple on any day of the week except Sunday between the hours of 12 and 3.

The Ministers repaired accordingly with their staffs to the Yellow Temple, where they were granted brief and very formal interviews with the Lama in the presence of Chinese officials.

On November 3, 1908, the following Imperial Decree was issued conferring new honours and titles on the Dalai Lama, appointing him to be the Emperor's loyal and obedient representative, laying down directions for his conduct on his return to Tibet, and bidding him memorialise the Throne on all matters through the Amban, and respectfully await the Imperial Will.

Imperial Decree of November 3, 1908.
(Translated from the *Government Gazette.*)

His Holiness the Dalai Lama, having come to Peking for Audience, has to-day invoked blessings upon Us, and has given expression to his innermost feelings in a manner which merits Our esteem. An additional Title of Honour is hereby conferred upon him as a mark of exceptional distinction.

His Holiness already bears, as a mark of the Imperial favour of former times, the Title of *Great Good Self Existent Buddha*. We now confer upon him the additional Title of Our *Loyal and Submissive Vice-Regent.*

Let the Boards of Ceremonies and Dependencies consult together as to the manner in which the grant of this Title is to be conferred. Let an

be fixed for an Imperial Audience. The Dalai Lama will familiarise himself with the ceremonies beforehand. He will enter the Palace Gate, and the Emperor will receive him standing. The Dalai Lama will respectfully greet the Emperor, and will prostrate himself kowtowing to thank His Majesty for the Imperial gifts. The Emperor will then ask after his health. A low couch will be prepared below the Throne on which the Dalai Lama may sit. After the Emperor has taken his seat, His Majesty will invite the Dalai Lama to be seated, after which refreshments will be taken, and His Majesty and the Dalai Lama will discuss Tibetan affairs."

annual allowance of ten thousand *taels* also be granted to him, the same to be paid quarterly from the Szechuan Treasury. Let His Holiness, having received his new Title, return forthwith to Tibet, and let the officials along his route provide escorts and afford him all the requisite travelling facilities.

When His Holiness has returned to Tibet, he must be careful to obey the laws of the Sovereign State, and must promulgate to all the goodwill of the Court of China. He must exhort the Tibetans to be obedient and follow the path of rectitude. He must follow the established custom of memorialising Us, through the Imperial Amban, and respectfully await Our will.

May peace be thus for ever preserved on the frontier, and the differences between priest and layman completely effaced. May Our desire to support the Lama Church and preserve the peace on the frontiers of the Empire never be disregarded.

Let the Board of Dependencies communicate this Decree to His Holiness.

The subsequent ceremonies attending the Dalai Lama's visit were abruptly cut short by the sudden and unexpected deaths of the Emperor and Empress Dowager. He eventually left Peking on December 21, 1908, and travelled through Honan, Shansi, Shensi, and Kansu to Sining, where he arrived in the spring of 1909. From Sining he crossed the Kokonor, and finally arrived back in Lhasa in November, 1909, after an absence of five years.

The reception accorded to the Dalai Lama by the Manchu Court during his visit to Peking was scarcely calculated to improve the relations between China and Tibet; and from this time it became apparent that it was the intention of the Chinese Government to assume full control over Tibet, hitherto, as far as its internal affairs were concerned, an autonomous State, and to deprive its Lama King of all temporal authority. This object was attained a few months after the Dalai Lama's return to Tibet at the end of 1909. Early in the following year a column of Chinese troops arrived in Lhasa, the Tibetans having been deceived by a ruse into withdrawing their opposition (as related in the following chapter), and the Dalai Lama only just made good his escape before the vanguard of the Chinese force reached the Tibetan capital. As he had fled north into Chinese territory on the approach of the British force five and a half years before, so he now fled south into British territory on the approach of the Chinese troops. He arrived at Darjeeling on February 24, 1910, where he was accorded the usual hospitality granted by the British Government to a political exile, on the understanding that he refrained during his stay in India from all political activities.

The Chinese Government were annoyed at the flight of the Dalai Lama, since they fully realised that the easiest way of subjugating the Tibetans was by controlling the Pontiff and King of Tibet, and special efforts had therefore been made by the advancing Chinese troops to effect His Holiness' arrest. Having failed to secure his person, the Chinese Government now issued an Imperial Decree on February 25, 1910, deposing the Dalai Lama on account of his "pride, extravagance, lewdness, sloth, vice, and perversity," and directing that a new Reincarnation be found to take his place.

Imperial Decree of February 25, 1910.

(Translated from the *Government Gazette*; this Decree was officially communicated to the British Government in a Note of the same date.)

The Dalai Lama of Tibet has received abundant favours from the hands of Our Imperial predecessors. He should have devoutly cultivated the precepts of religion in accordance with established precedent in order to propagate the doctrines of the Yellow Church.

But, ever since he assumed control of the administration, he has shown himself proud, extravagant, lewd, slothful, vicious, and perverse without parallel, violent and disorderly, disobedient to the Imperial Commands, and oppressive towards the Tibetans.

In July, 1904, he fled during the troubles, and was denounced by the Imperial Amban to Us as lacking in reliability. A Decree was then issued depriving him temporarily of his Titles. He proceeded to Urga, whence he returned again to Sining. We, mindful of his distant flight, and hoping that he would repent and reform his evil ways, ordered the local officials to pay him due attention. The year before last he came to Peking, was received in Audience, granted new Titles, and presented with gifts.

On his way back to Tibet he loitered and caused trouble; yet every indulgence was shown to him in order to manifest Our compassion. In Our generosity we forgave the past.

Szechuan troops have now been sent into Tibet for the special purpose of preserving order and protecting the Trade Marts. There was no reason for the Tibetans to be suspicious of their intentions. But the Dalai Lama spread rumours, became rebellious, defamed the Amban, refused supplies, and would not listen to reason.

When the Amban telegraphed that the Dalai Lama had fled during the night of February 12 on the arrival of the Szechuan troops, We commanded that steps be taken to bring him back. At present, however, his whereabouts are unknown. He has been guilty of treachery, and has placed himself beyond the pale of Our Imperial favour. He has shown base ingratitude towards his superiors, and has failed to carry out his duty towards his inferiors. He is not fit to be a Reincarnation of Buddha. Let him therefore be deprived of his Titles and of his position as Dalai Lama as a punishment. Henceforth, no matter where he may go, no matter where he may reside, whether in Tibet or elsewhere, let him be treated as an ordinary individual. Let the Imperial Amban at once cause a search to be made for male children bearing the miraculous signs and let him inscribe their names on tablets and place them in the Golden Urn[1], so that one may be drawn out as the true Reincarnation of previous Dalai Lamas. Let the matter be reported to Us, so that Our Imperial favour may be bestowed upon the selected child, who will thus continue the propagation of the doctrine and the glorification of the Church.

We reward Virtue that Vice may suffer. You, lamas and laymen of Tibet, are Our children. Let all obey the laws and preserve the Peace. Let none disregard Our desire to support the Yellow Church and maintain the tranquillity of Our frontier territories.

The Dalai Lama remained in India for more than two years, during which period the rule of the Chinese military officials in Tibet succeeded in uniting all the Tibetan factions in common detestation of everything Chinese. In 1912, after the collapse of the Chinese power in Tibet as a result of the revolution in China, he was unanimously requested to return. In July, 1912, he crossed the frontier into Tibet, where he received a triumphant welcome, and, after waiting in the neighbourhood of Lhasa until the last of the Chinese troops had been withdrawn, finally entered the capital towards the end of the year, thus peacefully resuming his place at the head of the government of autonomous Tibet after an absence of nearly two years.

It is doubtful whether the Imperial Decree of February, 1910, in any way impaired the Dalai Lama's position in Tibet and Mongolia, while it can hardly have failed to give great offence to, and thus prejudice the reputation of the Manchu Emperor amongst, all the lamaist peoples of Asia. In 1912, after the Dalai Lama's return to Tibet, the Government of China, now nominally a Republic, receded from their previous attitude, and issued the following Presidential Mandate recognising him once more as Pontiff of the Lama Church.

Presidential Mandate of October 28, 1912.
(Translated from the *Government Gazette*.)

The Dalai Lama has addressed a communication to the Head of the Department of Mongolian and Tibetan affairs in which he states that after his return from Peking to Tibet he did his utmost to arrange the affairs of the country satisfactorily. Later on, having been deprived of his rank,

[1] New Dalai Lamas were always chosen by lot in this way; see the Abbé Huc's description of the ceremony.

he resided for a time at Darjeeling. But, Tibet having remained in a state of unrest ever since the disturbances in Szechuan last winter, he now desires to protect the Buddhist Church and prays that the President of the Republic may take measures to this end.

Now that the Republic has been firmly established and the Five Races[1] united into one family, the Dalai Lama is naturally moved with a feeling of deep attachment to the mother country. Under the circumstances his former errors should be overlooked, and his Title of *Loyal and Submissive Vice-Regent, Great, Good, and Self Existent Buddha* is hereby restored to him, in the hope that he may prove a support to the Yellow Church and a help to the Republic.

[1] Chinese, Manchus, Mongols, Mahomedans, and Tibetans.

PART III

THE CHINESE CAMPAIGNS IN EASTERN TIBET DURING THE YEARS 1905 TO 1911, AND THE CHINESE ADVANCE TO LHASA IN 1910

Inauguration of China's forward policy in 1904 by the appointment of Feng Ch'uan to be Amban in E. Tibet—Revolt of Batang Tibetans and murder of Amban Feng in 1905—General rising of Tibetans on the Szechuan frontier—Despatch of Chinese punitive expedition under Chao Erh-feng and subjugation of the border country—Renewed revolt in Hsiangch'eng subdued by Chao Erh-feng—The Amban Lien Yü proceeds to Lhasa—Chao Erh-feng's reforms at Batang—Chao Erh-feng returns to Szechuan and is appointed Tibetan Frontier Commissioner—Introduction of Chinese administration on the Southern circuit of the frontier—Chao Erh-feng returns to the frontier in 1908—Introduction of Chinese administration in the Kingdom of De-ge—Tibetan Government memorialise the Manchu Throne against the Chinese advance in E. Tibet—Chinese occupation of Chamdo, Draya, and Markam—Tibetan Government appeal to the Manchu Emperor and to the foreign Powers to stop the Chinese advance—Chinese troops reach and occupy Lhasa—Protest by the British Government against overthrow of Tibetan Government—Chinese activities in S.E. Tibet on the borders of Assam—Subjugation of Kanze and the Hor States—Chao Erh-feng's proposals for the frontier between China and Tibet—Subjugation of Gonjo and Sangen—Chinese military operations in Bomed and Zayül—Expulsion of Tibetan officials from Nyarong—Chao Erh-feng appointed Viceroy of Szechuan—Memorial to the Throne proposing the conversion of E. Tibet into a Chinese Province.

THE immediate results of the British expedition to Lhasa and the opening up of direct relations between India and Tibet by the Anglo-Tibetan Convention of 1904 were to rouse the Chinese to make another attempt to impose their dominion on Tibet, and incidentally to extend the boundaries of China as far west as possible into Eastern Tibet in the event of their being unable to carry out the subjugation of the whole country[1].

China's new policy in Eastern Tibet was inaugurated in 1904 by the creation of a new post of Imperial Resident at

[1] Each of the three occasions on which China sent armies into Tibet followed on the invasion of that country by a third party (the Dzungarian Mongols in 1720, the Nepalese in 1790, and the British in 1904). As long as Tibet remained isolated and unvisited the Chinese were satisfied with a nominal control; but the opening up of relations between the Tibetans and their neighbours to the south immediately provoked the Chinese to action.

Chamdo, to which a *Taotai* named Feng Ch'uan was appointed, with instructions to curtail gradually the powers of the native rulers and lamas and bring the country under the more direct control of the Chinese Government. At the same time a start in the introduction of the new order of things was made by converting Tachienlu, hitherto the capital of the semi-independent Tibetan State of Chala, into the seat of a Chinese magistrate controlling a Chinese district.

Feng Ch'uan proceeded to the frontier towards the end of 1904, and travelling *via* Tachienlu and the main South Road, took up his residence temporarily at Batang. Here his activities in trying to interfere with the authority of the lamas soon caused disaffection and unrest, which were increased by the events occurring at the same time in Central Tibet and the loss of prestige by the Chinese resulting from the presence of the British Mission in Lhasa.

In April, 1905, the Tibetans of the neighbourhood and the lamas of the great Batang monastery rose in open revolt and attacked the Chinese. Feng Ch'uan himself, whose troops were quite insufficient to quell the outbreak, escaped through the back door of his yamen by the ingenious expedient of scattering rupees amongst his assailants. He then endeavoured to withdraw down the Litang road, but was killed with nearly all his followers in a narrow gorge just outside Batang, where the spot is still marked by a memorial stone. At the same time a French Catholic priest was killed while attempting to escape across the Yangtze below Batang, while another was murdered at the mission station of Yarragong (Chinese Yahaikung), three days' march to the south. The killing of these Catholic priests did not signify that the rising had any particular anti-foreign character. But, owing to their position as teachers of a strange religion amongst a population so deeply attached to their own religious beliefs, the Catholics had roused the bitter enmity of the lamas; while the fact that they took advantage of their Treaty right to claim the protection of the Chinese officials in their work resulted in their being to some extent identified with the Chinese in the eyes of the local Tibetans.

These events at Batang were the signal for a general rising of all the big monasteries on the borders of South-western Szechuan and North-western Yunnan, isolated Chinese garrisons were everywhere overwhelmed and put to the sword, and two more French Catholic priests were killed near Tsekou on the Mekong.

At the beginning of the outbreak the lamas and tribesmen had met with little resistance, but the Szechuanese Authorities now began to prepare a punitive expedition. General Ma Wei-ch'i, Commander-in-Chief of the Szechuan army, left Chengtu with troops in the early summer of 1905, and had little difficulty in reaching Batang and quelling the rebellion in that neighbourhood. The great Batang monastery, one of the largest in Eastern Tibet, was razed to the ground, such of its lamas as failed to escape were killed, the two native Chiefs were beheaded, and the surrounding Tibetans chastised with executions and burnings. In the meantime a *Taotai*, by name Chao Erh-feng, a Chinese Bannerman, was appointed by Hsi Liang, the Viceroy of Szechuan, to undertake the management of the punitive measures and the pacification of the border country. From this time on, up to his execution by the Szechuan revolutionaries at Chengtu in 1911, Chao Erh-feng remained the central figure in Eastern Tibet.

While the Szechuanese under Ma Wei-ch'i and Chao Erh-feng were engaged in chastising the Batang Tibetans, the Yunnanese forces were occupied with the same work in the Atuntze neighbourhood; and it was not long before the trouble appeared to have died down as suddenly as it had started. But the unrelenting severity with which Chao Erh-feng and his subordinates had been proceeding against the rebels, and the harshness of the measures by which he attempted to bring the country under the direct rule of Chinese officials, led to a renewed and fiercer revolt towards the end of 1905. Those of the Batang lamas who had managed to escape from the butchery which followed on General Ma's successes fled south to a turbulent district known to the Chinese as Hsiang-ch'eng (in Tibetan Chantreng), where they were joined by the monks who had survived the fighting in North-western Yunnan. Here, behind the massive walls and fortifications of a large monastery, they bid defiance to the Chinese. Chao Erh-feng took up the challenge and laid siege to the monastery with three thousand Chinese troops.

The siege of Hsiangch'eng monastery lasted for some

months, and only came to an end in the summer of 1906, when the Chinese, who were as exhausted as the besieged, and only kept to their work by Chao's indefatigable spirit, gained entrance by a ruse. The garrison of lamas, fighting to the last, were all put to the sword, the monastery looted and destroyed, and the resistance of the Tibetans of the neighbourhood overcome for the time being. But the feud between the Chinese and the people of Hsiangch'eng, which had begun long before, was not at an end, and the district was destined for many years to come to be the principal thorn in the side of the Chinese Authorities in Eastern Tibet and their chief obstacle in the subjugation of the border States.

With the fall of Hsiangch'eng the main South Road from Tachienlu up to Batang and the adjoining districts were in Chinese hands. Lien Yü, a Manchu, who had been appointed Amban at Lhasa to carry out China's new forward policy in Central Tibet, had been waiting on the frontier for more than a year for Chao Erh-feng to crush the revolt and open the road; he was now able to proceed to his post, and reached Lhasa in the autumn of 1906. He remained in Tibet for six years, eventually escaping with the Chinese troops *via* India after the revolution in China in 1912. Unlike his junior colleague, the Assistant Amban, Wen Tsung-yao, who was a gentleman of liberal ideas and popular with the Tibetans, Lien Yü made himself intensely disliked, and through his unwise and arrogant behaviour appears to have been largely responsible for the Chinese *débâcle* in Tibet which followed the revolution in China.

Chao Erh-feng now resumed his work at Batang. The large province of which this place was the capital had formerly been ruled by two native Chiefs and by the head lama of the monastery, the Chinese officials stationed there being merely charged with the forwarding of mails and supplies between China and Tibet and exercising no authority over the local Tibetan population. Chao Erh-feng abolished the office of native Chief, the last incumbents having been decapitated, appointed a Chinese magistrate in their place, introduced new laws limiting the number of lamas and depriving the monasteries of their temporal authority, and started various schemes for colonising the country with Chinese immigrants.

In November, 1906, Chao Erh-feng returned to Chengtu,

PLATE V

TWO VIEWS OF CHAMDO, THE PRINCIPAL CENTRE OF EASTERN TIBET, LOOKING NORTH AND SHOWING THE JUNCTION OF THE TWO BRANCHES OF THE MEKONG BELOW THE TOWN (LOW WATER SEASON)

PLATE VI

SUNRISE ON THE PEAKS OF THE MEKONG-SALWEEN DIVIDE IN SOUTHERN KAM

TRIBESMEN OF KAM IN ARMS

the capital of Szechuan, where he was received in state as a victorious general, and was subsequently granted the *Bataru* decoration, the Manchu Order of Merit, by the Emperor. He had shortly before been appointed to the newly created post of Frontier Commissioner (*Pien-wu Ta-ch'en*), with the rank of Vice-President of a Peking Board, the appointment being announced to be similar in scope to that of the Ambans at Lhasa and Sining. He was thus placed in independent control of a vast tract of country extending from the borders of Kansu and the Kokonor in the north to those of Yunnan, Burma and Assam in the south, and from Tachienlu in the east to the confines of Central Tibet in the west, with the duty of bringing under closer Chinese control the congeries of semi-independent Tibetan States, nomadic tribes, and lama principalities which occupied this region. It would appear, however, that while Chao Erh-feng had definitely determined to introduce the ordinary Chinese provincial administration in the whole of Kam, thus directly challenging the Priest Rulers of Tibet, the Throne had by no means committed itself to such far-reaching action. The history of the next few years, read in the light of the Imperial Edicts, Memorials to the Throne, and other State papers, shows the Manchu Court somewhat reluctantly acquiescing in the forward policy of its powerful Viceroy on the frontier.

Chao Erh-feng had intended to proceed to Batang, where a large yamen—still a landmark in the place—had been erected for his use, in the spring of 1907 to resume his work on the frontier. But in March of that year an Imperial Edict appeared transferring Hsi Liang, who had been Viceroy of Szechuan since 1903, to Yunnan, and appointing Chao Erh-feng to act pending the arrival of his successor. Chao Erh-feng remained in charge of the provincial government of Szechuan as Acting Viceroy for rather more than a year. By this time what was known as the Southern Circuit (*Nan Lu*) of the frontier, namely all the districts along the main South Road from China to Tibet as far as the old historical frontier line on the Bum La (Ningching Shan) just west of Batang, had been brought under direct Chinese administration, the native Chiefs of Tachienlu, Litang, and Batang had been deposed, and Chinese magistrates had been appointed to the newly created districts of Tachienlu (Dartsendo), Hok'ou

(Nyachuka), Litang, Batang, Sanpa (Taso), Taoch'eng, Hsiangch'eng, Tejung and Yenching (Tsakalo)[1]. All these districts, however, lay in territory which had always been under the influence of Peking rather than of Lhasa, and the more formidable task of subjugating the Lhasa-controlled parts of Eastern Tibet remained still to be accomplished.

In March, 1908, two Imperial Edicts appeared, one appointing Chao Erh-feng to be Imperial Commissioner for Tibet, with the rank of President of a Peking Board, and the second appointing his brother, Chao Erh-hsün, to be Viceroy of Szechuan. A further Edict appeared a few days later, explaining that the object of these appointments was that the two distinguished brothers should co-operate in their work, the one in Tibet, and the other in Szechuan. The appointments were most successful from the Chinese point of view, and resulted in the complete subjugation of Tibet, for a brief period, to Chinese rule.

In the autumn of 1908, Chao Erh-feng left Chengtu with several battalions of new troops, and advanced by the North Road towards De-ge, which for various reasons he had chosen as his first victim amongst the powerful semi-independent Principalities of Kam. The frontiers of De-ge, the largest, wealthiest, and most important of the native States of Eastern Tibet, extended from the neighbourhood of Jyekundo in the north to within a few marches of Batang in the south, and from Chamdo and Draya in the west to Kanze and Nyarong in the east. It had existed as an autonomous State for a thousand years or more, and the family of the Chief were supposed to be able to trace their ancestry back for forty-seven generations. The administration of the country was carried on, under the superintendence of the Chief, by twenty-five hereditary district officials and the head lamas of the big monasteries.

As related in a previous chapter[2], Chao Erh-feng appeared upon the scene with his army at a time when the State was torn by internal dissensions, the younger of the two brother claimants to the chieftainship being in armed rebellion against the elder. Following the precedent set by the Chinese General who had deposed the old Chief fourteen years before,

[1] See map facing p. 35.
[2] See p. 7.

Chao Erh-feng offered the elder brother the assistance of his troops against the younger. The offer was accepted with the same results as before. The pretender and his followers having been expelled from the State, and Chao Erh-feng's troops having entered and occupied De-ge Gönchen, the capital, the Chief was deposed, Chinese administration introduced, and the State subsequently cut up into the five Chinese districts of Shihch'ü (Seshü) and Dengk'o in the north, Teko, or Tehua, in the centre, Paiyü in the south, and T'ungp'u in the west.

The following is a *précis* translation (from the Peking *Government Gazette*) of the Chinese text of the Memorial submitted to the Throne by the Reform Council advocating the incorporation of De-ge State in China Proper. It is dated January, 1910, a year after Chao Erh-feng had already deposed the Chief.

His Excellency the Frontier Commissioner Chao Erh-feng reports that the Chief of De-ge, by name Dorje Senge, is a man of no ability, and that he has repeatedly petitioned to be allowed to surrender his territory to Chinese rule; also that the feud which has existed for the past ten years between him and his brother over the question of the chieftainship has caused great suffering to the people of the State. The Frontier Commissioner further points out that the territory of De-ge occupies a position of great strategic importance, and that only by controlling the same can the situation in Tibet be rendered secure and the frontiers of Szechuan be protected.

When in the past the wild tribes of the border lands submitted to China, native States were created in various provinces and titles and ranks were given to the Chiefs. It is, however, laid down in the Institutes of the Dynasty that when these native rulers misbehave themselves they must be replaced by other Chiefs or their lands must be taken over by Chinese officials.

The State of De-ge having been the scene of internal disturbances, troops have had to be sent to pacify the country. Moreover the territory in question is of great strategic importance to Szechuan and Tibet.

In view of the above, and of the fact that the Chief and the headmen are all anxious to come under Chinese rule, the Frontier Commissioner's proposal to incorporate De-ge in China Proper might advantageously be adopted.

As the said Chief of De-ge is willing to surrender his lands to Chinese rule, he should receive, as a mark of Imperial favour, a pension of two or three thousand *taels* a year, and the right to wear the Button of the Second Rank.

The question of whether De-ge ought or ought not to come under direct Chinese rule is hereby submitted for the Imperial decision.

The following Imperial Edict on the subject has now been received:—
The matter has been noted.

The elder brother was duly granted a Button of the Second Rank and an annual pension of 3000 *taels* (which, however, ceased when China became a Republic), and lived for some years as a state prisoner at Batang. In 1917, all being quiet on the frontier, he was permitted to return to De-ge Gönchen (the capital) as a private individual, and was found there when the Lhasa troops expelled the Chinese from De-ge a year later. The younger brother, fleeing from Chao Erh-feng, took refuge amongst the nomads of Seshü in the north of the State. On being pursued by the Chinese he fled still further north to the country of the wild Golok nomads, where even Chao Erh-feng did not dare to follow him. Thence he found his way to Lhasa, was attached to the Dalai Lama's suite during His Holiness' exile at Darjeeling in India, and eventually received an official appointment in Central Tibet on the Dalai's return to Lhasa.

In the autumn of 1908, the Tibetan Government, who were by this time much alarmed at the rapid advance of the Chinese in Kam, memorialised the Throne through the Amban Lien Yü claiming that the realm of the *Deba Shung*[1] extended to the borders of the district of Ch'iungchou (near Chengtu in Szechuan), and requesting that the Chinese should revert to the old *status quo* in Eastern Tibet. Though the Tibetans appeared to be justified, from their point of view, in protesting against the uncalled for Chinese aggression which was taking place, their territorial claims were somewhat extravagant; and the only result of the Memorial seems to have been to hasten the Chinese forward movement in Kam.

Having secured De-ge, Chao Erh-feng was now in a position to carry out the next step in his plans and advance on Chamdo, the most important centre in Kam and a strategical point at the junction of the main roads from Yunnan, Szechuan and Kansu to Central Tibet. Towards the end of the year 1909 some thousands of Chinese troops were concentrated at Batang and De-ge Gönchen, and soon after first Chamdo, and then Draya and Markam, were occupied without difficulty, the local Tibetan levies, who did not know whether to fight or not, dispersing before the superior forces of the Chinese.

Chao Erh-feng's evident intention to advance on Chamdo, an autonomous lama-ruled State in close relations with Tibet

[1] The Lhasa Government.

Proper, and the news that a fresh army of Chinese Imperial troops had left Chengtu in the late autumn of 1909 with the avowed intention of marching on Lhasa, created consternation in the minds of the Dalai Lama and his government, who were uncertain whether or not they should resist the invasion of the Chinese with whom they had so far no quarrel. The local people of the Tibetan frontier States, including Chamdo, Draya and Markam, petitioned the Lhasa Government for permission to oppose the Chinese advance by force of arms. The latter, reluctant to take up arms against their powerful Suzerain, refused, and attempted to stop the advance by negotiation with the Amban. Lien Yü temporised, assured the Tibetans that Chao Erh-feng himself would not advance further, and that if any Chinese troops entered Tibet it would be merely for the purpose of doing police work on the main roads. In desperation the Tibetan Government in December, 1909, sent out the following telegraphic appeals through India to the foreign Powers of Europe and America and to the Chinese Government at Peking.

Message from the Dalai Lama and the Tibetan Government to Great Britain and the foreign Powers.

Though the Chinese and Tibetans are of one family, yet the Chinese officer Chao and the Amban Lien are plotting together against us, and have not sent true copies of our protests to the Chinese Emperor, but have altered them to suit their own evil purposes. They are sending troops into Tibet and wish to abolish our religion. Please telegraph to the Chinese Emperor and request him to stop the troops now on their way. We are very anxious and beg the Powers to intervene and cause the withdrawal of the Chinese troops.

Message from the Dalai Lama and the Tibetan Government to the Chinese Government.

We, the oppressed Tibetans, send you this message. Though in outward appearance all is well, yet within big worms are eating little worms. We have acted frankly, but yet they steal our hearts. Troops have been sent into Tibet, thus causing great alarm. We have already sent a messenger to Calcutta to telegraph everything in detail. Please recall the Chinese officer and troops who recently arrived in Kam. If you do not do so, there will be trouble[1].

After the occupation of Chamdo and the expulsion of Tibetan officials and chief lamas, who fled into Central Tibet, the way was clear for the column of Imperial Chinese

[1] From the *Tibet Blue Book of* 1910.

troops to continue their march on Lhasa. This force, consisting of a mixed column of infantry, cavalry and light artillery, and totalling only some 2000 men, was equipped in the most up-to-date way and commanded by a young General with modern training named Chung Ying. It is said that when the latter reached Chamdo he refused to proceed any further with his young and untried men; so that in the end Chao Erh-feng had to provide an escort of his own ragged veterans, which accompanied the column to within a few marches of Lhasa. Although the Tibetans were massed in considerable numbers west of Chamdo, they offered little or no resistance to the Chinese advance in consequence of the indecision of the Lhasa Government and the diplomatic persuasiveness of the Amban. The column finally marched into Lhasa on February 12th, 1910, the Dalai Lama effecting his escape across the river down the road to India within sight of the Chinese advance guard, who had special orders to effect his capture. The whole affair took the Tibetans completely by surprise, and eyewitnesses report the amazement, consternation, and confusion in Lhasa when the first Chinese modern drilled troops rode into the capital.

Thus, for the third time in the history of the two countries, a Chinese army marched into the sacred city of Tibet. Chung Ying's column had accomplished a remarkable performance in crossing Tibet from east to west in the middle of the winter along one of the highest and most arduous roads in the world, including the passage of a large number of passes from 14,000 to 16,000 feet and more in height. The advance was, however, practically unopposed, and the success of the expedition was due not so much to the military arrangements as to the astute diplomacy of the Amban at Lhasa, who assured the Tibetan Government that less than 1000 Chinese troops were entering Tibet, and that the sole object of their coming was the policing of the main roads and Trade Marts. In the result more than 2000 troops appeared and proceeded to subvert completely the government of the country. It is said that the Assistant Amban, Wen Tsung-yao, resigned on realising the breach of faith towards the Tibetans to which he had been a party.

The Chinese Government in Peking had similarly given formal assurances to the British Government that troops were being despatched to Tibet solely for the purpose of preserving order and that under no circumstances would the political situation and status of Tibet created by the Treaties of 1904 and 1906 be altered in any way. It is possible that the Peking Government were not able to exercise proper control over their representatives in Tibet; in any case, after the arrival of the Chinese troops at Lhasa the Dalai Lama was formally deposed, and the administration of the country to all intents and purposes taken over by the Chinese. These events evoked the following Note, addressed by the British Government to the Chinese Government on February 26th, 1910, protesting against China's action in forcibly overthrowing the Tibetan Government and thus upsetting the *status quo* established under the Treaties concluded between Great Britain, China and Tibet.

> Great Britain, while disclaiming any desire to interfere in the internal administration of Tibet, cannot be indifferent to disturbances of the peace in a country which is her neighbour and on intimate terms with neighbouring States on her frontier, and especially with Nepal, whom His Majesty's Government could not prevent from taking such steps to protect her interests as she may think necessary in the circumstances. In view of their Treaty relations with both Tibet and China, His Majesty's Government had the right to expect that the Chinese Government would at least have tendered friendly explanations before embarking on a policy which, in the absence of such explanations, cannot but appear intended to subvert the political conditions set up by the Anglo-Tibetan Convention of 1904 and confirmed by the Anglo-Chinese Convention of 1906.
>
> The Treaty of 1904 was negotiated with the Tibetan Government and confirmed by the Chinese Government, and His Majesty's Government consequently feel that they have a right to expect that an effective Tibetan Government shall be maintained with whom they can, when necessary, treat in the manner provided by the two above-mentioned Conventions[1].

The Chinese having by their sudden stroke secured practical control over the Government of Tibet, Chao Erh-feng was left free to carry on his work of bringing Eastern Tibet under direct Chinese rule without any possibility of interference from the side of Lhasa. Some of his troops, who had been waiting on the old Sino-Tibetan frontier at Yenching on the Mekong, south of Batang, now advanced into South-eastern Tibet, occupied and expelled the Tibetan officials from Sangachu Dzong, an important administrative centre in the country west of the Salween, pushed forward still further

[1] From the *Tibet Blue Book of* 1910.

into Zayül in the basin of the Brahmaputra, and appeared at Rima on the borders of Assam. The Chinese were even found to be penetrating into the country of the Mishmis in British territory, with a view to claiming their allegiance for China.

Chao Erh-feng passed the summer of 1910 arranging for the substitution of the rule of Chinese magistrates for that of the former Tibetan officials in Chamdo, Draya and Markam, which were turned into the Chinese districts of Ch'angtu (formerly Chamuto), Chaya, and Ningching (formerly Chiangka) respectively. At the same time a small military expedition was sent against Kanze, where the Tibetan rulers had defied him when he passed through on his way to De-ge two years before. Now, with practically the whole of Tibet under his thumb, he had no difficulty in dethroning the reigning family and establishing a Chinese district magistrate in his place. The submission of all the five Hor States, of which Kanze was the heart and centre, followed as a matter of course[1].

During the year 1910 Chao Erh-feng memorialised the Throne, proposing that Giamda (in Chinese Chiangta), beyond the Salween-Brahmaputra divide and within a few marches of Lhasa, should be the boundary between China and Tibet[2]. The Tibetans protested through Lien Yü, the Amban, who had perhaps his own reasons for objecting to such a limitation of his sphere of authority[3]. The Throne at first refused its consent, but appears to have agreed to the proposal a year later.

Towards the end of 1910, the Chinese garrison at Hsiang-ch'eng mutinied, and the local Tibetans rose again in revolt against Chinese rule. Chao Erh-feng suppressed the rising

[1] The five Hor States (in Tibetan Horsekanga, in Chinese Huoerh Wu-chia), consisting of Hor Beri, Hor Kangsar, Hor Mazur, Hor Drango and Hor Driwo, all in the basin of the upper Yalung and its tributaries, bore the same relation to the Lhasa Government as De-ge, that is to say, they had been placed under the protection of the Dalai Lama after the Nyarong rising of 1863 had been suppressed by Tibetan troops.

[2] See sketch-map facing p. 45.

[3] The jurisdiction of the Lhasa Amban appears to have extended originally to Tachienlu. When the Frontier Commissionership was created in 1906 the Amban's sphere of authority was cut down to correspond with the old limits of Tibet Proper as laid down in the reign of the Emperor Yung Cheng (1723–1736), including, but being limited in the east by, the States of Chamdo, Draya and Markam. Chao Erh-feng's Giamda boundary appears to have been an arbitrary line, probably drawn for strategic purposes, and unsupported by historical claims of any kind.

PLATE VII

CARAVAN ARRIVING AT A CHINESE REST-HOUSE IN EASTERN TIBET

A SMALL MONASTERY IN DE-GE (POLO GOMBA ON THE YANGTZE)

PLATE VIII

CANTILEVER BRIDGES IN EASTERN TIBET
(MAIN ROAD TO LHASA, NEAR DRAYA)

with his usual severity, leaving the natives of this turbulent district more than ever irreconcilable to Chinese rule.

There still remained at this time a district called Sangen (meaning in Tibetan *Bad Lands*, and transliterated by the Chinese as Sangai), which had not yet been taken over by the Chinese. This region consisted of the almost inaccessible valleys draining into the Yangtze immediately above Batang, and was inhabited by wild robber tribes, who had never recognised any constituted authority and lived by raiding the caravans on the surrounding roads. As a preliminary step to the subjugation of these tribesmen, Chao Erh-feng occupied Gonjo, a small Tibetan province lying between Draya and Sangen. Operating with several columns based on Batang, Draya and De-ge, he closed in on Sangen from five directions, and was as usual successful in overwhelming the tribesmen with little or no fighting. Gonjo and Sangen were thereupon converted into Chinese districts as Kungchüeh and Wuch'eng.

Early in 1911, the Chinese forces in Lhasa, under the control of General Chung Ying and the Amban, Lien Yü, were engaged in military operations in Bomed[1], which is a difficult country of heavy rains, dense forests, and precipitous snow ranges lying west of Zayül on the borders of Assam. The Chinese contemplated opening up a road through that region in order to provide a short cut between China and Lhasa *via* Batang and Zayül. An expedition was sent into the country from Lhasa *via* Gongbo under the command of Lo Chang-chi, Lien Yü's chief assistant, but met with serious reverses. Lien Yü was compelled to appeal to Chao Erh-feng for assistance, and the latter despatched troops from Batang and Shuopando, who advanced into Bomed through Zayül, defeated the Tibetans, burned their villages and executed their headmen. Chinese districts, to be called Pomi Hsien and Tsayü Hsien, were subsequently planned for Bomed and Zayül, but were never actually established owing to the outbreak of the revolution in China[2].

[1] *Boyül*, "the land of Incense," divided into Upper and Lower, *Bomed* and *Boto*.

[2] Some account of these events was given in a Chinese book, containing a collection of papers on frontier affairs, published at Chengtu after the revolution. The following is a translation of an extract from Chao Erh-feng's report to Peking regarding the despatch of troops to Bomed, which occurs amongst these papers:

"I have been requested by Lien Yü to send reinforcements to Bomed. Owing to

In the spring of 1911 Chao Erh-feng was appointed to the post of Viceroy of Szechuan, the most important and the most lucrative provincial office in the Empire. Only one task remained for him to accomplish before leaving the frontier to complete the subjugation of the Native States of Eastern Tibet to Chinese rule, and that was the expulsion of the Tibetan officials from Nyarong (in Chinese Chantui), the Tibetan province occupying the basin of the Yalung river from below Kanze to the neighbourhood of Hok'ou. The reason why Nyarong had not been dealt with earlier was not so much due to any unwillingness on the part of Chao Erh-feng to face the opposition of the natives as to difficulties connected with its status, which was not that of a Native State, but of a Tibetan province under the direct rule of the Lhasa Government. This rendered its occupation by the Chinese a direct challenge to the Tibetan Government, a course which it had been impolitic to pursue before the Chinese had made good their position in Lhasa itself. The Manchu Court may also have been reluctant to sanction its occupation and thus break faith with the Dalai Lama, whose claim to rule the country was indisputable.

Nyarong seems to have been annexed by the Dalai Lama, with the approval of the Emperor, after the events of 1863, and its cession was later on formally confirmed in 1898[1]. The Manchu Court, adhering to their engagements with the Tibetan Government, had twice rejected Chao Erh-feng's proposals, made in 1908 and 1909, to take over the administration of the province. It appears that an offer of a sum of money for the country had been made to the Dalai Lama through the Amban at Lhasa, but on this being refused, no further steps were taken in the matter by the Peking Government. Eventually Chao Erh-feng, when on his way back to China to take up his post of Viceroy of Szechuan in the summer of 1911, acted on his own responsibility, entered the country with troops, expelled the Lhasa officials and

the great difficulties of the country and in view of the fact that General Chung Ying's Lhasa troops have already been beaten back, it is feared that two battalions will be insufficient for the expedition. I am therefore arranging for a battalion of the Kam force to advance from Shuopando apart from the battalion already despatched. Another battalion from the Chamdo reserves will be sent *via* Tsawa Dzogang. Feng Shan will proceed to Shuopando to take command.

I intend to arrange with the Chantui tribes before returning to Szechuan.

Dated Chantui, June, 1911."

[1] See pp. 5 and 6.

installed a Chinese magistrate in their place. Before the Throne could express their approval or disapproval of his action, the revolution broke out, Chao Erh-feng himself was put to death, and the Manchu Dynasty disappeared. The forcible annexation of Nyarong by the Chinese was always strongly resented and opposed by the local Tibetans, the Dalai Lama and the Tibetan Government.

When Chao Erh-feng finally left the frontier in August, 1911, the work, begun in 1905, was outwardly completed, and there was not a Tibetan ruler left in Eastern Tibet. From Tachienlu up to the Mekong the country was actually being administered by Chinese district magistrates, while west of the Mekong and the Salween several districts had also been planned but not actually established. The Amban Lien Yü and General Chung Ying ruled at Lhasa, the Dalai Lama was an exile in India, and the Tibetan Government had to all intents and purposes ceased to exist. The whole edifice of Chinese control was, however, but a hastily constructed framework, imposed on an unwilling people taken by surprise, and the greater part of it collapsed completely when put to the test at the time of the revolution in China.

Chao Erh-feng's place on the frontier was taken by his chief assistant, General Fu Sung-mu. Amongst the first acts of this officer was the submission of a Memorial to the Throne proposing that Eastern Tibet should be converted into a new Chinese province, to be called Hsikang (Western Kam). The revolution against the Manchu Dynasty broke out in Szechuan shortly after this Memorial reached Chengtu on its way to Peking. The following *précis* translation of the document is taken from a book on the history of the Tibetan frontier compiled by General Fu Sung-mu and published at Chengtu in 1912. The Memorial is dated August, 1911:

The frontier Territory lies between Szechuan in the East and Tibet in the West and is bounded by the Kokonor Territory in the North and Yunnan Province in the South. It was formerly divided up into more than twenty Native States and Tribes, the inhabitants of which, while paying tribute to the Emperor, were not actually Chinese subjects.

In the reigns of the Emperors Hsien Feng and T'ung Chih (1851 to 1875) the Chief of Nyarong, by name Gombu, invaded and ravaged the Five Hor States, De-ge, and other neighbouring Principalities, with the result that the Tibetans possessed themselves of his country. In consequence of these events the Chiefs and Head Lamas of various States cast off the suzerainty of the Emperor and recognised the overlordship of Tibet alone.

Later on Hsiangch'eng and Draya joined Tibet, troubles broke out at Taining and Batang, where the Imperial Envoy was murdered, and rebellion and unrest became everywhere prevalent.

In 1906 His Excellency Chao Erh-feng, having conquered Batang and Litang, was appointed Frontier Commissioner. In 1908 he advanced against the rebels of De-ge, where Chinese administration was introduced; more than ten district magistracies were thus created.

In 1910 Sangachu Dzong, Zayül and Sangen were subdued; and subsequently Chinese administration was also introduced in Chamdo and other districts.

On Chao Erh-feng being appointed Viceroy of Szechuan he converted nine more Native States into Chinese districts, while I, his successor, dealt in a similar manner with the few that were left. So that there remain at present scarcely any places where districts have not been established.

The time has now come when this whole region should be converted into a regular province, which should be named Hsikang.

The frontier regions in question march with Tibet and beyond Tibet lies the territory of a mighty Power. This Power is closely watching Tibet, which it no longer regards as a dependency of China. By converting the frontier regions of Kam into a Chinese province we shall secure ourselves against territorial aggression.

As a result of the British expedition to Lhasa in 1904 the Tibetans ceased to regard China as of any importance. When Chao Erh-feng was preparing to send troops into Tibet, the Tibetan Government objected and memorialised the Emperor in the year 1908 claiming that Tibetan territory extended to Ch'iungchou in Szechuan. When, in the winter of 1909–10, Chinese troops advanced into Tibet, the Tibetans would have hampered their march had not adequate preparations been made. This year again, when the rebellion broke out in Bomed, the Chinese troops despatched thither from Lhasa were repulsed and the situation was only saved by the timely arrival of reinforcements from Batang. Only thus was a serious rising in Tibet averted.

The Frontier Territory extends from Tachienlu to the Danda Pass beyond Chamdo and from Yunnan to the Kokonor. There is room in this region for more than eighty district magistracies. Adequate control cannot, however, be exercised over this vast region by the Viceroy of Szechuan, whose seat is too remote.

The post of Frontier Commissioner should therefore be altered to that of Governor of Hsikang Province; the subordinate officers being similarly replaced by provincial officials.

The Szechuan Treasury has in the past furnished the necessary funds, to the amount of about one million taels annually, for the expenses of the frontier administration. This payment should continue, as a subsidy to the new province.

A list of the Chinese districts planned by Chao Erh-feng for the Province of Hsikang is given on page 35 and their distribution is shown on the map facing that page.

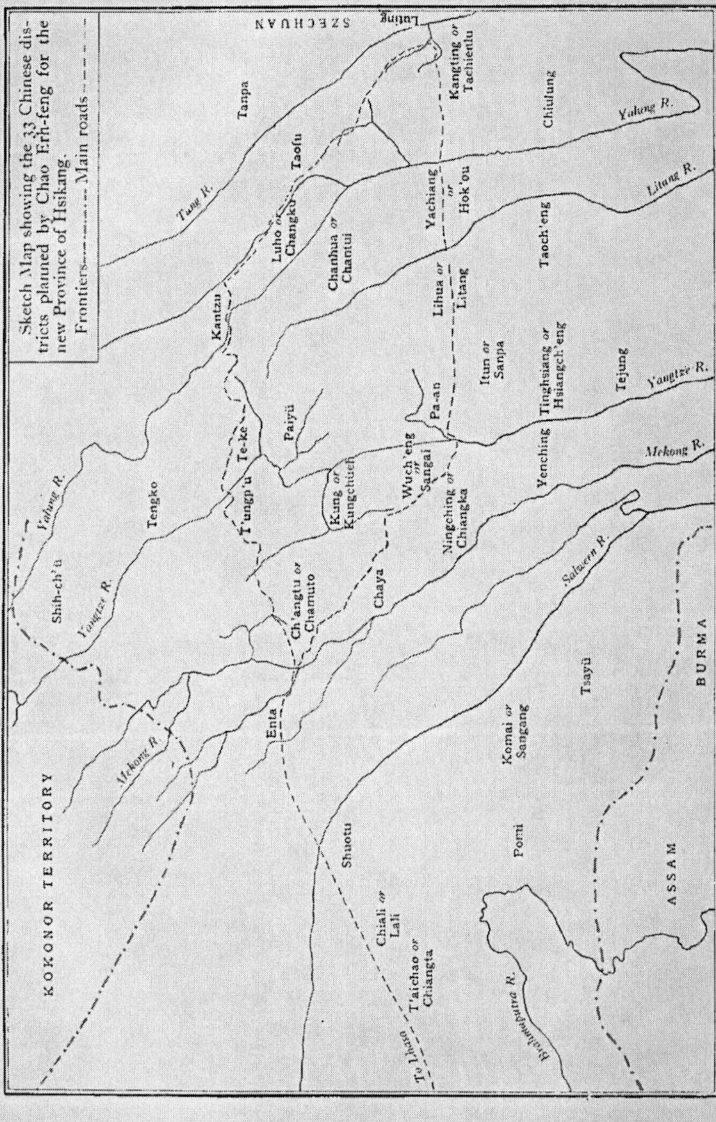
Sketch Map showing the 33 Chinese districts planned by Chao Erh-feng for the new Province of Hsikang.
Frontiers —·—·— Main roads - - - - -
KOKONOR TERRITORY
SZECHUAN
Luting
Kangting or Tachienlu
Tanpa
Tung R.
Taofu
Luho or Changku
Chanhua or Chantui
Yachiang or Hok'ou
Chiulung
Yalung R.
Litang R.
Lihua or Litang
Taoch'eng
Kantzu
Itun or Sanpa
Tinghsiang or Hsiangch'eng
Tejung
Yangtze R.
Pa-an
Paiyü
Te-ke
Wuch'eng or Sangai
Yenching
Mekong R.
Kung or Kungchüeh
T'ungp'u
Tengko
Yalung R.
Ningching or Chiangka
Shih-ch'ü
Yangtze R.
Ch'angtu or Chamuto
Chaya
Salween R.
Enta
Mekong R.
Komai or Sangang
Tsayü
BURMA
Shuotu
Pomi
ASSAM
Chiali or Lali
T'aichao or Chiangta
To Lhasa
Brahmaputra R.

MAP 3

Chinese Districts planned by Chao Erh-feng for the province of Hsikang (Tibetan names in brackets).

K'ang-ting Hsien, or Tachienlu (Dartsendo).
Lu-ting Hsien, or Lu-ting Ch'iao (Jazamka).
Chiu-lung Hsien (Jyetserong).
Tan-pa Hsien (Romidrango).
Lu-ho Hsien, or Chang-Ku (Drango).
Tao-fu Hsien (Dawu).
Kan-tzu Hsien (Kanze).
Chan-hua Hsien, or Chan-tui, or Huai-jou (Nyarong).
Ya-chiang Hsien, or Ho-k'ou (Nyachuka).
Ting-hsiang Hsien, or Hsiang-ch'eng (Chantreng).
Tao-ch'eng Hsien (Taotrin).
I-tun Hsien, or San-pa, or Ta-so (Dasho).
Te-ko Hsien, or Te-hua, or Keng-ching (De-ge Gönchen).
Pai-yü Hsien (Beyü).
Teng-ko Hsien (Denko).
Shih-ch'ü Hsien (Seshü).
T'ung-p'u Hsien (Tangpu or Rangsum).
Li-hua Hsien, or Li-tang (Letang).
Pa-an Hsien, or Ba-tang (Ba).
Yen-ching Hsien (Tsakalo).
Te-jung Hsien (Derong).
Ning-ching Hsien, or Chiang-ka (Markam Gartok).
Wu-ch'eng Hsien, or Sang-ai (Sangen).
Kung Hsien, or Kung-chüeh (Gonjo).
Cha-ya Hsien (Draya).
Ch'ang-tu Hsien, or Cha-mu-to (Chamdo).
En-ta Hsien (Ngenda).
Shuo-tu Hsien (Shuopando)[1].
Ko-mai Hsien, or Sang-ang (Sangachu Dzong)[1].
Tsa-yü Hsien (Zayül)[1].
Chia-li Hsien, or La-li (Lari)[1].
Po-mi Hsien (Bomed)[1].
T'ai-chao Hsien, or Chiang-ta (Giamda)[1].

[1] Trans-Salween districts planned but never established.

3—2

PART IV

THE COLLAPSE OF CHINESE POWER IN TIBET IN 1911, THE SUBSEQUENT CAMPAIGNS IN EASTERN TIBET IN 1912 AND 1913, AND THE TRIPARTITE NEGOTIATIONS IN INDIA IN 1914

Outbreak of the revolution in China and murder of Chao Erh-feng by the revolutionaries in Szechuan—Risings on the frontier—Mutiny of Chinese troops in Lhasa and withdrawal of Chinese from Central Tibet—Efforts of the Chinese Government to placate the Tibetans—Despatch of a Szechuanese relief force to E. Tibet and recovery by the Chinese of the frontier districts up to the Mekong—Hostilities on the border develop into open war between China and Tibet—The position on the frontier in 1914—Great Britain offers to mediate between China and Tibet—Chinese, Tibetan, and British Plenipotentiaries meet in India for the purpose of tripartite peace negotiations to settle the status of Tibet—Aims and objects of the Tibetan, Chinese and British Governments on entering the Conference—Conflicting Tibetan and Chinese boundary claims and British proposals for a settlement—The Conference breaks down over the boundary question—Truce between China and Tibet resulting from the tripartite negotiations of 1914.

CHAO ERH-FENG arrived in Chengtu in August, 1911, to take up his post as Viceroy of Szechuan. The revolution against the Manchu Dynasty, which began with popular risings in Western China, broke out almost immediately afterwards. The old warrior put up a determined resistance, and was besieged in Chengtu for three months. In November, however, the news of the murder of the Imperial Commissioner, Tuan Fang, by the revolutionaries and of the military risings at Hankow having reached the provincial capital, he surrendered on terms, and the republic of Szechuan was duly proclaimed. On December 23 he was treacherously beheaded by the revolutionaries. Thus died, tragically and ignominiously at the hands of his own countrymen, one of China's greatest Empire builders, and with him passed away Chinese ascendancy over Tibet.

Chao Erh-feng differed in many respects from the ordinary high Chinese official. Light and wiry in stature, and sparing in eating and drinking, he was always prepared to undergo the same hardships incidental to frontier campaigning as his officers and men. Unlike the somewhat effeminate and ease-loving Szechuanese, he disdained the sedan chair, and travelled all over Eastern Tibet on horse-back. He was universally successful in all his military operations in Kam, often attaining his ends as much by bluff and astute diplomacy as by force of arms. But, when he had to fight, his campaigns were always well planned and carried out. The key to his successes was the capture of De-ge by a sudden coup, followed by the rapid advance on Chamdo and the raid on Lhasa, the heart and centre of Tibet, after which he was in a position to eat up the rest of the country piecemeal without serious opposition. It must, however, be admitted, in justice to his successors, who were as conspicuous in failure as he was in success, that Chao Erh-feng always received the fullest support from his brother, the Viceroy of Szechuan, and that both had behind them the power and prestige of the Manchu Empire; whereas after the fall of the Empire and the establishment of the Chinese Republic, there was almost as little cohesion and unity of action amongst the various military leaders in Western China as there had formerly been amongst the Native States of Eastern Tibet.

Though he was known amongst the Szechuanese by the nickname of "Butcher Chao" owing to his alleged tendency towards wholesale executions, and though his proceedings were doubtless at times characterised by great severity towards the unfortunate Tibetans who objected to submitting to the Chinese yoke, his reputation was nevertheless that of a just man; and, while he did not hesitate to behead a recalcitrant Tibetan Chief or Headman, he was equally ready to decapitate offenders amongst his own officers and men. A remarkable man, of commanding personality, Chao Erh-feng's justice and fair-dealing are remembered to-day in Eastern Tibet as well as his severity; and his reputation in the former respect has grown of recent years owing to the weak inefficiency and cruelly oppressive rule of his successors. Amongst the lamas, however, his name is universally execrated as the arch enemy, the destroyer of monasteries and killer of monks. This anti-lama attitude adopted by Chao Erh-feng, and many of the local Chinese Authorities on the frontier since his time, was a reversal of the traditional policy of the Manchus, who had exercised their authority over Tibet and Mongolia largely through the instrumentality of the lama church.

The revolution in China was not immediately followed by risings on the frontier (though the new republican authorities in charge of the Szechuan government made an inauspicious start by circulating photographs of Chao's severed head in the border districts to demonstrate their victory and rise to power). Later on, however, as the Tibetan tribesmen began gradually to realise the relaxation of Chinese control, the trouble began, commencing, as was to be expected, in Hsiangch'eng, the centre of perpetual unrest. Revolts of the lamas and tribesmen in Sangen, Gonjo, Draya, Markam, and Chamdo followed.

By the summer of 1912, the Chinese had lost control of most of the frontier districts, their outlying garrisons being withdrawn to Batang and Chamdo, which became the centres of Chinese resistance. Chamdo, especially, was for a time hard pressed and stoutly defended by a Chinese commander named P'eng Jih-sheng; the latter was compelled in self-defence to destroy the huge Chamdo monastery, the largest in Kam, which contained 2000 to 3000 monks, and menaced the Chinese by its commanding position on a bluff immediately behind the town[1]. But the situation of the Chinese on the frontier at this time, though outwardly a very dangerous one, was in reality much less desperate than their situation at the time of the resumption of hostilities in 1918. In the first place, the Lhasa Government was not yet formally at war with China, and the issue thus still remained at this time one between the Chinese and the local lamas and tribesmen of Eastern Tibet, who were without cohesion or organisation and practically without arms; while, secondly, large stocks of rice and ammunition, carefully collected by Chao Erh-feng, were still in existence.

As soon as the news of the revolution in China filtered through to Lhasa trouble began in Central Tibet also. Following the example of the troops at Peking, Chengtu and other military centres, the Chinese soldiers mutinied and took to burning and looting. The same thing was happening at this time all over China Proper; but by acting thus in

[1] The same General P'eng was besieged in the same place by the Tibetans six years later and was compelled to surrender. The destruction of the Chamdo monastery, one of the most important religious institutions in Tibet outside Lhasa, greatly embittered all classes of Tibetans and was never forgotten or forgiven.

Tibet the Chinese destroyed any chance they may have had of maintaining themselves in the country. The Tibetans defended themselves and retaliated, and the situation soon developed into a struggle between them and the Chinese. Outside Lhasa the Chinese garrisons rapidly melted away, some being withdrawn to join General Chung Ying's force inside the capital, others being overwhelmed, and others again, stationed in the Chumbi valley and on the road to India, escaping into British territory. The Chinese force in Bomed, after mutinying against their officers, endeavoured to withdraw in a body, but were cut down almost to a man by the natives while struggling in single file across a big snow pass. Many a similar unrelated tragedy doubtless occurred in other outlying parts.

In Lhasa itself Chung Ying's force fortified themselves in the Tengye Ling[1] monastery and held out for some time, fighting and negotiating alternately in the Chinese fashion. Finally they were allowed to withdraw unmolested into India in accordance with the terms of an agreement made with the Tibetans through the mediation of the Nepalese Agent, and were subsequently repatriated by the British Authorities by the sea route to Shanghai. By the end of 1912 Chinese authority had ceased to exist in Tibet, and, the Dalai Lama having returned from his place of exile in India, the country became once more an autonomous State.

The new Republican Government of China, in the hope of placating the Tibetans and recovering their position in the country, proceeded to reinstate the Dalai Lama[2], who had been deposed by the Manchus only two years before, cashiered the Manchu Amban, Lien Yü, and appointed Chung Ying, a Chinese, as Amban in his place. General Chung clung on in the Chumbi valley for a time; but the Tibetans, intensely exasperated by the excesses committed by the Chinese troops, insisted that he and every Chinese official and soldier should leave the country, and refused to listen to the explanations of the republicans that Lien Yü and the Manchu Dynasty were responsible for all the trouble.

Lien Yü, having been made the scapegoat for the mis-

[1] One of the four great Lhasa monasteries, the others being Ganden Ling, Sera Ling, and Drepung Ling. It is said that Tengye Ling was subsequently destroyed by the Tibetans owing to the use made of it by the Chinese.

[2] See pp. 16 and 17.

fortunes of the Chinese, was permitted to retire into private life. Arrived at Peking in due course, he in turn proceeded to lay the blame for everything on General Chung Ying. A further attempt to placate the Tibetans was then made, this time by offering up the unfortunate Chung Ying, who was executed in Peking two years later, in the spring of 1915. The Presidential Mandate announcing his sentence is on record, having been published in the *Peking Government Gazette* of March 22nd, 1915:

Précis Translation of Presidential Mandate pronouncing sentence of death upon general Chung Ying, late Commander-in-Chief and Amban in Tibet. Dated March 19th, 1915.

The case of Chung Ying, former Amban in Tibet, having been referred to the High Military Court for examination, the following report has now been received on the subject.

According to the depositions of Lien Yü, a former Amban in Tibet, and others, General Chung Ying was in command of the army at Lhasa when the mutiny occurred, but, though invested with supreme military authority, he was unable to suppress the disturbances. He allowed the troops under his command to loot the Tibetans, which provoked the hatred of the latter against the Chinese. He permitted his mutinous soldiery to attack the Sera monastery. The whole of Tibet was thus thrown into confusion. He, being then Amban in Tibet, was ordered by the Government not to leave his post. But he disobeyed orders and left Tibet, thus rendering the situation past remedy.

According to other depositions General Chung Ying, fearing lest Lo Chang-chi would telegraph to the Government exposing the real cause of the disturbances in Tibet, executed him on the false charge of causing troubles[1].

Chung Ying being interrogated as to the correctness of the above statements could make out no case for his defence.

It is to be observed that after the suppression of the troubles in Bomed the whole of Tibet was at peace. But after the mutiny of the troops at Lhasa and the attack on Sera monastery widespread unrest ensued. Chung Ying was the cause of all these troubles. He has thus inflicted great misery on the Tibetans and created alarm on the frontier. Moreover, he murdered a faithful and loyal public servant and burned his remains.

Sentence of death is therefore hereby promulgated on General Chung Ying, to be carried out according to law.

This Mandate was accompanied by instructions to the Board of Mongolian and Tibetan Affairs to notify the Dalai Lama of the circumstances attending the execution of General Chung Ying and to cause proclamations to be issued through-

[1] Lo Chang-chi was Lien Yü's Chief Secretary and Commander of the Chinese expedition to Bomed.

RESIDENCE OF SMALL LOCAL OFFICIAL IN EASTERN TIBET
(AT JYEDAM IN WESTERN DRAYA)

TRAVELLING ACROSS THE PARK LANDS OF MARKAM

PLATE X

TYPICAL SCENERY IN SOUTHERN KAM, PINE FOREST AND SNOW MOUNTAIN

NEAR THE SUMMIT OF THE FIRST BIG PASS ON THE MAIN ROAD FROM CHINA TO TIBET

out Tibet explaining the facts of the case. But the Tibetans were not to be cajoled back into the Chinese fold by fair words. It is not unlikely that the new Republican Government of China had at this time an opportunity of coming to some arrangement with the Dalai Lama by which, in return for the grant of full autonomy to Tibet, the latter might have agreed to join the new Chinese Commonwealth as a junior partner. But the Chinese Government were badly served at this critical juncture in their relations with Tibet, and their frequent pronouncements regarding the equality and unity of the "Five Races" (Chinese, Manchus, Mongols, Mahomedans, and Tibetans) were unfortunately exemplified during the years following the revolution, as far as the Tibetans of Eastern Tibet were concerned, by the actions of a plundering soldiery and the oppressive and unjust rule of rapacious and inefficient officials, in comparison with which the régime of Chao Erh-feng came to be regarded as a golden age. As a result the Tibetans of autonomous Tibet became more and more determined as the years passed by to have nothing to do with the new China.

After the completion of the revolution by the formal abdication of the Manchu Dynasty matters began to settle down for the time being in China, and in the summer of 1912 a relief force, some 5000 strong, left Chengtu for the frontier to retrieve the Chinese position in Eastern Tibet. The expedition was under the command of a young Szechuanese General named Yin Ch'ang-heng, who had been the leader of the revolution and the head of the first republican government of the province. Inasmuch as he had been directly responsible for the execution of Chao Erh-feng, there was a certain justice in his being sent to reconstruct the work which had collapsed on Chao's fall. The reason of his going to the frontier was that he had been ousted from the governorship of the province by a rival revolutionary leader.

Yin Ch'ang-heng's plans were laid in imitation of those adopted by Chao Erh-feng, namely to converge on Chamdo by parallel advances by the North and South Roads. Arrived at Tachienlu, the expeditionary force proceeded to loot the city, burned down the palace of the ex-Chief of Chala, and decapitated his brother, the Chief himself having made good his escape into the inaccessible mountain regions of the interior of his former State. Batang and Chamdo were duly reached and relieved, and Draya, Markam, and other frontier districts fell again into Chinese hands. De-ge and Kanze, on the North Road, had never been lost. Lengthy military operations in Hsiangch'eng, accompanied by the usual atrocities, which appeared to grow worse with each rebellion and subsequent campaign of suppression, resulted in the reduction of that district during 1913. At Dawu (Chinese Taofu), on the North Road between Tachienlu and Kanze, a local rebellion, which nearly cost a Catholic priest his life, was easily quelled, and by the end of 1914 Chinese control had been to a great extent re-established in the frontier regions as far as the Mekong. These short-lived rebellions left behind, however, a greater feeling of bitterness on the part of the natives towards the Chinese than any of Chao Erh-feng's campaigns owing to the absence of order and restraint amongst General Yin's ill-disciplined republican soldiery.

The Lhasa Government, having regained their autonomy and being determined to retain it, viewed the advance of the Szechuan expeditionary force with some alarm, and the Kalon Lama, the Commander-in-Chief of the Tibetan army, was sent with troops into Kam to stop the Chinese advance wherever he might meet it. As a result the advancing Chinese forces were brought definitely to a halt on the line of the Mekong and the Mekong-Salween divide, where they came into contact with the newly-raised regiments from Central Tibet. From now on the situation on the frontier changed its aspect, and the confused border warfare between the tribesmen and lamas of Kam developed into a war between China and Tibet Proper over the question of the Sino-Tibetan frontier.

Towards the end of 1913, Yin Ch'ang-heng left the frontier for Peking, where Yuan Shih-k'ai was then engaged in establishing his control over China with a view to becoming, first, President Dictator, and then Emperor of a new Dynasty. Arrived in Peking, General Yin, instead of receiving honours and high military rank, was immediately arrested, but after languishing for a time in prison, and narrowly escaping execution for the murder of Chao Erh-feng, was released and relapsed into obscurity.

The commencement of the year 1914 found the position

beginning to stabilise itself. The Chinese front extended along the Mekong river from the Yunnan border northwards to the neighbourhood of Chamdo, whence it ran north-west along the Mekong-Salween divide up to the southern border of the Kokonor Territory (Chinese Ch'ing Hai)[1]. Batang and Chamdo were as before the principal Chinese military bases, while outlying Chinese garrisons were scattered up and down the frontier watching the Tibetan forces under the Kalon Lama, the latter's troops being centred on Shuopando and Sha-yi Zamka (Chinese Chiayü Ch'iao) in the Salween valley. This line remained the frontier for the next few years, thanks to the truce resulting from the Sino-Tibetan negotiations which had in the meantime taken place in India. The country between the Tung river in Szechuan Proper and the Mekong, which remained in Chinese hands, was constituted into a Special Military Territory dependent on Szechuan with its capital at Tachienlu, on the same lines as the territories of Suiyan and Chahar on the borders of North China and Southern Mongolia, and a Hupei officer named Chang Yi was appointed by Yuan Shih-k'ai as Governor, to reside at Tachienlu, with the title of Commissioner for the Szechuan Frontier Territory (*Ch'uan-pien Chen-shou-shih*). Two subordinate Generals, Liu Tsan-ting and P'eng Jih-sheng, were placed in charge at Batang and Chamdo respectively.

In the summer of 1914 there was more trouble with the ever-restless natives of Hsiangch'eng. At the same time a serious revolt broke out in Draya. Both risings were duly suppressed, the latter ending in a large body of Tibetans being surrounded in a large Draya monastery called Yemdo (Chinese Yent'ait'ang), where they were exterminated, and the monastery burned. Like Hsiangch'eng, Draya suffered very severely in this frontier warfare, the country-side being still depopulated and the villages and monasteries lying in ruins several years later.

* * * * *

Ever since the conclusion of the Lhasa Convention in 1904 and the subsequent withdrawal of the British troops, Great Britain had stood aside watching the ebb and flow of China's attempts to restore her position in Tibet by force of arms. At length, however, after the Chinese had been expelled

[1] See map facing p. 45.

from Lhasa and the situation had developed into open warfare between China and Tibet, which showed every sign of dragging on for years to the great detriment of Indo-Tibetan trade and the peace of the North-east Frontier, the British Government came forward to assist in settling the dispute. After some preliminary discussions for the purpose of ascertaining the general lines which the negotiations were to follow, namely, the establishment of an autonomous Tibet under Chinese suzerainty, Chinese, Tibetan, and British plenipotentiaries eventually met in India towards the close of 1913 for the purpose of negotiating a tripartite convention regulating the mutual relations of the three countries and establishing the status of Tibet.

The position at the time the conference met was briefly as follows: Lhasa-governed Tibet, which had discarded all vestige of Chinese control, extended east, roughly speaking, to the river Mekong, and north to the southern watershed of the Yangtze. In Kam, east of the Mekong, the framework of Chinese control created by Chao Erh-feng had been re-established, while in the north the Kokonor region, which had been unaffected by the events of the past ten years, remained as before under the nominal control of the Amban at Sining in Kansu.

The Tibetans entered the conference with the object of securing the recognition of Tibet as a practically independent State, with boundaries enclosing all those regions of High Asia inhabited by persons of Tibetan race.

The Chinese entered the conference with the object of recovering as far as possible the position they had held in Tibet at the time of Chao Erh-feng's conquests.

The British Government entered the conference with the object of restoring peace between China and Tibet, preferably on the basis of the restoration of the old status of Tibet as an autonomous State under Chinese suzerainty, and of securing the establishment at Lhasa of a stable Tibetan Government, with which friendly relations might be maintained by both China and Great Britain, and which should be free from all interference in its internal affairs from the side of China, Great Britain, or any other outside party.

After discussions lasting some months the three parties came to terms on all the points at issue with the exception of the question of the boundaries of Tibet. It was thus agreed by all concerned that Tibet Proper should be an autonomous State under Chinese suzerainty, that the Chinese Amban should return to Lhasa with an escort of Chinese troops suitable to his rank and position, and that both China and Great Britain should abstain from all interference in thc administration of the country. When, however, the question of the boundary between China and autonomous Tibet came up for settlement, it became apparent that the Chinese and Tibetan points of view were so widely divergent as to make an agreement almost impossible.

The Tibetans claimed all Tibetan-inhabited territory up to Sining in Kansu in the north and Tachienlu in Szechuan in the east, and produced whole libraries of historical evidence from Lhasa in support of their claims.

The Chinese, ignoring the old records and the Manchu settlement of 1727, went back no further than the time of Chao Erh-feng's greatest successes, and claimed the neighbourhood of Giamda (Chinese Chiangta), within a few marches of Lhasa, as the boundary between China and Tibet.

The British representative, in his character as middleman, proposed, as a compromise between the divergent claims of the two sides, that Tibet, that is to say, the country generally marked as such in European atlases, should be divided up into two zones, namely, Inner and Outer Tibet, on the lines of Inner and Outer Mongolia; Inner Tibet to be under more direct Chinese control, and Outer Tibet to be under the autonomous Government of Lhasa, where a Chinese Amban would be stationed in charge of Chinese interests; the boundary between the two zones should, it was suggested, follow in the main the old historical frontier line laid down by the Manchus in 1727 between the Dalai Lama's realm and the semi-independent States of Eastern Tibet.

The Tibetans objected to the proposed settlement as being too favourable to the Chinese, especially with regard to the placing of De-ge, Nyarong, and the former Hor States under Chinese control.

The Chinese objected to the proposed settlement as being too favourable to the Tibetans, because it entailed the surrender to Tibetan rule of certain districts which had been nominally incorporated in China by Chao Erh-feng and of a portion of the Kokonor Territory which was regarded as a dependency of Kansu Province, and still more so because the Batang-Litang region, which they considered to lie in Szechuan, had been labelled as part of Inner (namely Chinese) Tibet.

After much discussion, however, a draft Convention, embodying a boundary as proposed by the British representative, was initialled in April, 1914, by the three Plenipotentiaries preparatory to signature. But the Chinese Government refused to proceed further in the matter, and the Conference finally broke up in the summer of 1914 without an agreement having been reached.

Though no settlement had been arrived at, China formally notified Great Britain as middleman that the only point in the draft convention which she was unable to accept was that affecting the boundary, and gave an assurance that the Chinese troops stationed on the frontier would not advance beyond the positions they then held, provided they were not attacked by the Tibetans, both sides awaiting a final settlement by diplomatic means. The frontier truce, which lasted for the next few years, was based on this understanding.

The boundary proposals of 1914 appeared on the whole to represent a fair compromise between the widely divergent claims of the two parties to the dispute, and the objections of the Chinese thereto were perhaps largely based on the nomenclature employed. Thus the Chinese, though they were apparently to exercise a measure of control in Inner, or Chinese, Tibet, objected, as stated above, to the inclusion therein of the Batang-Litang region, which (though inhabited solely by peoples of Tibetan race) had for long past been regarded by the Chinese as lying, not in Tibet, but in Szechuan Province, and of portions of the Kokonor Territory, which they claimed had never been a part of Tibet.

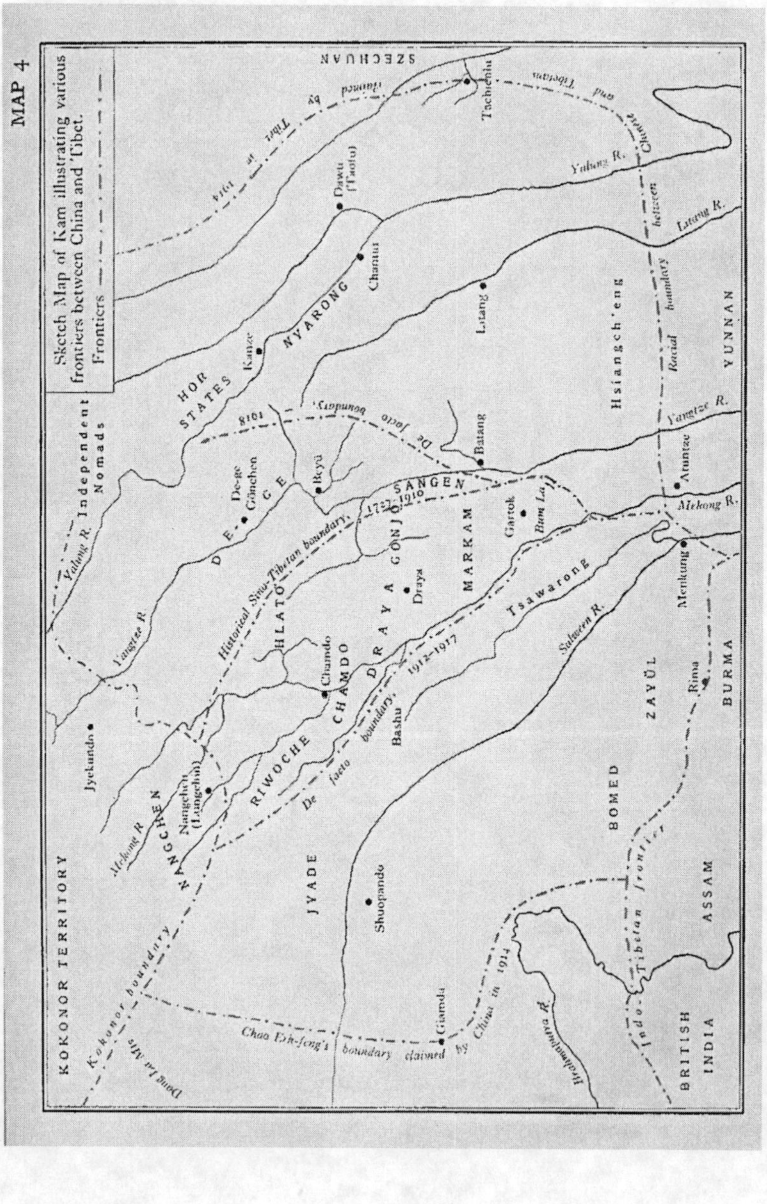
MAP 4
Sketch Map of Kam illustrating various frontiers between China and Tibet.
Frontiers
KOKONOR TERRITORY
Independent Nomads
HOR STATES
NYARONG
SZECHUAN
DE GE
HLATO
SANGEN
GONJO
DRAYA
MARKAM
CHAMDO
RIWOCHE
NANGCHEN
JYADE
Tsawarong
BOMED
ZAYÜL
Hsiangch'eng
YUNNAN
BURMA
ASSAM
BRITISH INDIA
Jyekundo
Nangchen (Lhangchin)
Chamdo
Draya
Bashu
Shuopando
Giamda
Kanze
De-ge Gönchen
Beyü
Batang
Litang
Chanlui
Dawu (Taofu)
Tachienlu
Gartok
Bum La
Atuntze
Menkung
Rima
Yalung R.
Yangtze R.
Mekong R.
Salween R.
Litang R.
Brahmaputra R.
Kokonor boundary
Dang La Mts
Chao Erh-feng's boundary claimed by China in 1914
Historical Sino-Tibetan boundary, 1727-1910
De facto boundary, 1918
De facto boundary, 1912-1917
1914 Tibet as claimed by
Racial boundary between Chinese and Tibetans
Indo-Tibetan frontier

PART V

THE TRUCE BETWEEN CHINA AND TIBET FROM 1914 TO 1917, THE RESUMPTION OF HOSTILITIES AND THE TIBETAN ADVANCE IN 1918, AND THE SUBSEQUENT RESTORATION OF PEACE THROUGH BRITISH MEDIATION BY LOCAL NEGOTIATIONS ON THE FRONTIER

Renewed rising in Hsiangch'eng in 1914—Forward movement in the Kokonor Territory by the Chinese Mahomedans of Kansu—Yuan Shih-k'ai ascends the Throne of China as Emperor at the end of 1915—Outbreak of anti-monarchical rebellion in S.W. China early in 1916 and resulting domination of Szechuan and the frontier by the Yunnanese—Hostilities between Szechuan and Yunnan break out in 1917—Neglect of Chinese frontier garrisons owing to continued civil wars in China—Hostilities between Szechuanese and Lhasa Tibetans provoked by the Chinese Commander on the frontier against the orders of his Government—Tibetans capture Draya and lay siege to Chamdo—Fall of Chamdo—Tibetans overrun De-ge and threaten Batang and Kanze—Chinese relief force despatched to Kanze to check Tibetan advance—Fighting between Szechuanese and Tibetans at Rongbatsa near Kanze—British mediation and peace negotiations on the frontier—Peace restored between China and Tibet at the end of 1918.

DURING the three years following the close of the conference in India peace reigned on the frontier between China and Tibet, though civil war and political strife in Western China, reacting on border affairs, prevented the Chinese from making any progress in consolidating their position in the Tibetan inhabited districts left in their hands. Towards the end of 1914 trouble broke out again in Hsiangch'eng, where the Chinese garrison joined the natives in rebelling against Chinese authority. The situation soon got out of hand, and by the spring of the following year the rebels, led by a Chinese officer, gained sufficient strength to advance on and capture Tachienlu, whence they emerged on to Szechuan Proper, and eventually dissolved amongst the hordes of brigands preying on that rich province. Tachienlu was then reoccupied and order restored by a Colonel named Ch'en Hsia-ling (who some years later became Frontier Commissioner).

General Chang Yi, who had fled from his post during the Hsiangch'eng rebellion, was now cashiered by President

Yuan Shih-k'ai, who appointed a Szechuanese named Liu Jui-heng to be Frontier Commissioner in his place.

In the summer of 1915 President Yuan Shih-k'ai, who was then at the height of his power and about to ascend the Throne as Emperor, made certain important alterations in the administrative arrangements of the Kokonor Territory. This vast expanse of elevated grass country, which, including the whole of the upper basins of the Yangtze and the Yellow river and part of that of the Mekong, covers all the north-eastern quarter of what is usually labelled *Tibet* on European maps, had hitherto been governed by an old Manchu Amban residing at Sining in Kansu, whose control was purely nominal. This official was now removed by Yuan Shih-k'ai, and the administration of the Kokonor was handed over to the Mahomedan General of Sining. The reasons for this change were connected with the fact that since the revolution of 1911–12 the Mahomedans had become the dominant power in Kansu Province. Up to this time, the Kokonor Territory had been left in peace under the rule of the native Tibetan Chiefs and Mongol Princes, and had thus escaped the fighting and constant unrest which had disturbed the Szechuan frontier ever since the days of Chao Erh-feng. From now on, however, the Kansu Moslems, a hardy race of horsemen who were much more suited to Tibetan campaigning than the soft Szechuanese, began to interfere more and more in the affairs of the Kokonor region. The following document, a *précis* translation of a proclamation issued by the Mahomedan General of Sining in the spring of 1916, is of interest as the first sign of a forward policy on the part of the Kansu Mahomedans in the southern part of the Kokonor Territory bordering on Tibet Proper. It is apparently addressed to the people of Jyade (the "Country of the Thirty-nine Tribes," situated in the basin of the upper Salween on the Tibetan side of the frontier), warning them of the intention of the Kansu Mahomedans to assert their authority in Nangchen (the "Country of the Twenty-five Tribes," situated in the basin of the upper Mekong on the Chinese side of the frontier), which had hitherto, though nominally under Sining, enjoyed practical independence:

A Proclamation by General Ma, Officer of the Second Class of the Order of the Striped Tiger, Frontier Commissioner of the Kansu Border, General Officer Commanding at Sining and in the Kokonor.

You, people of Jyade, were originally of Chinese stock[1], and friendly relations have existed between you and the Chinese Authorities for centuries. During the later days of the Manchu Dynasty ignorant persons on the Szechuan border destroyed your monasteries, killed your lamas, and oppressed the people[2]. Thus you became enraged, and a feud began which has lasted until to-day. But you have no quarrel with Sining, or with Nangchen, the country of the Twenty-five Tribes. Formerly, when the people of the Szechuan border attempted to seize the country of the Twenty-five Tribes[3], the Great President at Peking and the Governor of Kansu sent deputies to Jyekundo, who made a careful investigation, with the result that the country of the Twenty-five Tribes was again placed under the jurisdiction of Sining. The Great President gave orders that the Yellow Church should be respected, the lamas protected, and the *ula* service abolished.

The benevolent attitude of the Great President towards the people of the Twenty-five Tribes is known to all.

I, the Kansu Frontier Commissioner, have been instructed to protect the Tibetans of the Kokonor. Good people will be rewarded and evil doers punished.

The monastery of Kumbum is the birth-place of your great reincarnated Buddha. All must have heard of the manner in which the Authorities of Sining protect this monastery and its monks of the Yellow Church[4].

You, people of Jyade, come to trade at Sining, and the people of Sining go to trade in your country. Passports have been issued to you, and you have been protected like members of one family.

I have often exchanged letters with the Dalai Lama, with whom I am on the friendliest terms. You should therefore follow the Great Lama's example and remain at peace with us.

I am responsible for the protection of Nangchen, the country of the Twenty-five Tribes, and I am sending troops to guard those lands. They are under the jurisdiction of the Sining Authorities, and you, people of Jyade, must not interfere with them. No man can serve two masters, and no country can have two kings. You are well acquainted with the contents of the Scriptures, and the rules laid down therein. Repent therefore of your evil ways and follow righteousness. If you respect the Frontier and pursue your affairs in peace, you may be assured of my forgiveness and of favourable treatment.

Let all obey.

Dated the 26th Day of the 3rd Moon of the 1st Year of the Reign of Hung Hsien.

[1] The people of Jyade, who are nowadays entirely Tibetans, are supposed to have been originally immigrants from China or Mongolia; whence the name Jyade, or Chinese Lands.

[2] This appears to refer to the campaigns of Chao Erh-feng and his successors.

[3] In 1915 General P'eng Jih-sheng of Chamdo, acting either on his own behalf or for the Szechuan Authorities, attempted to appropriate Nangchen, and some fighting occurred between his men and the Kansu Mahomedans near Jyekundo.

[4] The monastery of Kumbum (Chinese T'a-erh Ssu), near Sining on the Kansu-Kokonor border, was the birth-place of Tsongkaba, the reformer of Tibetan Buddhism, and the founder of the *Gelugba* sect. The place was formerly known as Tsongka, hence the reformer's name. He was born in the middle of the fourteenth century.

At the end of 1915 Yuan Shih-k'ai ascended the Throne under the new dynastic title of Hung Hsien, and almost immediately the anti-monarchical rebellion, which was to overthrow him and drive him broken-hearted to a premature grave, broke out in distant Yunnan. One of the results of the success of this rebellion in South-western China was the domination of Szechuan by the Yunnanese; and in October, 1916, a Yunnanese Frontier Commissioner, named Yin Ch'eng-hsien, accompanied by Yunnanese troops, arrived at Tachienlu to take over charge of the frontier.

Yin Ch'eng-hsien was one of the band of able young Japanese trained officers with whose assistance General Tsai Ao was successful in overthrowing the great Yuan Shih-k'ai. He had had previous experience on the frontier, having commanded the Yunnanese column which had operated in the neighbourhood of Atuntze in the campaigns of 1913; and, backed as he was by a Yunnanese Government in control of the rich resources of Szechuan, he might perhaps have been able to restore the Chinese position in Eastern Tibet, which had become yearly more precarious since the revolution of 1911 owing to the neglect of the frontier garrisons by the Szechuanese Authorities.

Unfortunately for the Chinese, hostilities broke out between the provinces of Yunnan and Szechuan soon after, and the early summer of 1917 saw the Yunnanese armies retreating from the burning ruins of Chengtu, the capital of Szechuan. The position of General Yin and his Yunnanese troops at Tachienlu, cut off from their base in Yunnan and surrounded by their enemies, the Szechuanese, soon became desperate, and he eventually withdrew with great difficulty across the mountains *via* Mili to Lichiang in Yunnan. His place as Frontier Commissioner was taken by a Hunanese officer, General Ch'en Hsia-ling, who had been on the border since the days of Chao Erh-feng, and who was not at that time implicated in the dispute between Szechuan and Yunnan.

In the meantime, owing to the fact that both the provincial government of Szechuan and the central government at Peking were too preoccupied with the internal civil wars in China to pay any attention to the Tibetan border, the unfortunate Chinese garrisons on the frontier were completely neglected and left, without supplies of rice, silver, clothing, or ammunition, to shift for themselves and to live on the country as best they could. As a result they had degenerated into little better than brigands, helping themselves to food and money by plundering the natives of the localities where they chanced to be stationed. Nor was it to be expected that respectable Chinese officials would consent to remain in the country under such circumstances; and the administration of the frontier districts thus lapsed into the hands of a number of ex-brigands and military adventurers, who misgoverned and oppressed the natives until rebellion was rife from end to end of the border.

Autonomous Tibet, on the other hand, freed from Chinese rule, had been enjoying years of internal peace and prosperity, and had reorganised and strengthened her frontier army. By the year 1917 the Tibetan Commander-in-Chief, the Kalon Lama, who had faced the Chinese four years previously with untrained and ill-equipped levies, had at his disposal several regiments of comparatively efficient troops, who were as superior to the worn-out Chinese frontier forces as Chao Erh-feng's men had been to the tribesmen and lamas of Kam ten years before.

* * * * *

The Tibetans could scarcely fail to realise that the Chinese were utterly demoralised, that the frontier was open to them, and that their compatriots across the border, suffering under the oppressive yoke of the Chinese military, were but waiting for them to advance, to rise and join them in arms. But they were bound by the understanding of 1914 not to attack unless the truce were first broken by the Chinese, and they could be relied on to keep their word. The local Chinese on the frontier, however, acting on their own authority, and without the sanction of the Chinese Government, deliberately provoked a resumption of hostilities, and paid for doing so with overwhelming defeat.

The Chinese frontier forces were at this time divided into three independent bodies, under the commands of the local generals at Chamdo and Batang and the Frontier Commissioner at Tachienlu respectively, each of whom controlled civil and military affairs in his own sphere, and regarded one another, and the various provincial authorities of Western China, with mutual distrust and suspicion.

4—2

The Chinese general commanding at Chamdo, named P'eng Jih-sheng, had been on the frontier since the beginning of Chao Erh-feng's campaigns, and for the past few years had been absolute autocrat of the northern districts of the border under his control, appointing and dismissing civil and military officials, and collecting and disposing of the revenues of the country. He was notorious for his intolerant attitude towards the Tibetans, who in turn held him responsible for the destruction of the great monasteries of Chamdo, Draya, and Yemdo in previous campaigns, and who therefore regarded him as the arch-enemy after the disappearance of Chao Erh-feng.

Towards the end of 1917 General P'eng, chafing under the continued neglect of himself and his troops by the Chinese Government and the Authorities of Szechuan, which had indeed reduced his command to the direst straits, apparently conceived the idea of breaking the truce and advancing on Lhasa on his own responsibility, with the two-fold object of securing loot and supplies, and of obtaining the post of Frontier Commissioner, or of Resident in Tibet, by bringing off a striking victory against the Tibetans. Imbued, perhaps, with the recollection of Chao Erh-feng's easy victories against the ill-armed lamas and tribesmen of Kam and Chung Ying's unopposed march to Lhasa, he and his advisers played directly into the hands of the Tibetans, and gave them the opportunity they wanted to recover some of the country of which they had been deprived by Chao Erh-feng.

A pretext for resuming hostilities was easily found in an incident which occurred between the opposing Chinese and Tibetan outposts beyond Riwoche, a few marches north-west of Chamdo. A trivial dispute arose over the cutting of grass for fodder on the mountain which served as a boundary between the two sides, and the Chinese seized a subordinate Tibetan officer and carried him off to Chamdo. The Tibetans attempted a rescue and some skirmishing took place. The Chinese thereupon claimed that the truce was at an end, and prepared to advance.

It appears that the Kalon Lama, commanding the Tibetan frontier army, did all he could in reason to avoid a resumption of hostilities, and that he wrote to General P'eng on several occasions, demanding the surrender of the Tibetan officer and reminding the Chinese that both sides had agreed in 1914 to keep the peace pending a final settlement by diplomatic means with the mediation of Great Britain. His first communication was left unanswered; the reply to his second was a letter filled with dung; and he was finally informed in answer to his third appeal that the Chinese were advancing on Lhasa. The following is a translation of a letter addressed to the Kalon Lama by General P'eng on this occasion; it was apparently dated early in January, 1918:

> I have received your letters. You must be aware that Tibet, which was formerly subject to the Emperor of China, is now subject to the President of the Chinese Republic. You Tibetans have rebelled, as servants revolting against their masters. Evil thoughts have entered your hearts and your lips have uttered falsehoods. The Chinese Emperor can protect his own dominions and has no need of British mediation. The Chinese soldiers who have advanced from Riwoche are travelling in their own country and can go where they please. The Chinese forces are now about to advance on Lhasa, and you are ordered to make all the necessary preparations for their march.

At the same time the Chinese troops did actually advance from Riwoche, and killed a high Tibetan officer in the resulting fight. The Kalon Lama thereupon declared the truce at an end and called his men to arms.

General P'eng's plans appear to have been to advance in three columns, one by the North Road from Riwoche, one by the main road from Enda, and one by a road from Draya leading across the Mekong into the Tibetan district of Bashü. All three columns duly advanced, and the first two were driven back, fighting stubbornly, on Chamdo. The Draya column crossed the Mekong, met the enemy, and fled precipitately in such confusion that the Tibetans followed on their heels and captured Draya, together with two mountain guns and several hundreds of Chinese soldiers with their rifles, within a short time of the opening of hostilities.

The fall of Draya cut the main road in General P'eng's rear, and the two big passes on the De-ge road being seized by the Tibetans immediately afterwards, Chamdo was completely invested. South of Draya the Tibetans advanced into Markam, captured or dispersed all the Chinese troops stationed in that neighbourhood, and reached and occupied the old historical frontier line on the Bum La (Chinese Ning-ching Shan).

General P'eng managed to get messages out from Chamdo

by the North Road and summoned an outlying battalion garrisoning Kanze, the only one of his battalions still intact, to his aid. These troops advanced rapidly to the neighbourhood of Toba, two marches short of Chamdo, where they were surrounded by the Tibetans in a monastery and surrendered after a short fight. Another small relief force, bringing up supplies and ammunition from the direction of Tachienlu, only reached De-ge Gönchen, where they learned of the Tibetan victories and whence they fled precipitately back to Kanze.

Chamdo was now completely cut off. The Chinese garrison inside, however, about a thousand strong, put up a strong resistance, unlike the other battalions of the frontier force, which had in each case been surrounded and had surrendered with scarcely a fight. At length, after a siege lasting several months, in the course of which more than half of the garrison were killed or died of disease, General P'eng capitulated towards the end of April, 1918.

The following is a *précis* translation of a Chinese account of the events which led to a resumption of hostilities between China and Tibet towards the end of 1917, of the surrender of the Chinese relief force at Toba, and of the siege and fall of Chamdo. It was written by the Commandant of the battalion of General P'eng's Frontier Force which surrendered at Toba, and was printed and published at Batang in the summer of 1918. A full translation, from which this summary is taken, was published in the *North China Herald* of Shanghai.

During the autumn of 1917 an officer of the artillery stationed at Riwoche took some soldiers to cut grass on the mountain side, where he happened to meet two Tibetan soldiers, whom he caused to be seized and taken back to Riwoche. When the Kalon Lama heard of this he wrote to General P'eng requesting that the affair be settled by negotiation. General P'eng, however, ordered the two Tibetans to be sent to Chamdo.

The Tibetans then placed men in ambush and fired on our troops, who withdrew to Riwoche. But T'ien, the Commandant of the Riwoche battalion, sent reinforcements which drove off the Tibetans. General P'eng thereupon ordered Chang, Commandant of the 7th battalion, to advance from Chamdo to Riwoche.

At that time I strongly advised the General to proceed with caution in this matter, and to enter into negotiations with the Kalon Lama before sending reinforcements. But he would not agree, and ordered me to proceed with my battalion also to Riwoche. There we held a conference, myself and Commandants Chang and T'ien, as a result of which we wrote

PLATE XI

LOCAL TIBETAN HEADMEN IN KAM (DRAYA STATE)

TIBETAN OFFICIALS FROM LHASA IN KAM

PLATE XII

TIBETAN HEADQUARTERS AT CHAMDO, 1918

TIBETAN VILLAGERS PETITIONING AN OFFICIAL ON THE FLAT ROOF OF A FARM-HOUSE IN KAM

to the Kalon Lama proposing negotiations, and suggesting that each party should keep to their own boundaries and punish their own offenders. But Commandant Chang, unknown to the others, secretly wrote a private letter, and wrecked the whole affair.

Again I suggested to General P'eng that the matter be settled by negotiation, since the Tibetans had agreed to that course and to both sides keeping to their own boundaries and punishing their own offenders. Subsequently I received orders to return to Chamdo, where I informed the General of Chang's secret designs. The very next day a despatch was received from Commandant T'ien to the effect that Chang had advanced during the night with his battalion, had been surrounded, and was in great danger.

The General then ordered me to advance on Riwoche with two companies. Again I made representations, entreating him to refer to the Governor of Szechuan for instructions before taking further hostile action against the Tibetans. But he insisted on fighting, and I had to proceed towards Riwoche.

Later on I received orders to leave the front in order to arrange certain matters on the North Road. When about to depart I repeatedly warned the General not to fight the Tibetans, and advised him to instruct Commandant Chang not to advance without orders. But he only replied that he was not afraid of the enemy.

I accordingly left Chamdo for Tachienlu, whence I wrote to the General telling him of civil war raging in China and of the impossibility of securing the requisite supplies of arms and ammunition, and advising him to negotiate peace with the Tibetans.

At the end of the year I was appointed with my battalion to Kanze. No sooner had I taken over the seals of office there than I received an urgent despatch from General P'eng ordering me to proceed with all haste with my troops to aid in the defence of Chamdo, and to raise local militia levies everywhere for the same purpose.

I wrote to the General from De-ge Gönchen, telling him that the relief force I was bringing was too small to be of any use. Advancing further to T'ungp'u I received another message from the General urging me to hasten on, and directing me to advance to Toba and fight my way through to Chamdo on a certain day on which he would send troops to fight their way out to meet me. I thereupon determined to attack Toba and Reya.

Again a further special courier reached me from the General with a message to the effect that a concerted effort was to be made on a fixed day to effect a junction of our forces and overcome the enemy.

Accordingly I started in due course from Chorzhung for Beri monastery. On arrival there I found the enemy in force ahead, and so decided to hold the monastery. The battle then began, the Tibetans pressing closely on the building, climbing through the windows and on to the roof. Just as I was considering the advisability of ordering a retreat, my revolver was seized and I was made a prisoner. Some of the soldiers were killed, others were wounded, and the rest surrendered. General P'eng had agreed to make a sortie on that day, but had failed to do so.

Shortly afterwards I was sent to Olo Ch'iao as a prisoner, and was subsequently removed to Chamdo. All the others were sent into Tibet.

The following are the details of the siege and fall of Chamdo.

Before the Szechuan bridge and the hills overlooking the town were captured the Kalon Lama wrote on several occasions urging that the matter be settled by negotiation. But in reply General P'eng filled his letters with dung, reviled the Kalon Lama, and challenged him to fight. The Tibetans captured the hills behind the town. The Szechuan bridge was hard pressed and then captured. Thereupon the General surrendered. Two guns and over 1,400 rifles were given up. Commandant Chang committed suicide by jumping intc the river.

General P'eng placed his private treasure, over 40,000 rupees, in a coffin and buried it; but the Tibetans were informed by spies, and dug it up. This naturally led to their digging up all the graves of the soldiers honourably killed in action.

General P'eng's actions were throughout influenced by a letter he had received holding out hopes that he might secure the post of Frontier Commissioner.

During the siege General Nieh, second-in-command, suggested the advisability of arranging a truce. He was accused of being in communication with the Tibetans, and General P'eng caused him to be summarily shot. His secretary was decapitated.

After the surrender the captured soldiers were sent off into Tibet. The wounded men, when about to start, vainly begged General P'eng for a few rupees. Whereupon the Kalon Lama, hearing of this, gave to each man some rice and eight rupees.

Then the Kalon Lama came himself to Chamdo, and General P'eng gave him presents, and petitioned for a post under the Lhasa Government. But the Kalon summoned the General to his presence, and asked him whether he represented the Central Government of China, or the Governor General of Szechuan Province, or the Frontier Commissioner; why had he killed the Tibetan messengers; why had he replied with letters filled with dung; why had he refused to negotiate a peaceful settlement; what were his present intentions? General P'eng replied laying all the blame on his subordinate officers, who, he explained, had insisted on fighting. The Kalon remarked that he, General P'eng, had executed his second-in-command; why had he not also dealt in like manner with his disobedient subordinates. The General then begged for mercy.

With the fall of Chamdo the greater part of the old Szechuan Frontier Force (*Pien Chün*), which had garrisoned the border since the days of Chao Erh-feng, had ceased to exist. Two or three thousand Chinese prisoners of war were marched off to Lhasa, where they were well treated, judging by oriental standards, and whence they were subsequently repatriated to West China as in 1912 with the assistance of the British Authorities, *via* India, Burma, and Yunnan.

The Chinese troops, still left to defend the frontier against the advancing Tibetans, consisted of a few worn-out and demoralised battalions, the remnants of the Frontier Force, at Batang and other stations on the South Road, and the Frontier Commissioner's own brigade at Tachienlu. No move was made by either of these commands to save General P'eng and his troops in Chamdo. The troops at Batang were in any case incapable of making an offensive movement owing to lack of arms, ammunition and supplies, while General Ch'en Hsia-ling, the Frontier Commissioner, apart from his probable reluctance to assist a dangerous rival who had brought on his own destruction by his own acts, was at that time engaged (after the fashion of the various semi-independent military leaders in Western China) in a private campaign against another Szechuanese general, named Chang Wu-lan, in the Chiench'ang valley south-east of Tachienlu. When, however, having defeated and put to death Chang Wu-lan, and possessed himself of the latter's stores of ammunition, silver and opium, it became apparent that the Tibetan advance would, unless promptly checked, reach Tachienlu itself, General Ch'en Hsia-ling found himself compelled to turn his attention to the frontier, and hurriedly despatched two to three thousand troops along the North Road to Kanze with orders to meet and check the Tibetan advance. In the meantime, however, the Tibetans, assisted by the entire native populations of the newly-recovered territories, had overrun Chamdo, Draya, Markam, Gonjo and De-ge, and were approaching Kanze and Nyarong (Chantui) in one direction, and Batang in another.

By the middle of the summer of 1918 the Tibetans, advancing on Nyarong and Kanze from De-ge, had reached the village of Rongbatsa, a long day's march west of Kanze, which was held by the main body of the Frontier Commissioner's troops. Heavy fighting at Rongbatsa ensued, with the result that the Chinese, while holding their entrenched positions in the village, found their communications with their base at Kanze in danger of being cut by the more mobile Tibetan forces, who were also working round into Nyarong, and thus threatening to cut off the entire Chinese army from Tachienlu. At the same time a large Tibetan force was massed on the old Bum La frontier line for an advance on Batang; while another Tibetan column, marching south from De-ge, had surrounded a battalion of the Batang command thrown forward to meet them at a place called Gaji. Another month or two would possibly have seen several thousand more Chinese prisoners in Tibetan hands, and the Lhasa forces in possession of all the country up to Tachienlu.

At this juncture, however, the local Chinese leaders on the frontier invoked the mediation of the British Consular Agent stationed in Western China, whose duty it was to watch events on the border with a view to keeping the peace between the two parties pending a final settlement of the dispute by diplomatic means, and, the Tibetan leaders having been persuaded to stay their advance, the fighting ceased. The truce, however, was only just effected in time; for the further the Tibetans advanced towards Tachienlu, into regions like Batang, Litang, Kanze, Nyarong, and Chala, the more difficult a settlement became; since it would have been equally difficult to induce the Tibetans to withdraw from regions they had once occupied as to persuade the Chinese to surrender their claim to districts which they had long regarded as part of Szechuan province.

Peace negotiations followed between the various Chinese and Tibetan frontier authorities, the British representative acting as middleman, and arrangements were eventually concluded providing for a general cessation of hostilities, and the mutual withdrawal of the troops of both sides out of touch with one another. The provisional boundary between Szechuan and Tibet resulting from these frontier negotiations chanced to coincide to a considerable extent with the old seventeenth century line of the Manchus, the Chinese remaining in control of Batang, Litang, Nyarong, Kanze and the country to the east of those States, while the Tibetans retained Chamdo, Draya, Markam and De-ge, and the country further west. By the end of 1918 the frontier regions had settled down after the conclusion of the truce, the trade routes had been reopened, and peaceful relations generally had once more been resumed between China and Tibet[1].

[1] The journeys described in the following chapters were made in connection with these peace negotiations.

MAP 5

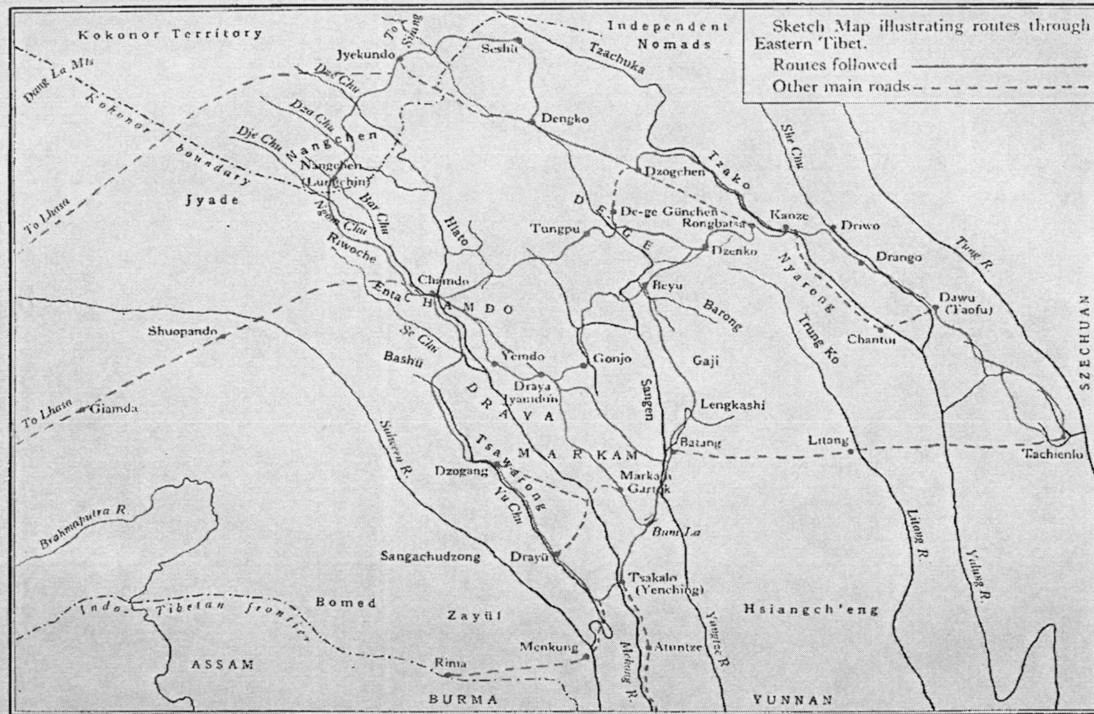

Sketch Map illustrating routes through Eastern Tibet.
Routes followed
Other main roads
Kokonor Territory
Independent Nomads
Dang La Mts
Kokonor boundary
To Lhasa
To Siling
Jyekundo
Seshü
Tzachuka
Dengko
Dzogchen
Tzako
Dza Chu
Dza Chu
Dje Chu
Nangchen
Nangchen (Lungchin)
Jyade
Bar Chu
Ngom Chu
Riwoche
Hlato
D E G E
De-ge Günchen
Rongbatsa
Kanze
Driwo
Drango
Tung R.
She Chu
Dawu (Taofu)
Tungpu
Dzenko
Nyarong
Trung Ko
Chantui
Beyu
Barong
Chamdo
Enta
C H A M D O
Shuopando
Se Chu
Bashü
Yemdo
Gonjo
Gaji
Draya Lyandum
D R A Y A
Sangen
Lengkashi
To Lhasa
Giamda
Salween R.
Tsawarong
M A R K A M
Batang
Litang
Tachienlo
SZECHUAN
Dzogang
Markam Gartok
Yu Chu
Bum La
Litang R.
Yalung R.
Brahmaputra R.
Sangachudzong
Drayü
Tsakalo (Yenching)
Bomed
Zayül
Hsiangch'eng
Indo-Tibetan frontier
Menkung
Mekong R.
Atuntze
Yangtze R.
ASSAM
Rima
BURMA
YUNNAN

TRAVELS IN EASTERN TIBET

CHAPTER I

FROM TACHIENLU TO KANZE BY THE MAIN NORTH ROAD

Departure from Tachienlu—The first big pass on the road to Tibet—Taining and Gata Gomba—Tea and *tsamba*—Nadreheka Dzong and the forests of Sunglink'ou—Silver pheasants and stags—A caravan from Tibet—Dawu—Reforming the caravan—Catholic Mission at Dawu—Racial types of Eastern Tibet—The *Horba*—Tibetan houses—Catholic settlement at Sharatong—Chinese colonists in Tibet and Mongolia—Hor Drango—Resemblance between Lamaism and Roman Catholicism—Collecting subscriptions for the Buddhist Society of Tachienlu—Hor Driwo—Snow mountains of the Yangtze-Yalung divide—Kanze and its monastery—Rumours of Chinese reverses—Difficulties of proceeding west of Kanze.

March 6. At TACHIENLU[1].

All our preparations are now complete and we leave for Tibet to-morrow. Our party will be a very mixed one, consisting of myself, three Pekinese servants, four Tibetans, a Chinese Mahomedan, a local Chinese-Tibetan half-caste (who acts as interpreter in the various dialects of Eastern Tibet and superintends the caravan), and also three Tibetan retainers of the ex-Rajah of Chala, who are accompanying us part of the way on business of the latter. The caravan consists of twenty odd animals, ponies for ourselves, and mules for the baggage and tents.

[1] The little border town of Tachienlu (a Chinese transliteration of the Tibetan name *Dartsendo*) lies in a narrow cleft in the snow-capped range which in this neighbourhood forms the racial boundary between Chinese and Tibetans. Coming from Szechuan, the traveller will up to this point see scarcely any signs of a Tibetan population; but proceeding west and crossing the big range, he will find himself, though a long way from the political frontier of Tibet Proper, in purely Tibetan country, without any signs of a Chinese population. In Tachienlu itself, which is nowadays a Chinese town, the two races meet and mingle. Kalgan, which lies north of Peking just on the Chinese side of the Mongolian plateau, and Sining, which lies west of Lanchow in Kansu just on the Chinese side of the Kokonor grass-lands, are border cities of the same type. Two main roads lead from Tachienlu into Tibet, the South Road *via* Litang and Batang, and the North Road *via* Kanze. The former used to be better known, as it was the route usually taken by Chinese and foreign travellers. At present, however, it has fallen into disuse owing to the disturbances which have prevailed of recent years on that part of the frontier, and the North Road presents for the time being the best way into Tibet. Tachienlu, now the seat of a Chinese magistrate, was formerly the capital of the semi-independent Native State of Chala.

March 12. At TAINING.

We left Tachienlu on the 7th and marched for three days up the northern branch of the Tachienlu river to a camp near the foot of the pass. There is some beautiful scenery in this valley, which consists of forest, cultivated fields, and park-like grass-lands. Numerous farms and hamlets and good camping grounds are passed, and one can make the stages as long or as short as one pleases. It is all good country for pheasants, both the ordinary Tachienlu variety and the beautiful long-tailed bird[1].

On the 10th of March we crossed the big pass, the Zhara La (in Chinese Haitzu Shan, i.e. Lake Mountain, about 14,000 feet high). On the summit of the pass, which is flat, there is a small lake, now a sheet of ice. Immediately overlooking the pass on the left hand is a peak of ice and snow, probably 20,000 feet or more in height, which is a prominent land-mark and a useful map bearing for a long way round. The descent is at first by easy gradients, past another small lake, and then by a steep drop into a flat well-timbered valley where we camped.

Our camping ground here was a delightful spot, a small grassy clearing in the forest of pines, junipers and rhododendrons, by the side of a clear streamlet, lying underneath the glaciers of the great Haitzu Shan, whose northern face presents a huge wall of ice. The only drawback was the fact that the locality was notorious for *Chagba*[2] and horse thieves, as is usually the case in forested country in these parts. During the night some horsemen were heard approaching along the main trail a hundred yards or so away; whether they were brigands or not we never knew. Our watch dog, a fine Tibetan mastiff called Domna ("Black Bear," a most appropriate name), woke everyone up, and our men proceeded to discharge their rifles into the air, which, as in China, is the recognised and usually effective method of scaring off robbers.

On the next day we marched to Taining, down the wooded valley to a point where the stream bends east, then up a

[1] For particulars of these pheasants see pp. 219 and 220.

[2] Mounted brigands are called *Chagba* all over Tibet, from Ladak to Tachienlu. It is very difficult to hunt them down, as, with small bags of *tsamba* attached to their saddles for food, they are independent of commissariat and supplies and can move rapidly from place to place through the most inaccessible mountains.

PLATE XIII

THE FRONTIER TOWN OF TACHIENLU, LOOKING DOWN THE VALLEY ALONG THE MAIN ROAD LEADING TO CHINA

THE FRONTIER TOWN OF TACHIENLU, LOOKING UP THE VALLEY ALONG THE MAIN ROAD LEADING TO TIBET

PLATE XIV

VALLEY LEADING UP FROM CHINA TO THE SNOW RANGE OVERLOOKING TACHIENLU, THE RACIAL BOUNDARY BETWEEN CHINESE AND TIBETANS

VALLEY LEADING DOWN INTO TIBETAN COUNTRY ON THE REVERSE SLOPE OF THE SAME RANGE

narrow ravine through more pine forests, and finally over a small pass and down the other side into an open valley.

Taining consists of a large monastery and a small village lying in the middle of a treeless valley plain, probably an old lake basin. In winter the scene much resembles the western hills at Peking, a bleak, dusty and windswept landscape. The monastery (*Gelugba* sect, three or four hundred lamas) is called Gata Gomba. In the central temple are statues of two former Dalai Lamas. One was a native of the locality; the other was deposed by the Chinese and interned in this neighbourhood. When we called, the lamas were making ready for some religious ceremony by preparing intricate patterns of coloured sand, the usual wheels and other devices, on the floor of the temple, the sand being poured out of hollow tubes in a very ingenious way.

Taining used to be a gold-washing centre, but the neighbourhood is now worked out. The abandoned workings, in the shape of pits in the gravelly soil by the streams, are everywhere to be seen.

The weather has so far been very fine, hot sun and cloudless skies during the day, and mild frosts at night. But we are warned that the snowy season is approaching, and that we must expect a bad time on the big passes during the next month or two. In view of the long distances ahead we are travelling very easily. Starting every morning at day-break we march ten or twelve miles and then camp, usually before midday, so as to give the animals the whole of the afternoon to graze. This is the usual method of travel followed by the Tibetans.

As I write these lines the Tibetan members of our party are preparing their evening meal in full view. First a fire is quickly lit between three stones with the help of the Tibetan bellows, an indispensable adjunct to travel in these parts. It consists simply of a metal pipe attached to a skin bag. Every Tibetan can operate this contrivance, which is useless to a Chinese or European unless he has discovered the peculiar knack of working it. A handful of pressed leaves and twigs is broken off the brick of Yachou tea and boiled in a copper bowl over the fire, and the tea is then poured through a strainer into a churn, a pat of butter (usually rancid) and some salt are added, and the whole churned up until it resembles *café au lait* in appearance. This concoction in no way resembles the European idea of tea; but it is not so bad if one is cold, hungry and thirsty, and regards it as a kind of gruel. The Tibetans at any rate cannot do without it, perhaps because they so seldom eat vegetables. Indian tea, which does not stew well, is not suitable for making a brew of this kind. When the tea is ready it is mixed by means of one's fingers with *tsamba* (the flour of roasted barley) in a small bowl which every Tibetan carries in the folds of his gown, and is eaten in the form of damp lumps of dough. Chinese who are unaccustomed to it say *ch'ih pu pao* ("impossible to satisfy one's hunger on it"), and that would probably be the verdict of most foreigners too.

March 17. At DAWU.

Leaving the Taining valley, the road runs north-west across a series of grassy ridges and ravines on the side of the range which serves as the watershed between the Yalung and the Tung rivers. On the left-hand side is a deep valley, beyond which rise the grassy mountains of Nyarong. Twelve miles out the trail descends into this valley near the hamlet of Jyesodrong (Chinese Chiehsechung), where the main road *via* the Ji La (Chinese Cheto Shan) is joined. Following up the wooded valley, the junction of two streams is reached, where an old Tibetan fort, called Nadreheka Dzong by the Tibetans, and Kuan Chai[1] by the Chinese, lies on a grassy bluff between the two ravines. It was built by the Rajah of Chala at the time of the war between Chala and Nyarong in the early nineties, and is now used by the Chinese as a rest-house.

From here the trail ascends very gradually over a flat plateau of grass-land for a few miles to reach the pass (elevation 13,500 feet), the top of which is so flat as to be imperceptible from this side. One only realises that the summit has been reached when the trail drops abruptly over the edge of the plateau into a wooded gorge. In the forest below the pass there is a camping ground and a ruined rest-house, lying at the confluence of two streams, called Mejesumdo[2]. De-

[1] The words *Dzong* in Tibetan, and *Kuan Chai* in Chinese, mean an official fort.

[2] The Tibetan name termination *do* means the confluence of two streams, as in Dartsendo, Jyekundo, Chamdo, and hundreds of other place names in Kam: a variation is *sumdo*, i.e. "three stream confluence."

scending through the forest, one finally emerges on to an open valley with farms and cultivated fields called Chyapa.

The wooded gorge leading down from the pass is called by the Chinese Sunglink'ou ("Pine Forest Valley"), and the neighbourhood is greatly feared as a haunt of *Chagba*, who ambush travellers from amongst the pine trees. The passage of time seems to make but little difference to conditions in Eastern Tibet. In 1882, the Indian explorer[1], A. K., wrote, with reference to this gorge: "The route passes through heavy forest, and the robbers from the Nyarong district generally plunder travellers in the neighbourhood of the pass."

Between Nadreheka Dzong and the pass a trail leads off to the left over another pass to a valley called Muru, an outlying district of Chala on the borders of Nyarong, in which the Chala Chief took refuge in a small monastery called Hoti Gomba, during the troubles of 1912, when the Chinese burnt his palace in Tachienlu and executed his brother. The Chinese either did not know where he was, or did not dare pursue him and his bodyguard of faithful retainers into such a difficult country of narrow forested valleys and high snow mountains. Later on he made his peace with the Chinese, and has since rendered them much assistance from time to time when they are in difficulties with the natives in their administration of the country. Muru appears to lie in or near the valley of the She Chu, probably near the latter's junction with the Yalung, and can also be reached by following the valley down from Dawu. Although this main road is well known, the country on either side is all entirely unexplored.

Sitting on the flat roof of the headman's house at Chyapa in the evening I watched a large flock of big silver pheasants[2] emerge one by one out of the forest on to the ploughed fields. They are always to be seen in the morning and evening feeding in the cornfields on the edges of the forests. But immediately anyone approaches them they run up hill amongst the pine trees. The only way to shoot them is to descend on them from above.

[1] The Indian explorer Krishna was sent out by the Government of India in 1879, and returned in 1882, having performed a journey through the length and breadth of Tibet which will always remain one of the greatest feats of exploration ever accomplished.

[2] See p. 220.

These forests round Chyapa harbour also a fine stag, a sort of sambar[1], with heavy three-tined antlers. The Tibetans say they are easily shot with the help of dogs.

From Chyapa to Dawu is a march of twelve miles down the valley by a good road. On the way we met one of the large Tibetan caravans, consisting of hundreds of mules, carrying wool, hides, deers' horns, musk, medicines and other Tibetan produce, to Tachienlu. At this time of the year we ought to be meeting these caravans daily, and their absence is a sign of the disturbed conditions prevailing in the interior owing to the resumption of hostilities between Szechuan and Tibet.

Dawu (in Chinese Taofu Hsien) is the seat of a Chinese magistrate established here by Chao Erh-feng. It lies in a small cultivated plain sloping down towards the river at an elevation of about 10,000 feet. The soil of the valley appears to be a kind of loess, of much the same nature as the famous yellow earth of Shensi and Kansu. Earthquakes are a special feature of the place. The river is called the She Chu. It takes its rise somewhere on the unknown grass country of the north, and here turns west through a gorge in the mountains to join the Yalung at some spot unknown.

In view of the long distances ahead we are resting here a couple of days to refresh and reform the caravan. Three of our mules have to be replaced by new purchases; in each case they were too young, so that their backs were not hardened to the load. One learns by experience, and we already know considerably more about Tibetan mules than when we started. They should be of the thickset, short-legged type, and preferably too old than too young; incipient sores on the back, under the girth, and under the root of the tail must be constantly watched for. If a swelling appears on the back of a young animal, the only cure is to let him run free for two or three weeks; otherwise the swelling bursts, and a large festering sore results which will take months to cure.

Yesterday we shot some duck on the river, and also a goose.

The Tibetans of Dawu belonged formerly to the Chiefs of Chala, Drango, Ge-she, and Mazur. The boundaries of these

[1] See p. 217.

PLATE XV

THE FIRST OF MANY CAMPS

TIBETANS OF KAM MAKING TEA

PLATE XVI

IN THE SHE CHU VALLEY, NEAR DRANGO

DRIWO, CASTLE OF THE NATIVE CHIEF

old States were most intricate, the jurisdictions of the Chiefs being over families rather than fixed territories. The representative of the family of the former Mazur Rajah lives in a village close by.

Dawu consists of a large *Gelugba* monastery with many hundreds of monks and a Tibetan village. We called on the monastery to-day, and saw some fine but odoriferous base reliefs of butter made in honour of the New Year festivities.

There is a Catholic Mission at Dawu, one of the stations of the *Mission du Tibet*, and for a short time the Protestant China Inland Mission had a branch here too. The Catholics established themselves here in Chao Erh-feng's time, shortly before the revolutionary troubles of 1911. In 1912, at the time of the widespread risings against the Chinese in Eastern Tibet, there was serious trouble at Dawu, and the Catholics, who on this frontier are compelled by force of circumstances to identify themselves with the Chinese, though their Mission is supposed to be a purely Tibetan one, suffered very severely.

The language spoken at Dawu (perhaps akin to that used in the Gyarong States further east) is a very corrupt form of Tibetan, if indeed it is Tibetan dialect at all. There is a curious mixture of racial types amongst the Tibetans of these borderlands, including the flat-faced Mongolian type, the tall thin-faced Aryan type, and a curly-haired and almost negroid type. The man I bought two mules off here had a strong beard, and a Turkish cast of countenance. In this connection it may be mentioned that the word Hor (referring to the Five Hor States, *Horsekanga* in Tibetan, which lie in this neighbourhood a little further north) means, according to Sarat Chandra Dass' Tibetan Dictionary, a Dzungarian Mongol of Turkestan. It is possible that these *Horba*[1] represent the remnants of the hordes of Dzungarian Mongols who overran Tibet and occupied Lhasa some two centuries ago.

March 22. At Drango.

On the 18th we marched up the She Chu valley, partly through gorges and partly through cultivated fields, to some farms called Tromne in Tibetan, and Tachai in Chinese. A few miles out a trail branches off north to the Erhkai gold

[1] The termination *ba* or *wa*, means native of, e.g. *Bōba*, a Tibetan, *Horba*, a man of Hor, *Nyarongwa*, a man of Nyarong.

mines, which, together with some in Nyarong (Chantui), are said to be the most productive on the frontier at the present time; further on another path leads up a branch valley northwards to Yuko, the seat of a small Chief deposed by Chao Erh-feng.

There are no inns in Eastern Tibet, and the traveller must either camp or quarter himself on the villagers. The houses of the wealthier inhabitants are very good, and offer much better accommodation than the homes of similar villagers in China. They are all of the same style of architecture, square built, with mud or stone exteriors, and are usually lined with clean wood inside. On the ground floor are the stables and cowsheds; on the first floor the living rooms; and on the second floor the granaries. The doors and windows, the latter generally of solid wood, slide horizontally in and out; and communication from floor to floor is usually by means of a notched pole. Tibetan houses have nothing in common with Chinese buildings; and in this, as in so many other respects, one passes from one civilisation to the other with startling abruptness on this border[1].

On March 19, a cold raw day with falling snow, we continued up the She Chu valley to a hamlet called Gara (in Chinese the locality is known as Jentakou). About half-way a tributary stream is crossed by a bridge, called by the Chinese Chiangchün Ch'iao ("The General's Bridge"), presumably in commemoration of some incident in the old Manchu campaigns. Here the river bends west, and the road crosses a *col* 1000 feet high to rejoin the valley at Gara.

There is a skin coracle[2] at Gara, and a trail leading west up a gorge and across the mountains to Nyarong (Chantui in Chinese) in the valley of the Yalung river, about two and a half marches distant.

From Gara we marched up the open valley to Sharatong (Chinese Chiachilung). The Catholics (*Mission du Tibet*)

[1] In the tribal country immediately west of the lowlands of Szechuan, the inhabitants, who are not of pure Tibetan race, construct peculiar towers, always of the same type, in their villages, apparently for purposes of defence. These towers, which are characteristic of the Gyarong States (lying just west of the Chengtu plain in Szechuan) are never seen in real Tibetan country further west.

[2] The skin coracle is in universal use on the rivers of Eastern Tibet, where boats are never seen. The Tibetan coracle is usually circular and is made of yak hides stretched over a frame-work of wood. It will hold three to five men in the water and is at the same time so light that it can be carried on a man's back. See Plates Nos. XXXVIII, XLVI and LVII.

have an establishment here, their most advanced post on the North Road, but, as elsewhere on this border, their work lies mainly amongst the Chinese. They have here founded an agricultural colony where Chinese settlers are engaged in ploughing up the grass prairie of the She Chu valley. The general appearance of the place reminds one of the agricultural colonies on the Mongolian grass-lands north of Chihli and Shansi provinces in China. All previous attempts, made by Chinese officials, to settle Chinese on the land in Eastern Tibet have failed, and the apparent success of this Catholic colony is therefore of interest. The explanation appears to be that the settlers are for the most part semi-tribesmen from the border country, and not pure Chinese. Generally speaking, the Chinese, and especially the Szechuanese, seem incapable of settling on the bleak uplands of Kam, perhaps because they cannot stand the climate. The position on this frontier is in this respect quite different to that on the north China-Mongolian border, where the sturdy natives of Chihli, Shansi, and Shantung are constantly pushing the Mongol further back and ploughing up his pastures[1]. For one thing the Mongol lets himself be pushed back, whereas the Tibetan does not. Then again the Tibetan is just as much an agriculturalist where elevation permits as he is herdsman; whereas the Mongol lives exclusively by his flocks and herds and never takes to agriculture. An interesting point in connection with the expansion of Chinese into Tibet and Mongolia is the fact that whereas in Mongolia the second generation of the Chinese immigrant's half-caste family is usually to all intents and purposes Chinese, in Tibet the half-caste children of Chinese are to all intents and purposes Tibetan.

The North Road from Tachienlu to Jyekundo fringes most of the way the grass-lands of the independent nomads of the north, *Yeh Fan* (Wild Barbarians) as the Chinese call them. Sharatong suffers from the raids of a tribe of these nomads called Seta, over whom neither the Chinese officials nor anyone else has any control. Chao Erh-feng was about to take these particular nomads in hand when he left the frontier in 1911.

[1] I am inclined to think that many parts of Eastern Tibet are practically full up, that is to say, that most of the land which can be cultivated has already been ploughed up by the Tibetans, while the grass-lands too high for cultivation already support as many flocks and herds as they are capable of feeding. Many parts of Mongolia, on the other hand, are far more empty.

Round about Sharatong we shot a good many duck, including some of the large orange-coloured sheldrake (yellow body with white and green-black wings and tail); these are quite edible if well stewed.

On March 21 we marched the remaining ten miles to Drango. The road follows up the valley for a mile or two, crosses the river by a cantilever bridge built by the Catholics, and then ascends the side of a mountain spur past a Tibetan village, crosses the ridge, and descends gently across grassy downs to the village and monastery of Drango.

The Tibetan name for this place is Hor Drango, corrupted by the Chinese into Huoerh Changku (a Tibetan *dr* or *tr* always becomes *ch* in Chinese). The new Chinese name for it is Luho Hsien, from the name of the old military colony Luho Tun, founded at the time of Viceroy Lu Ch'uan-lin's forward move in Eastern Tibet in 1894, at which period the family of the native Rajah became extinct. The place consists of a Tibetan village clustering round the old castle of the former Chief (now the Chinese magistrate's yamen), and is built, at an elevation of about 11,300 feet, on the hillside a few hundred feet above the river. The great Drango monastery lies higher up. Below is a small cultivated plain formed by the junction of a stream called the Ni Chu (Chinese Nipa Kou), with the She Chu; the former flows down from the Seta country in the north. All around are grassy mountains with here and there a patch of pine forest. There is said to be much gold up the Ni Chu[1] valley, but the neighbourhood is considered dangerous owing to the proximity of the Seta nomads.

To-day we called on the monastery, a large *Gelugba* establishment with more than a thousand lamas. The main courtyard was crowded with wild-looking nomads from the north, who had come in for some special occasion. In the central temple a service was going on before a congregation of some

[1] This river gave rise to a curious mixing up of names by that very reliable observer Mr W. W. Rockhill (*Land of the Lamas*): he writes:

"The Nya Chu flows out of the mountains to the North of Chango, a broad river, quite as wide and swifter than the Za Chu above Kanze."

In a footnote he wonders why Nyarong, the valley of the Nya, is the name given to the valley of the Yalung, or Za Chu. The explanation is that the Yalung is called Tza Chu at and above Kanze, and Nya Chu in Nyarong; the Driwo Drango river is the She Chu, joined at Drango by the Ni Chu.

hundreds of lamas presided over by a *Ge-she*[1] sitting up in a pulpit. The intoning of the monks, and the general appearance of the dim interior of the vast hall lit up by rows of little butter lamps, combined to make up an impressive scene, wonderfully reminiscent of a Catholic service. It is a well-known fact that there are many remarkable points of similarity between the ritual of Tibetan Buddhism and Roman Catholicism, concerning which there has been much speculation. I have been re-reading *The Cloister and the Hearth*, and have been much struck by the resemblance between the European monasteries, monks, and monastic life generally of those days as depicted therein, and the lamas and lamaseries of Tibet as I see them to-day. Both in Europe in those days and in Tibet at present the monasteries are the centres of wealth, power and learning, and all educated laymen, including my admirable half-caste Tibetan secretary, are monastery bred[2].

The two lamas attached to the suite of the Chala Chief, who have accompanied us so far, and have done us many small services, leave us here. They are engaged in the peculiar and somewhat delicate mission of collecting a sum of one rupee per head from each monk in every monastery on behalf of the *Fo Chiao Hui* (Buddhist Society) recently started by the Chinese Frontier Authorities of Tachienlu. The scheme is but one of the many shifts invented by the Chinese officials for raising money from the Tibetans, and can naturally only be enforced on the monasteries lying on and near the main road which are well under the Chinese thumb. The Chinese Authorities at Tachienlu are probably not really greatly concerned with Tibetan Buddhism. The ex-Rajah of Chala and a noted monk, called the Draga Lama, have, owing to their prestige and influence amongst the local Tibetans, been honoured by the Chinese officials with the appointments of President and Vice-President respectively of the Buddhist Society. The Draga Lama has to be held a prisoner at Tachienlu to keep him at his post. He is well known through-

[1] A *ge-she* is a monk who has graduated from the clerical colleges of Lhasa with the highest degree, the various ranks of monastic graduates being from the lowest up, *draba*, *genyen*, *getsül*, *gelong*, *ge-she*; only the higher graduates are really *lamas*.

[2] Perhaps the early Buddhists of Tibet came into contact with Armenian or Nestorian Christians.

out Tibet as a monk of profound learning, and until a year or two ago used to live in a small nunnery near Drango[1].

March 24. At DRIWO.

From Drango we descended gradually to the She Chu, leaving a trail to Nyarong up a side ravine on the left-hand side (followed by the French traveller Bacot), and then marched up the open valley to a group of farms called Dangka lying on a spur some hundreds of feet above the river. After spending the night here, we crossed the top of the spur, and, rejoining the She Chu, marched up its valley for the rest of the way to Driwo. Two villages are passed, Chalang and Shochiling (Chinese Sungchiling); near the latter gold washing was being carried on in the gravelly cliffs of the river below the level of the valley floor. On the way we shot some silver pheasants, by making a long détour and getting above them and between them and the depths of the pine forest, on the edges of which they are always found. These remarkable birds are just like white turkeys; nature evidently intended them to simulate patches of snow on the hillside, which they exactly resemble in the distance.

Driwo, in Chinese Chuwo, consists of a Tibetan hamlet clustering round the castle of the former Rajah of Hor Driwo, one of the Five Hor States. The buildings lie on the hillside beyond the river, which is here spanned by a good cantilever bridge. The ex-Chief still resides in his castle, part of which, however, is used by the Chinese as a rest-house.

There are no signs of spring yet, and not a vestige of green is to be seen on the mountains. Eastern Tibet, like North China, is a country of two seasons, winter and summer.

March 28. At KANZE.

Near Driwo the road leaves the She Chu, which comes down from the unknown grass country in the north (and more immediately from a district called Tongkor, where there is an important monastery), and turns up a gully to the west. Passing a village, where the drying of cowpats (*chowa*, the universal fuel where wood is unobtainable) by

[1] Returning along this road a year later we found Chinese proclamations posted calling upon the Tibetans to arrest the Draga Lama, who had escaped from Tachienlu and had fled to the country of the Golok nomads in the north, where he was safe from Chinese interference.

PLATE XVII

JORO GOMBA, WITH PARTLY FROZEN LAKE BELOW

VIEW LOOKING WEST OVER THE YANGTZE-YALUNG WATERSHED RANGE FROM THE LATSE KA PASS NEAR KANZE

PLATE XVIII

PUYULUNG VILLAGE, NEAR KANZE

KANZE GOMBA, ONE OF THE LARGEST MONASTERIES IN KAM

plastering them on the house walls seemed to be the principal industry, we reached the large *Gelugba* monastery of Joro Gomba. This monastery lies on the edge of a grassy basin overlooking a small lake swarming with wild fowl; to shoot them, however, would have been to cause grave offence to the lamas of the *gomba*[1]. Passing Joro, the trail tops a rise and emerges on to rolling grass-lands now patched with snow. Here we saw many gazelle (*gowa* in Tibetan, *chitzu* in Szechuanese). A long pull up hill with occasional short descents brought us to the top of the She Chu-Yalung divide, only about 13,000 feet high. As one tops the last rise, the great range beyond the Yalung bursts into view, a glittering mass of ice, snow and rock, culminating in the snow-clad mass of Kawalori ("peak of everlasting snow"), a sacred mountain of Nyarong, and one of the highest peaks in Eastern Tibet. This great range is here pierced by the Yalung, and glimpses of it are occasionally caught from the She Chu valley below Driwo. From the pass the trail descends across a side valley to reach the cultivated plain along the Yalung and a hamlet called Puyulung, where there is an old fort which now serves as a rest-house. Near by is a monastery.

From Puyulung to Kanze is only about eight miles by a good level road across the plain. The approach to Kanze on a morning of brilliant sunshine is too magnificent to be adequately described. The buildings of the great monastery, a blaze of varied colours, in which white and red predominate, cluster round the gilded roofs of the principal temple. The huge square castles of the former Chiefs of Hor Kangsar and Hor Mazur lie below. All around are mountains of dazzling whiteness; for at this time of the year not only the great barrier range of rock and ice on the south side of the river, but also the low grass downs to the north, are covered with snow.

Kanze[2] lies a mile or so back from the Yalung in the mouth of a ravine in the loess hills which here close in on the river and bring the cultivated plain to an end. It consists of a large *Gelugba* monastery, really a combination of two, housing

[1] Even Tibetan laymen will not usually eat wild fowl or hares.

[2] Kanze is called Kanzego by A. K. and appears in that form on most maps of Tibet; he presumably meant this as an abbreviation for Kanze Gomba; the abbreviation *gon* is often used in Kam for *gomba*.

more than a thousand lamas, the two castles of the former Rajahs, and a small Tibetan village. The elevation is about 11,200 feet. One castle, that of the former Mazur Chief, is now used as the yamen of the Chinese magistrate of Kanze district; the other is still occupied by the ex-Chief of Kangsar, who is now a wealthy trader. Kanze is an important trading, political and religious centre, and may be considered the capital of the former Five Hor States, Hor Kangsar, Hor Beri, Hor Driwo, Hor Drango, and Hor Mazur.

Since the destruction of the great Chamdo monastery, Kanze Gomba is probably the largest in Eastern Tibet. Numerous other small *gomba* are dotted about in the neighbourhood[1].

The Yalung (this being the Chinese name) is called Tza Chu by the Tibetans at Kanze and higher up; whence arise the names Tzako and Tzachuka for regions in its upper basin. Below Kanze the Tibetans call it the Nya Chu, whence arise the names Nyarong (Valley of the Nya), and Nyachuka (Chinese Hok'ou, on the Batang road). A bad trail leads down the Yalung, through the big range, to Nyarong.

Two companies of Chinese troops are at present quartered at Kanze, in the castle of the Kangsar Chief, waiting to be sent west against the Tibetans. One company went forward some time ago, and is rumoured to be surrounded somewhere near Chamdo. The news of events on the border is not reassuring for the Chinese at present. A refugee Chinese soldier from the frontier has just turned up here with the story that he is the sole survivor of the Chinese garrison of Draya, which he reports annihilated by the Tibetans. Chamdo is said to be invested, Chinese authority west of the Yangtse non-existent, and De-ge ripe for revolt.

The Horba States were, before the days of Chao Erh-feng, in close touch with Lhasa, the Chiefs being to some extent under the superintendence of the Lhasa-appointed Governor

[1] Monasteries in Tibet are called either *ling*, *gomba* or *chö-de*; the oldest foundations appear to be the *ling*, the word meaning literally "an island," and being perhaps applied to monasteries as places separated from their surroundings by their holiness (cf. the four great monasteries of Lhasa, Ganden Ling, Sera Ling, Drepung Ling and Tengye Ling). The ordinary monastery in Tibet is called a *Gomba* (literally "a desolate or unfrequented spot"). The *Chö-de* ("religious places") are rather theological colleges. There are also *Hlakang* (literally "Godhouses"), which are temples rather than monasteries, and *Ani Gomba* (nunneries).

of Nyarong[1], and the news of the victorious advance of the Lhasa troops beyond the Yangtze cannot but cause a feeling of restlessness amongst the Tibetans here. The Chiefs, and the more intelligent amongst the lamas and people, however, probably view the situation with considerable uneasiness and alarm. They would doubtless welcome the Lhasa Tibetans if the latter reach these parts; but in their hearts they must feel that they are too near China to be either comfortable or safe under Lhasa rule. They know that though the Chinese may be overwhelmed this year, they are sure to reorganise and return next year, or the year after, or at some later period; and the memories of the campaigns of Chao Erh-feng and Yin Ch'ang-heng are still fresh in the local mind. The purpose of our mission is to stop the advancing Tibetan wave, which threatens to submerge all the country up to Tachienlu. If we are unsuccessful in doing so, years of bitter border warfare will ensue; for the Chinese will never agree to surrender their claims to these districts, which they profess to regard as part of Szechuan; while the Lhasa Tibetans, once they have seized all the country up to Tachienlu, will never retire willingly from regions which they hold to be part of Tibet. The best course would appear to be to endeavour to stop the fighting on, or as near as possible to, the old historical frontier line between the Yangtze and the Mekong; in which case there might be a reasonable chance of inducing both sides to accept the situation.

The principal reason why the Chinese troops here do not advance, at least as far as De-ge, where their presence is urgently needed, is that the nomads of the Yilung grasslands, through which the main road passes just west of Kanze, have become restless under Chinese rule, and have decamped with all their yak and ponies into the Golok country to the north. There is, therefore, no *ula*[2] (forced transport) available for the Chinese troops across the grass country between Rongbatsa, just west of Kanze, and the Yangtze. Without *ula* the Chinese soldier in these parts is completely immobilised.

Although we are travelling with our own animals, and are therefore independent of *ula*, the country further west is, according to Chinese reports, so disturbed and dangerous as

[1] See p. 5. [2] See p. 223.

to make it impossible for us to proceed any further along the main road to Chamdo. Communication even with De-ge Gönchen is now interrupted, the last Chinese couriers sent from here having been shot on the way. The problem has, therefore, resolved itself into finding a way of getting through to the lines of the regular Tibetan forces without passing through the country behind the Chinese front which is more or less in a state of rebellion. The only solution appears to be to make a détour to the north through the neutral territory of the Kokonor, and drop down from the neighbourhood of Jyekundo to the Tibetan headquarters on the upper Salween, or wherever they may be. We are accordingly leaving to-morrow for Jyekundo in the Kokonor by a road up the valley of the Yalung river. The Chinese and Tibetans here, who are both equally anxious that our mission should be successful in restoring peace, have done everything possible to facilitate our journey.

So far, from Tachienlu to Kanze, we have followed a well-beaten track. From here on, however, we shall be making a plunge into country which is more or less unexplored and unknown to European geography.

CHAPTER II

FROM KANZE THROUGH THE TZACHUKA GRASS COUNTRY TO JYEKUNDO IN THE KOKONOR

The plain of Horko—Marching up the Yalung—The *Lao Shan* of E. Tibet—The Golok country—The *Podrang* (castles) of E. Tibet—Denchin Gomba and the Bön, or Black, Sect of Lamaism—Nando and Dzogchen Gomba—The various sects of Lamaism—A snowstorm, and shelter in a nomad's tent—The Native State of Lintsung—A Lhasa caravan—Nojeling Gomba—Dissecting deceased lamas—Dengko and Drölma Hlakang on the Yangtze—Plight of Chinese officials in E. Tibet—Merchants from Kansu—The road to Tzachuka—Crossing the Dzi La (16,000 feet) in a snowstorm—A camp in the snow—Gazelle and wild asses—Seshü district and the grass country of Tzachuka—Seshü Gomba—A Golok raid—Entering the Kokonor Territory—Crossing the Yangtze—Jyekundo—The wool trade—Chinese control over the Kokonor Territory—Kansu Mahomedans at Jyekundo.

March 31. At DEJI PODRANG.

We left Kanze two days ago in fine sunny weather. The trail led south-west across low hills of loess for a mile or two down to the Yalung, and then turned up the left bank between mountain and river. A few miles out a *Sajya* monastery called Nyara Gomba is passed, picturesquely situated on a spur overlooking the river, and painted with the usual stripes of red, white and black by which the monasteries of this sect can always be distinguished. Just beyond Nyara Gomba the village of Beri is reached, clustering round the castle of the former Chief of Hor Beri (Paili in Chinese). Having passed Beri we emerged from the narrow valley on to another large cultivated plain, and soon reached our destination, a group of farms called Dumbugo.

This valley plain, usually called by the Tibetans Horko (valley of the Hor), extends from here to Rongbatsa, a day's march distant to the west, and is the largest tract of level cultivated land in the whole of Eastern Tibet. The elevation is a little over 11,000 feet. The Yalung river winds through the middle of it, and farms, hamlets, and monasteries are thickly dotted about. The inhabitants are prosperous and wealthy, being engaged in the lucrative Chinese-Tibetan tea trade, as well as in agriculture. On the south side of the valley rises the same rocky snow-capped range as at Kanze, while to the north are rolling hills of grass.

The territories of the former Hor Chiefs were most confused as regards situation, and their jurisdictions were over families rather than lands. This village belonged of old to the Driwo Chief.

On March 30 we continued on our way in a snowstorm. For six miles the road lay west across the open plain, and then turned north, following the Yalung up a narrow gorge in the mountains for the rest of the way to a group of farms called Shetanda; a small nunnery lies on the opposite side of the river[1].

The main road, which we left when we turned up the Yalung gorges, continues west across the plain on the other side of the river past Darjye Gomba to Rongbatsa. The Yalung can be crossed by coracle ferry either near Kanze, or at Beri, or near Darjye Gomba.

The Yalung at Shetanda is at this time of the year a deep dark green stream, fifty yards or so wide, swirling with blocks of ice, and flowing with a swift current between mountains rising from the water's edge.

On this march we saw plenty of small game, duck on the river, and hares, small partridges, and silver pheasants on the mountain side.

To-day we made a longer march, travelling all the way up the Yalung, to Deji Podrang. Rather more than half-way we passed the confluence of the Yilung river (Yi Chu) with the Yalung, the former issuing out of a similar narrow cleft in the mountains. Further on the gorges open out into a valley.

This place consists of an old fort, Deji Podrang, formerly the seat of a Tibetan official under the Drango Chief, and a *Gelugba* monastery called Sangdru, or Samdru, Gomba, lying in a small cultivated plain.

The Yalung valley from here up for several days' march is called Tzako (Valley of the Tza).

Except for the half-caste interpreters (*T'ungshih*) practically no Tibetans in the interior of Kam speak Chinese, and I was therefore surprised when a man, to all appearances a Tibetan, came up to me on the flat roof of Deji Podrang and

[1] Nunneries, called *Ani Gomba* in Tibetan, are not uncommon in Kam.

VIEW OVER THE BIG SNOW RANGE (YANGTZE-YALUNG DIVIDE)
LOOKING SOUTH FROM KANZE

CARAVAN OF *DZO* (HALF-BRED CATTLE YAK) RESTING NEAR KANZE

PLATE XX

TIBETANS IN CAMP, UPPER YALUNG BASIN

TIBETANS IN CAMP, UPPER YALUNG BASIN (MANNER OF WEARING THE HAIR USUAL AMONGST THE WOMEN OF KAM)

addressed me in fluent Chinese. He turned out not to be a Tibetan at all, but a *Lao Shan* (a local term designating merchants from Shensi province). These hardy and courageous traders have been established in this valley, which is practically unknown to the ordinary Chinese, for many years for the purpose of tapping the trade of the grass-country nomads of the north, and of exchanging barley, tea and Chinese wares for the wool, skins, furs, deers' horns, musk, gold, and other Tibetan produce of the interior. They are completely Tibetanised in dress and customs, and the second and third generations appear to become Tibetans altogether. The *Lao Shan* are to be found all over the Szechuan-Tibet frontier carrying on the Sino-Tibetan trade in remote parts where no Szechuanese dare go. They have their counterpart on the Kansu border in the *Hsieh Chia*, the Mahomedan middlemen who monopolise the Kokonor trade in a similar way.

The Chinese have never exercised any control over the nomads of the grass-lands north of the Yalung valley above Kanze, which extend from here east to Sungp'an in Szechuan and north across the Yellow river basin to T'aochou and Labrang Gomba in Kansu. This vast extent of country is inhabited by the Golok and other wild nomad tribes, and, being a closed land to Chinese and foreigners, remains one of the least known parts of Asia. It is enclosed in a rough triangle formed by the following three caravan routes, Tachienlu Kanze Jyekundo, Jyekundo Sining, Sining T'aochou Sungp'an Tachienlu; all these roads are subject to raids from the nomads living inside the triangle they enclose. The Golokwa appear to recognise the temporal authority of the Lhasa Tibetans as little as they do that of the Chinese. They are, however, very religious (though adhering mostly to the unreformed red sects), and a Lhasa passport would probably see one through their country in safety. The possession of rifles, which they acquire in the course of trade from the Mahomedan merchants of Kansu, has made them far more formidable than they used to be.

We are quartered here in the old fort, called a *Podrang*. This word, which means, according to the dictionary, a castle or palace, appears to be confined in Central Tibet to the Dalai Lama's residence, i.e. the Potala Podrang at Lhasa.

In Kam it means the castle of a native Rajah, occupied either by the Chief himself, or one of his officials.

April 1. At TROTSANG PODRANG.

This is another old fort, surrounded by a few scattered farms. It was formerly the seat of an official of the Chief of De-ge, and we are now in that State. The road to-day lay all the way up the valley of the Yalung. Two small *Gelugba* monasteries were passed *en route*. The number of monasteries in this sparsely populated valley is remarkable, the explanation apparently being that they serve as religious centres for the surrounding nomads, who always build their monasteries in cultivated valleys if they can.

A few miles before getting in we passed the valley of a branch stream from the north, up which lies a trail to a celebrated *Nyimaba* monastery called Jala Gomba. All these branch valleys lead into unknown and unmapped country, and one would like to follow each of them in turn.

This road up the Yalung has not previously been used to any great extent by the Chinese, and the Tibetans along it are nervous of strangers. It appears that they have good reason to be so; for we learn that a small Chinese force, convoying ammunition to the front, has left Kanze, and, following our example, is travelling along this road to avoid the disturbed area on the main route. They are reported to be seizing transport animals, commandeering supplies, and beating, shooting and maltreating the natives, so that the latter are on the verge of revolt.

The scene on the flat roof of Trotsang Podrang, where I am writing up my diary, is a busy one. Our Chinese Mahomedan from Tachienlu, who acts as butcher to the party, is cutting up a fine sheep which we have just purchased (price, five rupees, returning the skin); one of our Tibetans is mending a saddle and another is buying a sword; the cook is making bread; and two Tibetan women are sifting barley (to eliminate the stones) for the mules' evening feed. Below, a party of Tibetans are crossing the river, three men and their loads in the frail coracle, with two yak swimming in the water tied on behind.

April 2. At BOME GOMBA.

Leaving Trotsang we continued up the open valley for a

few miles to reach another old fort called Dema Podrang, lying alongside a monastery of the Bön sect, Denchin Gomba. This is a celebrated place, reputed the largest monastery of that sect in Eastern Tibet, housing a couple of hundred lamas and a Reincarnation famous in Kam and Amdo for his powers of divination.

The Bön, or Black, sect of Lamaism is generally considered to be a relic of the old pre-Buddhist nature worship of Eastern Asia[1], whose followers in Tibet compromised with the invading Buddhism by adopting the Buddhist saints under different names, and much of the Buddhist ritual reversed, e.g. turning wheels and circumambulating holy places in the wrong direction.

Dema Podrang and Denchin Gomba lie in a sloping plain formed by the junction of the Di Chu, a large tributary from the north, with the Yalung. Up the Di Chu valley lies the main trail to the unknown Golok country. This was the road taken by the Yilung nomads, who recently decamped with their chief from their own grass-lands to the country of the independent nomads of the north, as a protest against the *ula* exactions of the Chinese troops.

Denchin Gomba appears on the latest *Survey of India* map of Tibet, and must have been visited by some foreigner, perhaps a Russian of Kozloff's party.

From Dema Podrang we continued up the Yalung, which here flows in a narrow pine-clad gorge between banks of ice and snow, finally emerging on to a more open valley at this place, another Bön monastery called Bome Gomba, and a few farms. The altitude of the valley is gradually rising, and is here over 12,000 feet. Cultivation is becoming scantier and barley more and more difficult to purchase as we proceed.

We are here in what was formerly the independent Native State of Lintsung, or Gö-ze Lintsung.

There are still several degrees of frost in the early mornings,

[1] Traces of this nature worship are to be found in the rites of the Lolo and Moso sorcerers, in tree worship in China, and in the practices connected with the temples of the Sun, the Moon and the Earth at Peking; and again in the religion of the Chinese Taoist, whose object it is to live in harmony with nature, all evil being a departure from this guiding principle, and who holds that everything in the universe is a constant interplay between the two great forces of nature, the *yang*, the light, active, male principle, and the *yin*, the dark, passive, female principle, the junction of these two elemental forces resulting in life, and their separation in death.

and ploughing has not yet been begun. The barley is sown towards the end of April, and has barely time to ripen before the winter sets in.

April 4. At RUNGU GOMBA.

Yesterday we only made a short march, being delayed at the coracle ferry across the Yalung, near Bome Gomba, by the Chinese ammunition convoy, which here caught us up. It took several hours to get the ammunition across, three coracles being in use all the time.

Last night we camped near a farm, and to-day continued on our way up the valley to Rungu Gomba, a small *Nyimaba* monastery. From here a more direct trail leads north across the Yalung and over the hills to Seshü and Tzachuka. We should have taken that road had it been summer, but the country through which it runs is reported to be very cold and bare of grass at the present time of the year. Moreover, we met a Tibetan from Tzachuka who said that there were rumours current of a Golok raid into Seshü. We have accordingly decided to make for Dzogchen Gomba on the main road, and enquire about our future route when we get there. I was reluctant to give up the direct road, as it would probably have been of some geographical interest in connection with the course of the upper Yalung in this neighbourhood. It is said to pass two large grass-country monasteries, Tsatsa and Gotsa (or Gonsar) Gomba. From local information about this road I gather that the Yalung must make some big bends in this neighbourhood; or perhaps it consists of two branches.

To-day we saw some marmots for the first time; they are said to come out of their hibernating earths on the second day of the second moon (say end of March).

April 5. At NANDO.

This, our last day's march up the Yalung, lay at first through pine-clad gorges, and then through an open grassy valley to this place, a miserable hamlet of half a dozen mud hovels surrounded by a few wretched-looking fields. From here up the Yalung basin is called Tzachuka, and contains only grass country. The elevation of the river is about 12,400 feet.

We found a couple of dozen rather unprepossessing Chinese and half-caste soldiers in occupation of Nando. They had been hurriedly sent down by the Chinese magistrate of Dengko when the news of the revolt of the Yilung nomads reached him in order to keep open his communication with Kanze by this road. As a result, the natives in this valley, hitherto unaccustomed to the exactions of the modern Chinese soldiery, are on the verge of revolt. One can feel rebellion in the air; and wonders how many of these Chinese will ever get out of the country alive.

Yesterday evening a party of pilgrims passed through, returning on foot from Lhasa to their homes in Nyarong. They had been two months or more on the road, and appeared very footsore and weary.

April 7. At DZOGCHEN GOMBA.

At Nando (which means confluence of the Nan river) we left the Yalung and marched up the valley of a tributary stream called the Nan, or Nam, Chu to Dzogchen. A large *Nyimaba* monastery called She-che Gomba is passed on the way. The valley finally debouches on to the open grass-lands of Dzogchen, with the dazzling snow-fields and glaciers behind the monastery in full view.

Dzogchen Gomba is the largest *Nyimaba* monastery in Eastern Tibet. It lies at an elevation of about 13,200 feet on the edge of a basin-like plain immediately underneath the glaciers of the Yangtze-Yalung watershed range. A number of streams flow down from these snows, water the plain, and drain away into the Nan Chu. The elevation is too great for cultivation, and the surroundings are bleak and dreary in the extreme. In front of the monastery is a small lake below a pine forest; and in the rocks under the snow and ice of the glaciers are the cells of some very holy hermits. Another celebrated hermit lives in a cell on a mountain near Nando[1]. Below the monastery is a hamlet of mud hovels inhabited by the laymen connected with the Gomba.

[1] Hermits living in caves, who pass their lives in contemplation and concentrated meditation on the Buddhist philosophy, are common in Eastern Tibet; they are sometimes walled in, and thus shut off from all communication with the world, for years on end, their food being pushed daily through a small opening.

Dzogchen Gomba lies in De-ge, in which State, as in Nyarong, and in the nomad country to the north, the unreformed red sects of lamaism predominate. The following are the principal sects of Tibetan Buddhism:—Black: the *Bönba*, representing probably the original religion of the country overlaid with Buddhism. Red: *Nyimaba*, the old unreformed sect, *Sajyaba* and *Garjyuba*, the early reformed sects. Yellow: *Gadamba* and *Gelugba*, the reformed sects, representing the established Tibetan Church of to-day, founded by the great reformer of Tibetan Buddhism, Tsongkaba.

We have here rejoined the main road from Tachienlu to Jyekundo (followed by Rockhill, A. K., and other travellers). Dzogchen Gomba and the neighbouring camping grounds are regular halts for the caravans going in and out of Tibet, and in normal times abundant yak transport should be available here. But at present the nomads and their animals have all disappeared.

April 9. At LINTSUNG.

Yesterday we made a long march in weather that was too Tibetan to be pleasant, falling snow accompanied by high wind and intense cold. Leaving Dzogchen the trail ran along the edge of the half-frozen marshy plain for a few miles, and then ascended a low pass, where the road to De-ge Gönchen *via* the Le La and Kolondo branches off over the big range to the left. We continued north-west, down one flat valley and up another, all the way in a blinding snowstorm, to reach another pass, the Latse Kare La (14,100 feet), the divide between the Yangtse and the Yalung. This is an easy pass, with a flat plateau-like top, an outlying shoulder of the big range. Descending from the pass into a valley we came upon a nomad encampment, and hastened to pitch our tents in the snow alongside.

The interior of a nomad tent, a rectangular structure of black yak hair cloth, packed round the bottom with walls of dried yak dung, is very comforting on a day of snow and wind. Seated on a rug on the ground in front of an earthen oven of glowing yak dung, one imbibes copious draughts of rich new milk, and envies the poor nomad his warm refuge from the cold. Our animals, however, were not so well off; for they were, as usual, without shelter, and had nothing to eat but the scanty pasturage round the tents, the grazing always being bad in the vicinity of an encampment.

To-day a short march down the valley brought us to Lintsung, which consists of a number of farms and a large *Sajya* monastery; the latter, a striking sight with all its buildings coloured with the usual red, white and black stripes, lies on a cultivated slope high above the stream, which can here be seen sinking rapidly westwards towards the great canyon of the Yangtze. Two small *Nyimaba* monasteries are passed on the way, one of which, Dzungo Gomba, is most picturesquely situated on the top of a bluff overlooking the river.

Lintsung is the seat of the former Rajah of the Native State of that name, whose ancestor, like the other Chiefs of Kam, was recognised by the Manchu Emperor Yung Cheng and granted a seal of office early in the eighteenth century. The present Rajah was deposed by Chao Erh-feng in 1910 or thereabouts. He held the Tibetan rank of King (*Jyelbo*), like the Rulers of De-ge and Chala, and must originally have been an important figure in Eastern Tibet; but at the time of his deposition his subjects consisted of less than a thousand families, mostly nomads in the basin of the Upper Yalung.

It is curious that neither Mr Rockhill nor A. K., both very careful observers, made any mention, when passing this place, of the State of Lintsung and its King. A. K. notes the monastery, which he calls Gainjo Gomba.

To-day we met a large caravan of some hundreds of mules and yak bound from Lhasa *via* Jyekundo to the Chinese border. They were carrying Lhasa cloth, rupees, and odds and ends of foreign goods from India to exchange for Szechuan tea, and were accompanied by forty or fifty horsemen armed with the usual motley collection of Russian, Chinese and Lhasa-made rifles. They reported all peaceful in Tibet and along the road they had traversed from Jyekundo. While the direct route from Tibet into Szechuan *via* Chamdo has remained closed for years, and is at present the scene of hostilities between Chinese and Tibetans, trading caravans have continued to come and go quite peaceably all the time by the northern route through Jyekundo and the Kokonor. The reason for this peculiar state of affairs is to be found in the fact that the quarrel has been strictly confined

6—2

to the Tibetans and the Szechuanese border troops, and has not affected the relations between the former and the Kansu Mohamedans, who are in charge of the Kokonor. The situation is much the same in the case of the Yunnan-Tibet trade further south.

These large Lhasa caravans always use mules, yak being hired every now and then from place to place to rest the regular caravan animals when passing through grass country where cattle are numerous and the grazing poor.

April 12. At DENGKO.

A short march up a grassy ravine and over a low *col* brought us to a *Garjyuba* monastery called Nojeling Gomba, lying high up on the mountain side overlooking the Yangtze, which flows in a deep canyon some 2,000 feet below. This appears to be A. K.'s Nagli, and Mr Rockhill's Nojyle.

On this march we passed a deceased lama being cut up and fed to the birds, a somewhat gruesome sight. Domna, our Tibetan mastiff, immediately galloped off to join in the feast, and was with difficulty recalled. This is the usual method of disposing of deceased lamas. The idea appears to be that a speedy reincarnation is secured by being thus fed to the birds (and each reincarnation is, it is hoped, a step towards non-reincarnation and the desired escape from the revolving wheel of earthly existence). Dead laymen are usually thrown into rivers, a practice which makes it inadvisable to drink unboiled river water in Tibet[1].

From Nojeling the road runs along the mountain side overlooking the canyon of the Yangtze far below for some twelve miles, and then descends into the cultivated plain of Dengko by the river.

Dengko consists of a Chinese yamen, which is the seat of the Chinese magistrate, a few scattered farms, an old Tibetan fort called Adu Podrang, the seat of the former native official, and a Tibetan temple called Drölma Hlakang, all lying on a

[1] We never came across a mummied lama in E. Tibet, but the mummy of Tsongkaba (the great reformer of Tibetan lamaism) is said to be preserved in a monastery at Lhasa. Mummies of priests and other celebrities are not uncommon in China, and there is one at Peking which is well known to foreign tourists. The Chinese make their mummies by starving the subject before his death (so that he may be as empty and dry as possible) and then placing the body in a sealed jar with charcoal, which absorbs the moisture; when the body is entirely dried it is removed from the jar and gilded.

flat plain along the river. On the further side of the Yangtze there is a large *Gelugba* monastery, Chunkor Gomba. Mr Rockhill does not appear to have noticed this place. A. K. calls Chunkor Gomba, Chingo, and with his usual accuracy names and refers to Drölma Hlakang as "a well-known temple." It is indeed quite a celebrated place. The temple contains a famous image of the goddess Drölma (Chinese Kuanyin, "Goddess of Mercy"), which is supposed to have flown here from Peking[1].

Chao Erh-feng intended Dengko to be the seat of a Taotai governing the northern districts of Eastern Tibet (while Batang was to be a similar administrative centre for the Southern Circuit), because he regarded the place as a suitable centre from which the wild nomads of the northern grasslands might be controlled. Hence the existence in this remote spot of a big Chinese yamen, similar to the one at Batang; it is the only Chinese building for hundreds of miles around.

The ex-chief of Adu (Adu Bön in Tibetan), in whose castle we are lodged, was an hereditary official, or subordinate Chief, under the King of De-ge; he controlled a number of scattered families here, in Tzako, and even at distant Rongbatsa. His house is a fine example of the Tibetan *Podrang*, all of which are built on the same principle, a many-storied structure with a flat roof, built in a square round an open court in the middle.

The Yangtze is here, at the present season, a clear blue stream a hundred yards or so in width, flowing through an open plain between two very high mountain ranges. A little further up lies Drenda Druka, the ferry where the main road crosses the river.

We spent the greater part of to-day in being hospitably entertained by the Chinese magistrate and his staff, who are all very alarmed at the advance of the Lhasa Tibetans. He is an official appointed by General P'eng of Chamdo, who for some years past has been ruling all this country as though it were his own property, dismissing and appointing magistrates and collecting the revenues entirely on his own account. The magistrate opines that General P'eng and his

[1] A Hlakang means a temple, literally "God-house," as opposed to a *Gomba* which means a monastery, literally "a solitary place" or "hermitage."

troops will never get out of Chamdo except as prisoners of the Tibetans, and he intends to withdraw with his small garrison of Chinese soldiers before the Lhasa troops arrive, if the advance of the latter is not stopped by peace negotiations in the near future. This seems to be the wisest thing he can do, seeing that he is in no condition to defend the place, and that the local people have unfortunately been very badly treated of recent years by their Chinese rulers in this neighbourhood. Chao Erh-feng's first magistrate here was a Mahomedan gentleman named La, who left a reputation for justice and fair-dealing behind him. But since the revolution in China and the subsequent neglect of frontier affairs by the republican authorities, the story here has been the same as in so many other parts of the frontier, and the conduct of affairs has been left in the hands of a few military adventurers of low origin, who have cruelly oppressed the people for their own enrichment.

There are many hares and partridges in this neighbourhood, the latter resembling the small partridge of North China, but without the black patch on the breast. They are very good to eat, but afford poor shooting, as they much prefer running to flying, and, when they do get into the air, remain only a very short time on the wing. They so exactly resemble the stony mountain side in colour that they are almost invisible until they move.

I have just had a talk with three Mahomedan merchants from T'aochou in Kansu, who arrived here yesterday with a caravan bringing Kansu brassware to sell to the Tibetans of Kam. They came by a route fringing the Golok country, probably the same as that followed by Miss Taylor on her remarkable journey in 1893.

A trail leads south from here towards Chamdo across a high pass over the big range which rises immediately south of the river. This is the same range which runs parallel to the main road, on the traveller's left hand, nearly all the way from Tachienlu to Jyekundo.

From Dzogchen to Dengko we have been following the main road. There is no reason why we should not continue along it all the way to Jyekundo, now only a few marches distant. But as there is an alternative route through Seshü and Tzachuka, which would take us through country unknown to European geography, we intend to proceed by this road to-morrow, in the hope of being able to locate at least the whereabouts of Seshü, which appears to be a centre of some importance. The main road leads north-west up the Yangtze valley; the Seshü trail turns north into the mountains and leads across the divide back into the Yalung basin.

April 16. At Jü Gomba (Shihch'ü Hsien).

We left Dengko on April 12, and marched up a narrow winding gorge in the mountains in a northerly direction to a ruined Chinese rest-house where we camped at an elevation of about 13,500 feet.

After a very cold night we broke camp on the following morning in falling snow, a bad beginning to a long hard day, for there was a big pass ahead. A couple of hours' march up the gorge brought us to the usual waste of rock and snow over which we scrambled to reach the pass, the Dzi La, 16,000 feet high. This pass probably presents no great difficulties in fine weather during the dry season; but what with the deep drifts of snow, in places over the animals' bellies, and a cutting wind which brought the temperature down to zero Fahrenheit, we found the ascent most difficult and arduous.

The descent on the northern side was very gradual, and we debouched on to a region of flat shallow valleys, at an average elevation of over 15,000 feet, divided up by low pyramid-shaped mountains; this is all good grazing land in the summer, but is now a foot or more under snow, with sheets of ice instead of streams. We struggled on for hour after hour down one of these flat valleys in a blinding snow-storm, our exhausted animals making very slow progress. At last our guides announced that we had reached our destination; but, to our disappointment, there were at first no traces to be seen of the Chinese rest-house, built by Chao Erh-feng in 1911, which we had hoped to find. We did discover it in the end; but it was a complete ruin hidden under the snow; and there was therefore nothing to be done but pitch our tents alongside. At first it seemed as though we should have to dispense with a fire for cooking and heating purposes, as, it being impossible to search for yak dung owing to the snow, there was apparently a complete absence of anything combustible. Some old timbers, however, were eventually unearthed from the ruins of the rest-house, and we soon had several fires alight. The worst sufferers were the mules and ponies, who got nothing to eat after their hard march but a ball of tea and *tsamba* apiece. Domna, our Tibetan dog, was the only member of the party really at his ease; he usually suffers from the heat, and rolls on every patch of snow and ice he meets on the road; now, curled up like a ball of wool in the snow, he seemed quite content.

An opium-smoking Chinese trader from Dengko, who is accompanying us on business of his own, refused absolutely on our long cold march to warm himself by occasional walks in the snow, and was so stiff with cold when we arrived that he had to be lifted off his pony like a log and thawed out by the fire. He must have been in serious danger of freezing to death in the saddle; many Chinese have a great aversion to taking bodily exercise if they can possibly avoid doing so, and I have often noticed them riding their animals along the most hair-raising precipices sooner than dismounting and walking a few steps.

In the evening the snow ceased and the weather cleared, and we found that we were encamped at the junction of two flat valleys; up the other, we were told, lay the direct Dzogchen-Seshü trail. The elevation was close on 15,000 feet. It was fortunate that our guides, two Tibetans from Dengko, were reliable men, well acquainted with the trail, for it would have been impossible to find the road without them. The country below the pass was a waste of snow, with flat valleys opening out in all directions.

We broke camp the next morning in fine weather but intense cold. The ponies were miserable, but all had survived; the mules, wonderful animals, seemed none the worse. The start, at 7 a.m., was a depressing affair, everything being frozen stiff, including the iron tent-pegs in the ground. One of the local Tibetans accompanying us was snow blind, and could not proceed. But he did not appear to consider it any particular hardship to be left behind with a bag of *tsamba*, a pot of tea, and a supply of firewood. The Tibetans, and more especially the nomadic Tibetans, must be one of the hardiest races in the world.

Soon after we had started several of the mules walked into

a deep drift of soft snow, and had to be unloaded before we could get them out. For the first half of the morning it was hard work, ploughing through the snow; then the sun's rays began to make themselves felt, the snow grew less with the decreasing elevation, and matters began to improve all round. Our road lay all the way down the same valley, surrounded by open downs. We saw hundreds of gazelle, and also several large herds of wild asses (*chyang* in Tibetan, *yeh lotzu*—"wild mules"—in Chinese). Wild yak are found just across the Yalung to the north. At last we reached some nomad tents, where we were met by the local headmen, and shortly afterwards arrived at our destination, a square mud fort, the residence of the Chinese magistrate of Seshü district (in Chinese Shihch'ü Hsien), lying in the open valley: near by is a small monastery, called Jü Gomba, consisting mostly of tents. The elevation is between 13,000 and 14,000 feet, and it is altogether a cold, dismal and desolate spot at this time of the year.

We received a warm welcome from the Chinese magistrate, who had prepared quarters for us in his mud yamen. The only discomfort here is the extreme cold, coupled with the absence of any fuel but yak dung. The latter, which is very smoky and gives off an unpleasant sickly odour, makes good enough fuel once it has stopped smoking and reaches the glowing stage; but unfortunately, unlike charcoal, it goes out almost immediately afterwards.

With the exception of this mud fort and a few monasteries, there are no houses, nor trees, nor cultivated fields in the whole of Seshü district, which consists entirely of rolling grass country from 13,000 to 15,000 feet in elevation. From here one may travel northwards to Labrang Gomba and T'aochou in Kansu, eastwards to Sungp'an in Szechuan, and westwards right across Tibet to Ladak, and never see a house or a tree. It is really a portion of the great Northern Plateau of Tibet (the *Jang Tang*). The only Chinese in the district are the magistrate and his staff. The native nomads here are remarkable for their good looks, both men and women; of course they are extremely dirty; but then the conditions of life on these uplands do not tend towards cleanliness. I have not had my clothes off since leaving Dengko.

We rested to-day at Seshü, and I took the opportunity to

climb a neighbouring hill to have a look at the country. But there was nothing of interest to be seen, the view being the same all around over bare hills. The stream flows north, and is said to join the Yalung ten or twelves miles off. There is a trail running east across the hills, leading to Rungu Gomba and Tzako, the most direct road from Seshü to Kanze.

The boundaries of the district of Seshü appear to extend northwards beyond the Yalung; but in fact that river seems to represent the southern boundary of the independent nomad country. In the summer, when swollen with rain and melted snow, it forms an efficient protection against the raids of the Golokwa; in winter the latter are able to ford it, or cross on one of the numerous ice bridges which form on the quieter reaches.

All is peaceful amongst the nomads of Seshü at present, in contrast to most of the other districts of the frontier, which are nearly all either in open rebellion or on the verge of revolt. This is due to the character of the magistrate, one of the few of the better class of Chinese official still left on the border, and to the absence of Chinese troops. Were the other magistrates of the frontier districts of the same type as this gentleman, the present troubles would never have arisen. If the Chinese Government were able to replace all the bad and corrupt officials by reasonably honest and well-meaning men, and if they would withdraw all their troops except for a few native police, they would be able to administer Eastern Tibet without difficulty and to the satisfaction of the people[1].

We are beginning to have trouble with our animals, whose loss of condition is manifesting itself by a tendency to girth and saddle sores and swellings on the back; there is only one cure for the latter, and that is complete rest; otherwise the swelling bursts and the animal becomes useless. Our loads have therefore to be cut down to the minimum, and now consist of nothing beyond the tents, bedding, and indispensable personal baggage. Although no mules are obtainable in these

[1] Later on in the summer the local headmen politely informed the Chinese magistrate of Seshü that they could no longer guarantee him protection if he remained. He accordingly retired, together with his staff, servants, baggage, and archives, to Kanze, being escorted as far as Tzako by a guard of his former subjects; the Chinese magistrates of De-ge and Dengko also escaped in safety, but in a less dignified manner and with the loss of all their effects; and the administration of the country was thereupon taken over by the former Tibetan officials of De-ge.

parts, ponies are abundant and cheap; unfortunately they are all in very bad condition at the present time of the year, which is the worst season for grazing.

The Golok nomads, a race of horsemen, use a peculiar kind of saddle, which is in general use in the Tzachuka grass country; it has a very high pommel, standing six inches or more off the pony's withers, and is an excellent saddle for use in a country where sore backs are a perpetual source of trouble to the long distance traveller.

April 17. At SESHÜ GOMBA.

To-day's march took us in a north-westerly direction across the same kind of grass country, up one valley, down another, and then over a low *col* giving access to a perfectly flat plain, evidently one of the numerous old lake basins of this region, watered by several streams, and opening on to the Yalung. Crossing this plain, we reached our destination, Seshü Gomba. This monastery is an important and well-known centre, and houses several hundreds of lamas of the *Gelugba* sect. Chunkor Gomba at Dengko is a branch of the same establishment. It lies under the mountain side bounding the northern edge of the plain. The Yalung is almost within sight a few miles off. The Chinese magistrate of Seshü used to live in this monastery until the mud fort at Jü Gomba was constructed for him. This accounts for Shihch'ü Hsien often appearing in different places on Chinese maps.

When debouching on to the plain in front of Seshü Gomba to-day we came on six fine stags[1] who were trotting unconcernedly across our front. Big game and wild animals of all kinds are remarkably tame near these big grass-country monasteries, where the power of the lamas is still paramount, and all hunting is prohibited, owing to the Buddhist principle of not taking life.

The country round Seshü Gomba could provide an unlimited number of perfect race-courses, polo grounds, cricket pitches, and golf links; but at this elevation (about 13,400 feet) one has no inclination to indulge in a gallop or take any violent exercise, and is only too content to crawl about at a walk.

I am told that the Yalung is here joined by a river called

[1] See p. 217.

the Marmu Chu from the north, a name which appears on the latest map of Tibet. It is a pity that we cannot afford the time to spend a few days examining the country, which is quite unknown from a geographical point of view. I am too tired even to go down to the Yalung and verify the exact position of its confluence with the Marmu Chu.

The Tzachuka grass-lands support large flocks of sheep and herds of yak. Hence Seshü is, in spite of its scanty nomadic population, quite a wealthy and prosperous district from the point of view of the officials, who levy a tax of so many rupees on every sheep and yak. The region is a great wool-producing country, though very little is exported, except for small quantities which find their way out to Tachienlu or Sungp'an. Further north the same wool country is tapped by the Tientsin trade at Sining and other centres on the Kansu border, whence the wool is transported by boats down the Yellow river and by camel caravans across the deserts of Mongolia to the coast. The wool of the Tzachuka grass country might perhaps be profitably exported in a similar way by coracle or raft down the Yalung to Szechuan.

An official (a sort of *Dzongbön*, or Tibetan district officer) appointed by the Rajah of De-ge used to administer this region from an encampment near Seshü Gomba. When Chao Erh-feng took over De-ge State, the younger of the two brothers who were then contending for the Chieftainship fled north into Seshü and took refuge with the Dzongbön and the lamas here[1].

While sitting in my room at Seshü Gomba this afternoon, a great hubbub arose amongst the lamas outside the monastery, accompanied by shots and blowing of trumpets. Going out to investigate, I saw a dozen or so armed horsemen driving a mob of ponies across the plain towards the Yalung. It appeared that the horsemen were Golok brigands from across the Yalung engaged in a raid, and that the herd of ponies they had lifted belonged to the stock of the monastery. At the request of the lamas we joined them for some time in taking long shots at the raiders, in the hope of inducing the latter to relinquish their prey, while others amongst the monks held a special service, but with no better results.

[1] See p. 26.

PLATE XXI

NOMAD CAMP ON THE SNOW-COVERED PASTURES OF THE TZACHUKA GRASS COUNTRY, UPPER YALUNG BASIN

CAMP OF TRAVELLING TIBETANS, UPPER YALUNG VALLEY

PLATE XXII

HERD OF YAK IN THE GRASS COUNTRY OF EASTERN TIBET

TIBETAN WOMAN WEAVING WOOLLEN CLOTH IN KAM

Eventually the raiders disappeared with their booty round the corner of the mountain in the direction of the river.

The Golokwa, being by all accounts very religious, had no business to be raiding the stock of a monastery; but it appears that they belong almost entirely to the old unreformed red sects, and have not a proper respect for a *Gelugba* establishment. But the lamas said that they expected to get their stock back after negotiation and payment of presents, when it had been established that the ponies belonged to them and not to laymen.

Incidents such as this are of constant occurrence in the country which fringes the grass-lands of the Golok and other independent nomad tribes; our animals are never allowed to graze unwatched, and are always picketed and guarded by Domna, the mastiff, at night-time.

April 19. At Dorgön Gomba.

We left Seshü Gomba yesterday, and, turning our backs on the Yalung, marched up a flat open valley in a westerly direction, eventually pitching our tents alongside a nomad encampment at an elevation of about 14,000 feet. On the way we saw hares, geese, storks with grey bodies and black legs and tails, and many gazelle.

The people of these grass-lands are very suspicious of strangers. On two occasions when we wanted to ask some horsemen the way they galloped off up side valleys. As one of the Chinese with us said—one man fears two, two fear three, and so on.

After a very cold night with a zero temperature we started again this morning and followed up one of the many shallow valleys to reach the pass, the Ngamba La, 14,600 feet. This is the boundary between Seshü district and the Jyekundo district of the Kokonor Territory (Ch'ing Hai). We found many partridges on the other side of the pass, but shooting between 14,000 and 15,000 feet is too much effort to be pleasant. From this pass there is a steep descent into a valley, which is followed down to a hamlet called Shewu (Hsiehwu in Chinese) and a *Sajya* monastery called Dorgön Gomba. Here for the first time since leaving Dengko we met with cultivation again in the form of a few stony fields, the elevation being a little under 13,000 feet.

We found a small official stationed at this place, a Kansu Mahomedan from Jyekundo, apparently a sort of tax collector. The local people used to pay their taxes to a *Bönbo* (official) of the Rajah of Nangchen State; but now pay them to the Kansu Mahomedans who have recently taken over the administration of these parts.

April 25. At JYEKUNDO.

Leaving Dorgön Gomba on April 20, we marched down a narrow winding valley which eventually debouched on to the Yangtze. After following up the river for a mile or two, we crossed by coracle ferry, and then continued up the right bank for a few more miles to a hamlet called Gala.

The Yangtze is here, at the present season, a clear blue stream, one to two hundred yards wide, hemmed in by steep mountains rising for thousands of feet from the water's edge, and flowing in alternate shallow rapids and still dark blue pools of great depth. The elevation is about 11,800 feet.

We were met at the ferry by an official sent to welcome us by the Jyekundo Authorities, a sturdy Kansu Mahomedan, about twice the size of the average Szechuanese.

Ploughing was going on in the Yangtze valley, and a few blades of green grass were even to be seen in sheltered spots, welcome signs of coming warmth. The dry stony nullahs in the hillside were full of partridges.

The men in this neighbourhood wear their hair cut in a fringe over the forehead and hanging down loose over their shoulders behind, giving them a rather wild appearance, though in reality they seem tame enough[1].

From Gala the trail leaves the Yangtze and ascends the mountain side to the west to reach the pass, the Ra La, 14,400 feet, from which there is a view over the Jyekundo valley in the foreground. We saw many wild sheep (*na* in Tibetan) in the neighbourhood of the pass, which is very

[1] We afterwards found this method of wearing the hair to be common all over the Southern Kokonor grass country. In most parts of Kam the men wear their hair in a queue which is usually wound round the head, and is sometimes lengthened by the addition of a false queue of tow and adorned with rings of ivory and other ornaments. The women throughout Kam wear their hair in the same way, namely hanging down their backs in a number of small plaits fastened together at the end; women from Central Tibet can always be recognised again by their peculiar head-dress, a sort of wide framework projecting on either side of their heads; rather similar styles can be seen amongst the Mongols. See Plate XX.

steep on both sides. The descent leads into the valley of the Jyekundo river, which is reached at the village of Manitung, consisting of a number of caravanserais and a huge pile of *mani* stones (flat stones inscribed with the sacred formula *o-ma-ni-pa-me-hum*), said to be one of the largest in Tibet. From here a short march up the valley brought us to Jyekundo.

A squadron of mounted Mahomedan braves was drawn up outside the village to receive us, and it was evident from their appearance that we had reached a new country. In the place of the Szechuanese foot soldiers, with their opium pipes, straw sandals, and thin cotton clothing, who always seem dissatisfied, home-sick and miserable on the bleak uplands of Kam, we here found a hundred or so burly Kansu Mahomedans, well armed and equipped, and mounted on well-fed Sining horses. In front of the squadron floated four large banners inscribed with the character *Ma*, representing a power now supreme from Ninghsia in Northern Kansu to Nangchen on the confines of Central Tibet[1].

Jyekundo (in Chinese Chiehku—pronounced Chaiku or Gaiku by the Szechuanese) is a mud-built village lying in a cultivated valley formed by the junction of two streams, the Dzashi Chu from the west and the Barung Chu from the south, which combine to flow east and south-east towards the Yangtze. There is a touch of Mongolia and the north about the place, and a complete absence of anything Szechuanese. On a spur above and overlooking the village is a large *Sajya* monastery containing four or five hundred lamas. Jyekundo has been visited by various foreign travellers, such as A. K., Rockhill, De Rhins (who was killed in the neighbourhood), and the Russian explorers under Kozloff. A. K. calls it Kegudo (the *n* does not appear in the spelling of the word any more than it does in *Dartse(n)do* and other placenames with the *do* termination) and makes its elevation 11,860 feet. Rockhill makes the elevation 12,940 feet. We made it above 11,900.

Though only a village of mud hovels, Jyekundo is the

[1] A large percentage of Moslems in China and nearly all the Mahomedan leaders in Kansu are named *Ma*; the Chinese ideograph for the word means "horse," which is appropriate enough in view of the horsey proclivities of the average Chinese Moslem.

most important trading centre in Eastern Tibet. Nearly all the caravans plying between Lhasa and China pass through it and usually rest a few weeks in the vicinity to enable their animals to recuperate on the surrounding grass-lands. Situated in the centre of the triangle Lhasa—Sining—Tachienlu, it is equally in touch with Tibet, Szechuan, Kansu and Mongolia. A big fair is held here in August, which attracts Tibetans from far and wide.

The following are the chief roads which radiate from Jyekundo; west to Nagchuka and Lhasa; north over the mountains and across the Yangtze to Sining; north-east to Labrang Gomba and T'aochou; east through the Golok country to Sungp'an in Szechuan; east and south-east *via* Seshü and Tzachuka to Kanze (the road by which we arrived)[1]; south-east down the Yangtze *via* Dengko to De-ge and Kanze; and south to Chamdo *via* Nangchen (the road by which we are leaving).

We found matches, cigarettes, candles, and other foreign odds and ends for sale at Jyekundo cheaper than similar goods at Tachienlu (which they reach from Shanghai); the explanation of this is apparently to be found in the cheap freight furnished by the empty tea caravans returning to Central Tibet. From the north come Kansu copper and brassware, Russian cloth, arms and Kansu vermicelli; from Szechuan, tea and silks, more especially Katas[2]; from Yunnan, Chinese sugar; and from India and Central Tibet, Lhasa cloth, dried fruits, and foreign sundries.

Apart from the troops and officials, the Chinese population of Jyekundo consists of a few families of *Lao Shan* (Shensi merchants) and Mahomedan traders from Kansu, engaged mostly in collecting Tibetan produce, such as hides, furs, wool, deers' horns, musk, medicines, and the like, for export to China. The place is a great centre for the collection of wool,

[1] This road is much used by the caravans in summer in preference to the main road down the Yangtze, as by following it they can avoid the agricultural valleys and secure good grazing all the way from Jyekundo to Kanze.

[2] The *kata*, or ceremonial scarf, plays a prominent part in every-day life in Eastern Tibet, and serves the purpose of a visiting card. Judging by our experience in Kam, the consumption of these scarves in the whole of Tibet must be very large and the trade in them one of considerable value. They vary from a flimsy rag to a fine silk wrap, and are manufactured in Szechuan. The traveller in Tibet should provide himself with a large stock of these indispensable articles.

and would become vastly more important in this respect were there reasonable facilities for getting produce out of the country. It is surrounded on all sides by great expanses of elevated grass country, the best wool-raising regions in Asia. The wool finds its way out to Sining and Kansu, thence to Tientsin, or to Tachienlu and Szechuan, and eventually to Shanghai *via* Chungking and Hankow, according as it is bought by the Mahomedan merchants of the Kansu border or the Shensi merchants of the Szechuan border respectively. The price here at present is 12 to 15 rupees per load of 60 to 80 Chinese pounds; but freight to Tachienlu costs at least 20 rupees a load, apart from probable taxation exactions, while there is always a good chance of the caravan being pillaged *en route*.

All over Eastern Tibet the wool is woven by the women in their homes, usually into a strong grey-white cloth marked with red and black lines, known in Chinese as *mutzu*[1]. Lhasa cloth, which is the best in Tibet—indeed its reputation extends even to Peking—is called *p'ulu* by the Chinese.

Jyekundo is the administrative centre for the southern portion of the Kokonor Territory (Ch'ing Hai in Chinese, Tso Ngombo in Tibetan—all meaning "Blue Lake"), which covers all the north-eastern quarter of what is usually labelled Tibet on European maps. This vast area, consisting for the most part of nomad grass country, much of it too high even to be inhabited, used to be controlled by a Manchu Amban residing at Sining (Tibetan, Ziling) on the Kansu border. In 1915 this official was suppressed by President Yuan Shih-k'ai, and the region handed over to the control of the Kansu Mahomedans, whose power had long been supreme in Kansu and in the Kokonor border country. Hence the Mahomedan officials and troops now in control here; they are an innovation not altogether appreciated by the local Tibetans[2].

The practice followed by European geographers of including the whole of the Kokonor Territory in the map of Tibet has given rise in the past to a great deal of confusion and misunderstanding. The region has never been a part of Tibet Proper, and in its northern portion is partly inhabited by Mongols, as was pointed out by A. K. as long ago as 1882. Probably the greater part of it was inhabited by Mongols

[1] See Plate XXII. [2] See p. 48.

once. But the Tibetans are nowadays much the more powerful of the two races, and they appear to be absorbing and pushing back the Mongols more and more every generation. The north-eastern portion, marching with the Labrang-T'aochou section of the Kansu border, is called Amdo by the Tibetans, and is inhabited solely by people of Tibetan race, including the Golok and other tribes of wild nomads. The whole of the southern half is also purely Tibetan from a racial point of view, while the south-eastern portion is filled up by the Tibetan State of Nangchen, the only part of the Territory where agriculture is carried on to any great extent. But it does not appear that any portion of it was ever under the temporal rule of the Deba Shung (the Lhasa Government of Tibet Proper).

Under the Manchus the control exercised by the Sining Amban over the Kokonor was merely nominal and of the same nature as that exercised by his colleague at Lhasa over Tibet Proper; and the Mongol Banners and Tibetan Tribes inhabiting the Kokonor were ruled by their own Princes and Chiefs. The Mahomedans, however, are tightening up their control, especially from Jyekundo as a centre, and are levying all kinds of new taxes, and propose to appoint their own Chinese Mahomedan magistrates.

At the time the Mahomedans were taking over the Kokonor two or three years ago, the Szechuanese, who then controlled the portion of Eastern Tibet up to and including Chamdo, advanced north from the latter place and endeavoured to seize Jyekundo, in order to be able to command the valuable revenues which can be collected from the trade passing through this centre. The Mahomedans objected, and some fighting, in which the Szechuanese were badly worsted, ensued in these remote wilds; subsequently President Yuan Shih-k'ai sent a Commissioner who delimited the frontier and assigned the whole of the Kokonor to the Mahomedans.

From Jyekundo to Sining is reckoned about a month's journey for a caravan; but the Mahomedan couriers cover the distance in very much less time by means of relays of ponies. No houses are passed on the road, which is none too safe, as it fringes the country of the wild Golok nomads[1].

[1] Later the Kansu Mahomedans sent a military expedition into the Golok country in order to eliminate this danger to their communications.

General Ma, who is in charge at Jyekundo, turns out to be an old acquaintance whom I had met some years ago at Sining. He has been most hospitable, and has presented us with gifts of sacks of barley and wheat flour, half a yak, and a case of Kansu *mien* (vermicelli), the latter a great delicacy in these parts. I could only make a poor return with an electric torch and some twelve bore cartridges for his shot gun.

Although heavy fighting is now going on between Chinese and Tibetans at Chamdo, General Ma appears to remain on the best of terms with the Kalon Lama, the Tibetan Commander-in-Chief. For the Kansu Mahomedans regard the quarrel between the Lhasa Tibetans and the Szechuanese as no concern of theirs.

These Kansu Moslems are a sturdy race of beef and mutton-eating horsemen, united and stiffened by their religion, and inured from youth up to the hardships of life in Tibetan country. Unlike the Szechuanese lowlanders, always pining for their opium pipes and bowls of rice and pork, these Mahomedans readily accustom themselves to Tibetan conditions and are satisfied if need be with a diet of buttered tea, *tsamba*, and dried meat. Their principal failing, here as in Kansu, is a weakness for "eating silver."

We leave to-morrow for Chamdo, another plunge into the unknown, both as regards the road, and as regards what we shall find when we get there. According to the latest news the besieged Chinese are still holding out. General Ma is sending two Tibetans and two of his Mahomedans, who have travelled the road, with us as guides; they will accompany us as far as the Kalon Lama's headquarters, wherever they may be. It appears that, by having made this détour through the neutral territory of the Kokonor, we shall be able to avoid all difficulties in regard to crossing the frontier between the two belligerents, the Lhasa Tibetans and the Szechuanese.

The Russian explorer Kozloff seems to have marched south-east from Jyekundo towards Chamdo; the route we are going to follow leads south-west. We are proceeding in the first instance to Nangchen, the seat of the Rajah of the State of that name, which is reported to lie a dozen marches north-west of Chamdo, and propose to enquire the whereabouts of the Kalon Lama when we get there.

7—2

CHAPTER III

FROM JYEKUNDO, ACROSS THE GRASS-LANDS OF THE UPPER MEKONG BASIN, TO NANGCHEN AND CHAMDO

Crossing the Yangtze-Mekong divide by the Shung La (15,800 feet)—The Dze Chu—Rashi Gomba and the Rijnhart tragedy of 1898—Pen picture of a nomad of Eastern Tibet—Kanda on the Dza Chu, the main branch of the upper Mekong—Bare spring pastures and exhausted animals—Ferry across the Dza Chu at Gurde Druka—Traces of the Russian explorer Kozloff—Pilgrims—Tibetan paper—Crossing the Manam La (15,500 feet)—The Native State of Nangchen—Tibetan turnips and a Chinese cook in Eastern Tibet—The Bar Chu—Big game—Meeting with emissaries from Tibetan headquarters—Crossing the frontier from the Kokonor into Tibet Proper—The Dje Chu—Two more big passes—Monkeys—Marching down the Ngom Chu to Chamdo—Chamdo after the Tibetan occupation—The Kalon Lama, the Tibetan Commander-in-Chief—The siege of Chamdo—Condition of the wounded—Proposed peace negotiations—Tibetan leaders at Chamdo—Departure for Batang.

May 2. At Kanda.

We left Jyekundo on April 26, and have been travelling for the past week across the grass country. Our first day's march took us over the mountains immediately south of Jyekundo. From the pass, the Ashu La (14,400 feet), we looked south across a valley to a great barrier range of rock, ice and snow, the Yangtze-Mekong divide. This appears to be a continuation of the big range which trends right across Kam from north-west to south-east, being pierced by the Yangtze below Dengko and by the Yalung below Kanze, to end in the snows south of Tachienlu. Descending from the pass across an undulating plateau, where we saw many gazelle, marmots and hares, and some kind of pheasant grouse with a whistling call, we reached a flat grass-covered plain, another old lake basin, watered by a stream flowing east to join the Jyekundo river. Crossing this plain, which was dotted with the black tents and flocks and herds of many nomads, we camped at an elevation of 12,800 feet at the entrance to a gorge leading into the barrier range ahead.

The next morning I was awakened by the sound of some-one beating on my tent, a sign of ill omen, meaning that the snow was being shaken off the flies, and a glance outside showed the ground to be covered with snow, which was still falling from a grey and leaden sky. A discussion with the guides ensued as to whether the big pass ahead would be feasible in such bad weather. The Tibetans advised against the attempt, and proposed that we should follow an alternative trail leading westwards up the open valley and then south across the range at a lower point. But the Mahomedans assured us it would be all right, and said that we should save at least a day's march by taking the direct road to the south. In the end we decided to risk it.

Starting at seven, we followed up the gorge into the heart of the big snow range. About ten o'clock we reached what might be considered the foot of the pass, and then followed a two hours' struggle up a very steep slope through deep snow. We eventually reached the summit of the pass, the Shung La, 15,800 feet, about noon, but found it covered by an impassable cap of ice, and had to climb to one side, a few hundred feet higher, to get across. From the pass we descended rapidly down a steep slope through the snow, and followed down another valley for several hours, until, having reached an altitude where the snow was less and some poor grass was showing for our exhausted animals, we camped near some nomads' tents at an elevation of 13,500 feet.

Owing to the deep snow we had great difficulty in getting our animals over the Shung La, and one of the two Chinese mules, which had been bought by mistake, gave out and had to be left to his fate. The traveller who has to penetrate Tibet from the Chinese side should be careful to secure only Tibetan mules for his caravan. The mules of Yunnan and Szechuan, which can be distinguished by their finer appearance, though sometimes used in the border country, are not hardy enough for travel in Tibet Proper. My big Amdo riding mule carried me up through the snow without difficulty. It would be very difficult to cross these high passes in snowy weather on foot, and everyone rides over them. As long as one remains on the animal the effect of the rarefied air is scarcely noticeable, except that the mule stops for breath every few yards; but immediately one dismounts and tries to ascend on foot, one's limbs feel like lead, and one gasps for breath with aching head and beating heart. We have had bad luck with the weather so far, meeting with snowstorms on the two biggest passes yet encountered.

We had broken camp that morning by the banks of a streamlet whose waters find their way into the Yangtze and so through Central China to Shanghai; in the evening we were camped on the banks of one of the headwater streams of the Mekong, which flows through Siam and Annam to Saigon.

The 28th of April was a brilliantly fine sunny day, though the thermometer registered fifteen degrees of frost when we broke camp. For several hours we marched down a valley, partly through limestone gorges, and partly through open grass country, passing a monastery called Rashi (also known as Lungshi) Gomba, until we eventually debouched on a large river flowing from north-west to south-east. This turned out to be the Dze Chu, one of the three principal rivers which go to make up the Mekong. It was about one hundred yards wide and was just fordable at the present low water season. Crossing this stream we followed down its right bank until we found a suitable spot to camp. The elevation was about 12,400 feet. All around were grassy mountains with snow ranges in the background.

Rashi Gomba, which we passed on this march, is a handsome-looking monastery with white buildings. It houses many hundreds of lamas, and ranks with Seshü Gomba as one of the principal monasteries of North-west Kam.

One of the most remarkable journeys ever made in Tibet was that of the Dutch missionaries, Mr and Mrs Rijnhart, in 1898[1]. Starting from Sining in Kansu, they eventually reached the neighbourhood of Lhasa where they were stopped and turned back along the Jyekundo road. Arrived at a camp on the banks of the upper Mekong, Mr Rijnhart left his wife to go and seek assistance from some nomads. Mrs Rijnhart watched her husband follow a path round a corner of rock, and never saw or heard of him again. From the spot where Mr Rijnhart disappeared Mrs Rijnhart travelled for seven days to a monastery she calls Rashi Gomba, whence she reached Jyekundo in three days. They left no geographical records of their journeys; but putting two and two together, I have little doubt that we are now, twenty years later, in the

[1] See Mrs Rijnhart's book, *With the Tibetans in Tent and Temple.*

neighbourhood of the scene of the Rijnhart tragedy, and that the Rashi Gomba we passed is the same place as the monastery of that name referred to in Mrs Rijnhart's story.

The country here is much more peaceful than the regions under the control of the Szechuan Frontier Authorities, and appears to be free from brigands and horse-thieves. We are even able to let our mules and ponies graze free at night-time, much to their advantage.

Our animals were very exhausted after their experiences on the Shung La, but we were fortunately able to obtain some *ula* yak from the nomads of the Dze Chu valley. The *ula* (forced transport system) is no hardship in these parts, as it is seldom demanded of the natives; whereas on the main roads of the Szechuan Frontier Territory the people are continually being harried by the Chinese military to provide animals for transport purposes.

On April 29 we made a short march across grassy downlands in a south-westerly direction, leaving the Dze Chu flowing south-east, and camped on the slopes of the low watershed dividing the latter from the Dza Chu, the largest of the three main branches of the upper Mekong. On the following day we crossed the divide by a small pass, and marched south across low hills with streams draining west towards the Dza Chu. Our animals were by this time getting so exhausted that even with the yak carrying most of the baggage we could not do more than ten miles a day; and we camped after a short march in another flat grassy valley where we found some nomad tents.

Marmots abound on these grass-lands. They are always exciting our dogs by sitting up in front of their holes and whistling, only dodging in at the very last moment as the dogs get up to them.

I am living on mutton, the Kansu vermicelli given me by General Ma, butter and milk. The complete lack of fruit and vegetables is becoming a hardship; but the milk is abundant and good. The butter is good when fresh, but is usually rancid to a greater or less degree. It is sewn up in bags made of leather or sheep's stomach, and is sometimes a year or more old.

On May 1, we made another short march, over a low subsidiary pass to a camp below a small monastery called Göche

Gomba on the banks of a stream flowing west through a limestone gorge to join the Dza Chu. The principal features of this neighbourhood are rugged and precipitous masses of limestone rising a few thousand feet above the grassy hills, the latter composed of red sandstone, a formation characteristic of the whole of the upper Mekong basin.

Sitting in the doorway of my tent below Gö-che Gomba I made the following pen picture of a typical nomad Tibetan of these parts who stood watching me as I wrote.

Features, regular and Aryan; skin, a dark brown and encrusted with much dirt; a square-cut fringe descending over the forehead to the eyes, and long straight black hair hanging loose over the shoulders behind; silver and coral ear-ring in the left ear; two charm boxes suspended round the neck; a straight sword thrust crosswise through the front of the girdle, from which hang a pouch, flint case, and other odds and ends; the sole garment a greasy sheep-skin robe gathered up at the waist and thrown back to leave the right arm and shoulder bare; no trousers; and long, coloured Tibetan boots of the usual pattern reaching to the knee.

To-day we made a rather longer march in order to reach this place, Kanda on the Dza Chu. A gradual ascent into an amphitheatre of rocky mountains brought us to a pass, the Ka La, 14,000 feet, across a rocky spur trending westwards from the main watershed range. From this pass we descended for several hours' march, at first through a grassy valley and then through a limestone gorge with perpendicular cliffs, debouching finally on to the Dza Chu at the hamlet of Kanda, elevation about 12,000 feet.

This place consists of half a dozen hovels surrounded by a few stony fields; but it is pleasant to come upon trees, houses and cultivation again after wandering for so many days in the bleak and empty grass country. We have, indeed, scarcely seen a tree since leaving the Yalung valley weeks ago. The barley here has been sown, and is even beginning to sprout in places, almost the first sign of green we have seen on our journey; on the same latitude in Szechuan the wheat is now being harvested. Silver pheasants and partridges are abundant in the neighbourhood.

A cultivated valley such as this is called *rong* by the Tibetans, and is regarded as a land flowing with milk and

PLATE XXIII

CAMP ON THE GRASS COUNTRY OF THE UPPER MEKONG BASIN

YAK CARAVAN TRAVELLING ACROSS THE GRASS COUNTRY

PLATE XXIV

LIMESTONE GORGES AND FORESTED VALLEYS BELOW THE LEVEL OF THE GRASS COUNTRY IN EASTERN TIBET

honey compared to the grass country; for us it means a house instead of a tent to sleep in, and straw and barley for our hungry animals.

The grass-lands across which we have been travelling will be covered with rich herbage in two or three months time; but at the present season, which is the worst time of the year for mule caravans to be crossing the plateau country, they are almost bare of last year's grass owing to the large numbers of yak, sheep and ponies belonging to the nomads which they support; while not a blade of new grass is yet to be seen. As a result our animals are now almost exhausted, the ponies especially being as thin as rakes and in much worse condition than the mules, and several have given out. Amongst the latter is a favourite black pony given to me in Sining three years ago. He has carried me all over North-western China, from Kansu to Peking and from Peking to Szechuan, to collapse finally in the middle of Eastern Tibet. I left him with some nomads, and suggested to our Mahomedan guides that they should pick him up on their way back if he had recovered by then; so that he may yet find his way back to his original home on the Kansu border. The ponies we have bought from the nomads to replace our foundered animals are cheap but in very poor condition. As soon as swellings appear on an animal's back one can be certain that he is done for and that he will be unable to travel much further even without a load.

The Dza Chu is here a shallow stream flowing in several channels in a broad, sandy bed. The valley is in places a mile across, with a fair amount of cultivation on the lower slopes of the red sandstone hills. The river is just fordable at low water in this neighbourhood, but we are to cross it by a ferry to-morrow lower down. Unlike the Yangtze, which we found two weeks ago crystal clear in the neighbourhood of Jyekundo, the Mekong is here already discoloured. It also clears, however, in the winter; the early discolouration being due to the red sandstone country through which it flows.

The Dza Chu has the best claim to be considered the main branch of the upper Mekong. The name carries on for a short distance below Chamdo. In sound the words Dza Chu (for the upper Mekong) and Tza Chu (for the upper Yalung) are identical; the difference in the romanised spelling is retained to avoid confusion; the Tibetan spelling of place names in Kam is apt to be rather variable.

May 7. At NANGCHEN.

We crossed the Dza Chu by coracle ferry at a spot called Gurde Druka[1] nine miles below Kanda, marched back up the opposite bank for three miles to a village called Shungda[2], and then turned up a side valley to the west for a few miles to reach Barmendo, a hamlet lying at the confluence of two streams below a small monastery called Barme Gomba. There was a small post of Mahomedan soldiers from Jyekundo stationed here, this being their most southerly garrison.

At the Dza Chu ferry I happened to converse with a native of more than average intelligence and was told by him that a large party of Russians had crossed the river at this point recently, coming from the north-east and proceeding by a trail due south across the mountains. Visions of a Bolshevik inroad into Tibet crossed my mind, but further enquiry elicited the fact that "recently" meant some ten or more years ago, such an event as the passage of a party of foreign explorers being naturally a matter of outstanding interest not soon to be forgotten in these remote parts. The intelligent native went on to volunteer the information that these Russians, who were a large and well-armed party with the best of horses and yak from the Kansu border, had had a fight with the Tibetans further south, and been turned back from their objective, which seems to have been Chamdo.

A comparison of my route survey with the map of Tibet showed that we had apparently reached a point touched by the Russian explorer Kozloff, and called by him Gurtu-tuka, which must be the same as our Gurde Druka (Gurde Ferry). Kozloff's party seem to have come by a route leading south-east from Jyekundo, whereas we had taken a road running south-west from the latter place. Our routes touched at this ferry, and then diverged again.

The Tibetans in these parts divide mankind into *Bŏba* (Tibetans), *Jyami* (Chinese), *Sobo* (Mongols), *Ka-che* (Ma-

[1] *Druka* means "boat place," i.e. "ferry."

[2] The name termination *da* is common in this neighbourhood; it appears to mean locally a point where a side ravine debouches on to a big valley; similar to, but not quite the same as *do*, which means the confluence of two streams.

homedans from Turkestan), *Urusugi* (Russians), *Jyagargi* (Indians) and *Pilingi* or *Chilingi* (British or foreigners generally)[1].

Crossing the river at the same time but in the opposite direction was a large party of pilgrims returning on foot from Lhasa to Labrang Gomba on the Kansu-Kokonor border. The poorer foot pilgrims travelling between Lhasa and Amdo[2] prefer this way to the main road *via* Nagchuka and Jyekundo, as they pass more monasteries, villages and nomad encampments on this route from which to beg food.

The Tibetans in these parts salute one by trotting up with their tongues hanging out and the palms of their hands uplifted like those of a gesticulating Hebrew. The tongue of a Tibetan nomad is a remarkable organ, rendered long and muscular by lifelong licking of the *tsamba* bowl.

We rested at Barme Gombe for a day, while I made a bag of geese, hare and partridges in the river valley. While so occupied I came across some Tibetans digging up the root of a kind of bush from which Tibetan paper is made. This paper is used all over Tibet. The Chinese locally call it *p'ichih* ("skin paper"—there are also other kinds of *p'ichih* made in China). It is very tough and strong, but, in Eastern Tibet at any rate, so roughly made as to be difficult to write upon with a steel pen; the Tibetan wooden pen, however, slides over the obstructions of unassimilated fragments of wood and straw more successfully.

We left Barme Gomba on May 5 for Nangchen, distant only one day's march. Following up the ravine and then ascending the mountain side we reached a pass at 14,000 feet after two hours' climb. This, however, turned out to be only a secondary pass over a spur, and we had another two hours' rough scrambling, the trail winding along the side of the range over a waste of rock and snow, before we reached the real pass, the Manam La (15,500 feet), the watershed between the Dza Chu and the Dje Chu, the two branches of the upper

[1] *Chilingi* really means "outsiders" or "foreigners"; the usual word for "English" in Tibet nowadays is *Yingi* (probably from the Chinese *Yingkuo*). Tibetans of the upper classes talk about other countries, France, America, and so on, by their English or Chinese names according as they happen to be from Central or Eastern Tibet.

[2] Amdo is the Tibetan name for the north-eastern portion of the Tibetan high lands, that is to say, the country west of T'aochou and Labrang Gomba in Kansu.

Mekong which unite at Chamdo. Near the pass we saw many wild sheep. The Manam La would be a difficult pass in bad weather; fortunately we crossed it in brilliant sunshine. It is practically the top of the range, the neighbouring peaks being not much higher; this is often the case with passes in China and Tibet, where the roads usually cross the ranges by the most direct rather than the easiest routes. The descent from the pass is very steep for a thousand feet or so, and the trail then runs south across two spurs, keeping close under the divide, with finally another steep drop to reach Nangchen.

Nangchen, in Chinese Lungch'in, consists of the *Podrang* of the Chief, a *Garjyuba* monastery called Tsepchu Gomba, a huge heap of *mani* stones, and a few mud hovels, lying at an elevation of about 13,500 feet in a ravine on the southern slopes of the range which separates the valleys of the Dza Chu and the Dje Chu. The elevation is too high for the cultivation of grain, but a few Tibetan turnips are grown.

The Native State of Nangchen, of which this place is the capital, covers a large area of grass country in the basins of the upper Mekong and Yangtze rivers. It is bounded on the east by De-ge and Hlato, on the south by Chamdo and Riwoche, and on the south-west by Jyade (in Chinese San-shih-chiu-tsu, or "Country of the Thirty-nine Tribes"). The population is mostly nomadic, and is said to consist of some 10,000 families divided up into twenty-five clans; hence the region seems to be also known as the "Country of the Twenty-five Tribes."

Nangchen lies nominally in the Kokonor Territory, that is to say, under the jurisdiction of the Kansu Frontier Authorities at Sining[1]. Under the régime of the Manchu Amban at Sining the State enjoyed practical independence under Chinese suzerainty. The Tibetan rank of the native Rajah was that of *Jyelbo*, or King, and his ancestor had been

[1] The French explorer, M. Grenard, who travelled from Central Tibet to Jyekundo with M. De Rhins, traversed a corner of Nangchen State, and writes in his book (*Tibet and the Tibetans*), referring to their arrival in the Nangchen grass country, perfectly correctly as follows:

"This tribe is dependent upon the Nanchen Gyalpo, a very venerable and lazy King, who pitches his camp in the basin of the Mekong between Jyekundo and Chamdo. We were now within the territorial jurisdiction of the Imperial Legate of Sining."

Apart from the Russian traveller, Kozloff, who also traversed Nangchen on his journey south from Chamdo, no other foreign explorer in Tibet appears to have noticed the existence of this important Native State.

recognised as such by the grant of a seal and a red button by the Manchu Court at the time of the settlement of Tibetan affairs in the reign of the Emperor Yung Cheng early in the eighteenth century. But since the transfer of the control of the Kokonor Territory to the Kansu Mahomedans the latter have interfered considerably with the authority of the native Tibetan officials, especially in the neighbourhood of Jyekundo, where they have taken over the administration.

The houses at Nangchen are the most miserable of hovels, lit by holes in the roof instead of windows. This is the style of house which is generally built in the grass country where tents are the usual habitations. Being constructed by a race of tent dwellers, they are doubtless built in imitation of the nomads' tents, which always have a hole in the roof to permit the escape of the smoke.

The Chief has presented us with the usual sheep and sacks of grain and dried turnips. The latter, called *nyungma* in Tibetan, and *yuanken* in Chinese, are grown at elevations which are too high even for Tibetan barley, and they are commonly cultivated in small quantities by the nomads. Dried in thin strips they form a valuable fodder for mules and ponies during the lean season (the spring), and they seem really intended for this purpose. But we felt so in need of vegetables that we soaked them in water and then cooked and ate them ourselves.

The Chinese are born conservatives and dislike change or innovation of any kind; but at the same time they have a genius for adapting themselves to changed circumstances and making the best of things when they have to do so. My cook comes from Peking. When we left Tachienlu he thought he could not possibly cook my food without charcoal; then he found that he could not do without firewood; then he complained when eggs and vegetables gave out; now he is reduced to a fire of yak dung, and flour, butter, mutton and dried turnips; yet he continues to produce excellent meals.

The prairies round Nangchen, as in many other parts of Eastern Tibet, are honeycombed with the holes of a small field rat; in places the ground is alive with them.

Going out yesterday to examine the surrounding country I discovered a river, the presence of which one would not suspect, flowing from north-west to south-east in a deep valley less than a mile from and about a thousand feet below Nangchen. This turned out to be a stream called the Bar Chu, a tributary of the Dje Chu. It is given undue prominence on most maps of Tibet. We found it only a few yards wide and a foot or so deep at the present season, and I doubt whether its sources can be more than fifty miles distant.

May 10. At Guzhi Gomba.

We finally left Nangchen on May 8. The trail dropped down through a ravine to the Bar Chu, followed down the gorges of the latter for a short distance, and then, after crossing the stream[1], turned up a side valley to the south, which led eventually to an easy pass, the Shigar La, 14,300 feet high. From this pass we dropped abruptly into one of the limestone gorges characteristic of this region, and following down the stream through a remarkable cleft where the trail lay for a space in the stream itself, hemmed in by towering walls of limestone rock not ten yards apart, we emerged on to a grassy valley where we camped at an elevation a little below 13,000 feet. This was one of our pleasantest camping grounds, near a clear streamlet flowing through a park-like valley, bounded by gentle grassy slopes of red sandstone, which were dotted with pine trees and abounded in silver pheasants. Near by were some hermits' caves.

On this march we met various kinds of big game, all of which were remarkably tame. This was due to the fact that Nangchen is a very religious place, no shooting or hunting being permitted in the vicinity. Soon after starting we met with some gazelle and a kind of large musk deer, which stood still and looked at us in the most unconcerned way; and further on, while following down the Bar Chu, we found a flock of half a dozen wild sheep wandering along the water's edge on the opposite side of the stream; they were so near that they could have been shot with a revolver. Later on, when I thought we had got sufficiently far from Nangchen, I let the men shoot for the pot, and they bagged two sheep,

[1] An alternative route to Chamdo runs down the Bar Chu valley; this was probably the route taken by Kozloff's party, who seem to have come straight over the mountains south from Gurde Druka without visiting Barmendo or Nangchen Podrang.

a young ewe and an old ram with a fine head. We ate the ewe in the evening and found the mutton excellent[1].

All over Tibet it is the custom to have prongs, usually made of antelope horns, attached to the native guns as rests to steady the aim. In Kam these prong attachments are often used on rifles also. The result is that a shot is seldom wasted when an animal has once been covered after a successful stalk.

On the evening of the 8th of May an important event occurred in the history of our travels. As it was getting dusk three horsemen galloped into our camp, and one of the Tibetans ran up crying *Debashungi mami* (Lhasa soldiers)! They turned out to be a lieutenant, a non-commissioned officer, and a private of the Tibetan army, who had been sent by the Kalon Lama to meet and escort us to his headquarters in reply to a letter I had sent him through General Ma from Jyekundo. They brought the news of the fall of Chamdo at the end of April, and of the surrender of the whole Chinese garrison to the Tibetans.

The fact that there are still eight to ten degrees of frost at night-time on these grass-lands, although we are getting on towards the middle of May, explains why there is no cultivation in these parts.

On May 9 we made a short march down a narrow gorge and debouched on to the Dje Chu, camping on the further bank after crossing by coracle ferry. The Dje Chu is here a swift muddy river, quite unfordable, and nearly a hundred yards wide; it flows from north-west to south-east in a cultivated valley between red hills dotted with pine trees; the volume of water appeared to be little if at all less than that of the Dza Chu[2]. There is a small red sect monastery, called Ne-de Gomba, on the hillside opposite the spot where we camped.

While marching down the gorge just before reaching the Dje Chu we crossed the southern boundary of Nangchen State and entered Riwoche territory; that is to say, we left

[1] This profusion of big game in Eastern Tibet is only found in the more remote parts in the grass country. In the agricultural valleys and on the more frequented main roads, as for instance, that between Batang and Chamdo, big game is seldom met with.

[2] The Dje Chu, lower down known as the Ngom Chu, joins the Dza Chu at Chamdo to form the Mekong.

the Kokonor (Ch'ing Hai) and the jurisdiction of the Kansu Mahomedans and entered Autonomous (Lhasa-controlled) Tibet.

To-day, May 10, after crossing a steep spur above the river, we followed down the cultivated valley of the Dje Chu, past several hamlets, to this place, a *Gandemba* monastery called Guzhi Gomba, also known as Tupde Dorjeling[1]. Below the monastery the river is spanned by a frail-looking iron suspension bridge, and the adjacent hamlet is naturally called Chazamka[2]. The elevation of the river is here about 11,800 feet. Perhaps this place is the same as Kozloff's Ga Gomba.

Our Chinese Mahomedan guides having accomplished their task of seeing us safe into the Tibetan lines, return to Jyekundo from here. They have been travelling for the past two days in the company of the Lhasa soldiers without the least friction, although the Chinese, or rather the Szechuanese, are at war with Tibet in the neighbourhood. These Kansu braves show much more aptitude than the Szechuanese for dealing with the local Tibetans of the country, and have the advantage over the Szechuanese of being thoroughly conversant with the language and customs of the Tibetans and acclimatised to the country.

May 14. At Śagang Gomba.

We left Guzhi Gomba on May 11, expecting to have an easy march down the valley, with villages and monasteries to stop in, for the rest of the way to Chamdo. But after following down the Dza Chu for a few more miles our trail turned south up a side ravine, the river here bending east through an impassable gorge; and, after crossing two small passes, we found ourselves camped again in the wilderness.

On the following day we marched up a long valley due

[1] Dorjeling, meaning "Place of the *Dorje*" (the latter the sacred emblem of the thunderbolt), is fairly common as a name in Eastern Tibet; there was formerly a monastery of that name on the Sikkim border, from which the Indian hill station of Darjeeling derives its name.

[2] Chazamka means "Place of the Iron Bridge"; this spot is marked on Chinese maps as "T'ieh So Ch'iao," meaning "Iron Suspension Bridge"; these bridges, made either of iron chains or bamboo ropes, are common in the Chinese border country, but this was the only one we met with in the course of our travels west of Tachienlu. Single rope bridges, to which the traveller and his baggage are attached by a sling (see Plate LXIV), are also common in the border country but not in Tibet Proper.

south-east to a pass called the Dongma La, 15,100 feet, and down through a pine forest to another camping ground in a grassy vale at the junction of two streams. From here we ascended again through forest to another high pass, the Jyola La, 14,800 feet, and followed down a wooded gorge the other side to a hamlet called Bangrushi near the Dje Chu, which from here down to Chamdo is called the Ngom Chu.

When crossing the Dongma La we found ourselves marching for a mile or two along the top of a bare ridge some 15,000 feet high, the watershed between the Ngom Chu and the Riwoche river, and looking down a ravine to the west could almost see the latter. The country between the Ngom Chu and the Riwoche river traversed on these marches is a pleasant region of grassy vales alternating with pine forest. Hares are remarkably numerous, and we have been living on them for the last few days. Coming down from the Dongma La through the pine forest we came upon a large flock of monkeys hanging like huge pieces of fruit from the branches of the trees at an elevation of over 13,000 feet.

Leaving Bangrushi we emerged on to the Ngom Chu valley almost immediately, presumably at a point just below its confluence with the Bar Chu. Here we seemed to have rejoined Kozloff's route, the latter lying on the opposite side of the river. For the next two days we marched down the valley, partly wooded and partly cultivated, past numerous hamlets and monasteries, including Nendo Gomba and Monda Gomba, to this place, a monastery called Sagang Gomba, a branch of the great Chamdo monastery destroyed by the Chinese some years ago[1]. The river, the elevation of which is about 11,200 feet, is here crossed by a big cantilever bridge in three spans.

The women in this neighbourhood have the unpleasant habit, common in most parts of Eastern Tibet, of smearing their faces with black grease, which renders their otherwise comely countenances perfectly hideous to look upon. I have read somewhere that they do this to render themselves unattractive to the lamas; but everyone here says it is done simply to protect their faces against the wind; which, if less

[1] Often pronounced Sagung: the final syllable *gang* is frequently pronounced *gung* or *gong* in Kam, as for instance Dzogang Gomba in Tsawarong, pronounced Dzogung.

romantic, is much more probable. At fairs and on other festive occasions, the nomad women appear with fresh rosy faces after ridding themselves of this protective coating of black grease.

We have at last reached spring in this valley, the trees are in bud, and the crops are appearing above ground. Yesterday it actually rained, for the first time on the journey.

May 21. At CHAMDO.

From Sagang Gomba to Chamdo is only two or three days' march by a good road down the valley of the Ngom Chu. Arrived at a small monastery called Yongda Gomba, however, we were delayed for a day or two awaiting messengers from Chamdo. From here on signs of the recent fighting between Chinese and Tibetans were numerous in the shape of ruined stone sangars, burned out houses, and huge vultures feeding on the dead bodies of horses, yak and men. The Chinese had retired, fighting stubbornly, step by step from Riwoche to Chamdo.

At the hamlet of Lamda we joined the main road from Lhasa[1]. Here we found great activity, caravans from Central Tibet with supplies for the Lhasa troops arriving and departing. Half-way between Lamda and Chamdo the river is crossed by a big cantilever bridge at the hamlet of Nguro Zamka (Chinese Olo Ch'iao). From here the road runs down the left bank of the Ngom Chu for the rest of the way to Chamdo, where we arrived on May 19, just three weeks after the Chinese garrison had surrendered to the Tibetans.

Chamdo (in Chinese Chamuto or Ch'angtu) consists of a few yamens and temples and a village of mud hovels built on a narrow spit of land between, and just above the confluence of, the Dza Chu and the Ngom Chu. The elevation is about 10,600 feet. On a sort of plateau immediately behind rise the gaunt ruins of the once great and splendid monastery, formerly the largest and wealthiest in Kam. The two valleys are so narrow as to permit of scarcely any cultivation. All around are bare and somewhat dreary-looking mountains.

Though a miserable place in appearance, Chamdo ranks

[1] From Lamda the Lhasa road runs up a gorge and over a high pass to Enda in the valley of the Riwoche river, whence it crosses another big pass, or rather plateau, called by the Chinese Waho Shan, to reach Sha-yi Zamka (Chinese Chiayü Ch'iao), the bridge over the Salween.

PLATE XXV

VIEW OF CHAMDO, LOOKING EAST UP THE NGOM CHU VALLEY: THE TOWN IN THE FOREGROUND, AND THE RUINED MONASTERY ON THE HIGH GROUND BEHIND

VIEW OF CHAMDO, SHOWING THE JUNCTION OF THE DZA CHU AND THE NGOM CHU (HEADWATER STREAMS OF THE MEKONG) BELOW THE TOWN (HIGH-WATER SEASON)

PLATE XXVI

THE "YUNNAN BRIDGE" ACROSS THE NGOM CHU AT CHAMDO

THE "SZECHUAN BRIDGE" ACROSS THE DZA CHU AT CHAMDO

with Jyekundo as one of the most important centres of Eastern Tibet. It was formerly the capital of the lama-ruled Tibetan State of the same name, and was the residence of the lama ruler, locally known as the *Tsangdruba*[1]. The small Chinese commissariat official stationed here in those days with a few Chinese soldiers kept very much to himself and was careful not to interfere with the lama rulers[2]. Chao Erh-feng seized Chamdo in 1909, expelled the Tibetan officials, and set up a Chinese magistrate. During the troubles of 1912–13 the Chinese attacked and destroyed the monastery, reducing the huge buildings to heaps of rubble. The Tibetans have never forgotten or forgiven this act of sacrilege.

Five main roads meet at and near Chamdo, namely those leading west to Lhasa[3], north to Jyekundo, east to De-ge Gönchen and Kanze, south-east to Batang, and south to Yunnan. The Ngom Chu and Dza Chu are each spanned by fine cantilever bridges, probably the largest of their kind in existence, called the Yunnan and Szechuan Bridges, because they lead to Yunnan and Szechuan respectively, and were built at the expense of Yunnanese and Szechuanese merchants many years ago.

We were accommodated in a dilapidated old yamen, formerly the residence of the Chinese commissariat officer who used to be stationed at Chamdo under the Manchu Dynasty. More recently it had been the residence of the

[1] A kind of Treasurer, or Prime Minister, to the nominal Ruler, the principal Reincarnation.

[2] General Bower, writing in 1894 (*Across Tibet*) refers to this officer as an *Amban*, which is inaccurate. The Abbé Huc writes of him more correctly as a *commissary* in charge of a magazine of provisions, his Chinese title being that of *Liang-tai*. The French traveller, M. Grenard (*Tibet and the Tibetans*), refers to the Chinese officials at Chamdo and Jyekundo as Consular Agents, that is to say, Chinese officials with jurisdiction over their own Chinese nationals but not over the Tibetans. This appears to have been an accurate definition of their position in those days.

[3] Chamdo is reckoned nearly a month's journey from Lhasa for ordinary travellers (being about half-way between Lhasa and Tachienlu) but the distance is covered by official Tibetan couriers in ten days. These official courier services in Tibet are somewhat remarkable, as the same messenger is supposed to ride right through night and day, changing ponies at the stages; his belt is stamped with an official seal (apparently to ensure that he does not loosen his robe to rest *en route*); and when the belt is unsealed at the end of the journey the man is naturally in a very exhausted state, having spent (between Chamdo and Lhasa) some ten consecutive days and nights in the saddle on one of the most arduous roads in the world. Perhaps only a Tibetan could accomplish the feat.

8—2

Chinese Second-in-Command, a Yunnanese General, who had been executed by the fire-eating General P'eng for advocating negotiations with the Tibetans early on in the siege. The Chinese said it was haunted by the spirit of the decapitated General, calling for redress; in any case it was infested with rats, which seemed to have grown and multiplied by feeding off the dead bodies of men and animals during the siege.

Chamdo has a strong religious and historical connection with Tibet Proper, and ever since the Chinese occupation in 1909 the Tibetans have been anxiously waiting and hoping for its ultimate restoration to Tibetan rule. Now that they are again in possession of this hideous collection of ruins and mud hovels, with its surroundings of rubbish heaps, old horns, dead dogs, and half-buried corpses, universal joy and satisfaction reign. Had the Chinese continued to administer the conquered regions of Eastern Tibet on the lines initiated by Chao Erh-feng, the natives would perhaps in time have become reconciled to Chinese rule. But ever since the Chinese revolution of 1911–12 the Government of Republican China, while formulating in theory an excellent policy providing for the unity and equality of treatment of the "Five Races" (Chinese, Manchus, Mongols, Mahomedans and Tibetans), have unfortunately been too preoccupied with other matters to pay any attention to Tibetan affairs and have left the administration of the frontier districts in the hands of a few military adventurers, who have misgoverned and oppressed the Tibetans of the regions under their control. As a result of years of tyrannous misrule, which has grown worse from year to year, scarcely a single native of Eastern Tibet, outside the staffs of the yamens, was to be found when hostilities were resumed last year who did not promptly desert the Chinese and welcome the advancing Lhasa soldiers as liberators. This was one of the principal reasons for the completeness and suddenness of the Chinese collapse.

Over the Kalon Lama's residence, a small Tibetan house, floats the banner of Tibet, a yellow flag bearing a device like a lion in green, with a white snow mountain and a sun and moon in the corner. The Kalon Lama himself[1], who has been at the head of the Tibetan army on the frontier for the past five or six years, is a middle-aged monk of commanding

[1] See Plate XXXI.

MAP 6

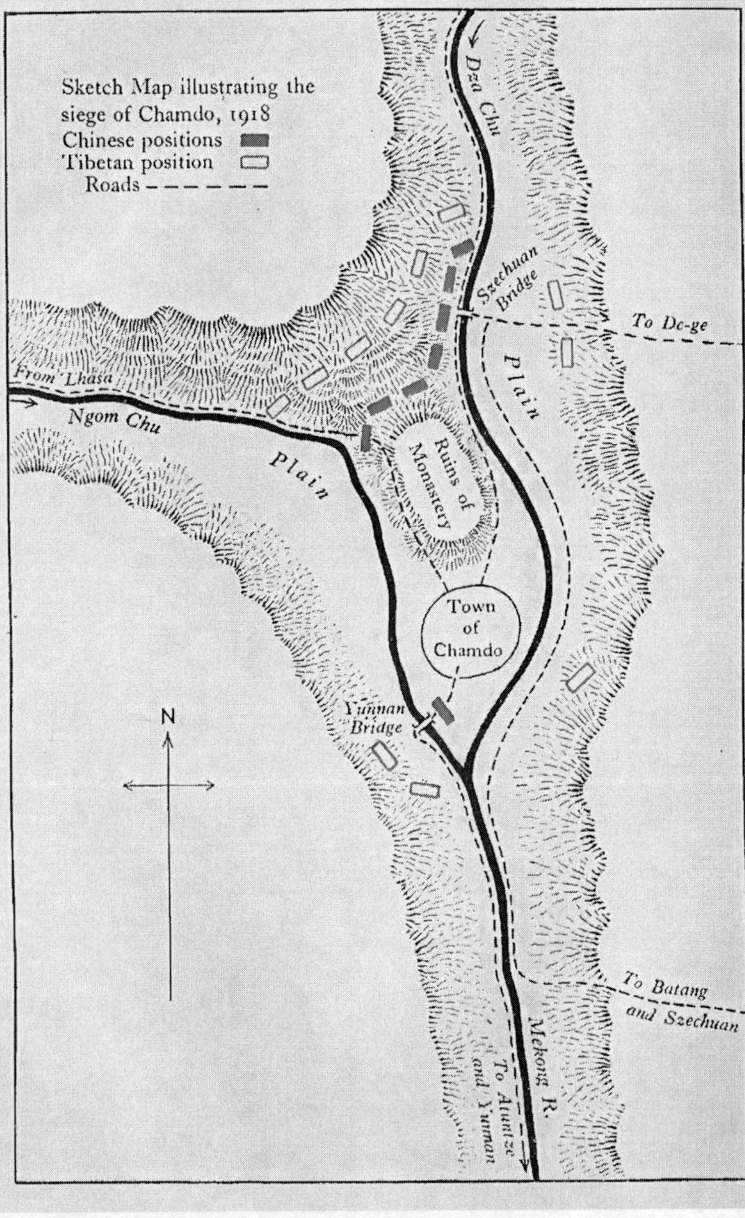

Sketch Map illustrating the siege of Chamdo, 1918
Chinese positions
Tibetan position
Roads
Dza Chu
Szechuan Bridge
To De-ge
Plain
From Lhasa
Ngom Chu
Plain
Ruins of Monastery
Town of Chamdo
Yunnan Bridge
N
To Batang and Szechuan
Mekong R.
To Atuntze and Yunnan

appearance and stature, with features showing great intelligence and refinement. He is at present absolute autocrat of all the Tibetan-controlled parts of Kam, which he administers with efficiency and justice, and where he is universally respected and obeyed without question[1].

The siege of Chamdo was a terrible tragedy for the Chinese, though a just retribution for the folly of their leaders in provoking a resumption of hostilities with the Tibetans. Once the investment was completed, the final surrender was only a matter of time. The position, surrounded as it is on three sides by large rivers, is a strong one against an enemy unprovided with artillery; its weak side is the north, where the hills slope down to the ruined monastery behind the town. After the investment had been completed in February the fighting was mostly confined to these hills, the commanding positions on which were stubbornly defended by the Chinese, only to be forced one by one by the Tibetans. Both parties fought behind stone sangars (*Dzingra* in Tibetan, *Chatzu* in Chinese) instead of in trenches. The Tibetans gradually advanced their stone barricades closer and closer, until they were almost within a stone's throw of the Chinese positions round the ruined monastery. Then they brought up a small mountain gun which they had captured from the Chinese at Draya (it was served by Chinese gunners, who were apparently quite ready to fight for anyone who paid and fed them). General P'eng, the Chinese Commander, thereupon surrendered unconditionally, and the Tibetans entered the town.

Of the garrison, consisting of about a thousand Chinese soldiers, more than half were killed or died of disease, while the unwounded remainder have been marched off to Lhasa as prisoners of war in the wake of their colleagues of other battalions captured earlier[2]. General P'eng is being detained

[1] The Government of Tibet is largely in the hands of a Council, called the *Kasha*, composed of four councillors, called *Sha-pe*, of whom three are laymen and one a cleric. This cleric councillor is known as the Kalon Lama, the word meaning "Commanding Minister Priest"; he is usually addressed as *Sawang Chempo* ("Great Lord of the Land"), and is one of the most important personages in Tibet.

[2] All these prisoners were subsequently repatriated by the Tibetan Government safe and sound *via* India, Burma and Yunnan to their homes in Szechuan; it was typical of the confused situation that they should have been loud in their praises of the good treatment and attention they received on the journey until they crossed the Burma-Yunnan frontier into Yunnan, where they were pillaged and robbed by soldiers and brigands on the road.

with his Tibetan wife and family in a monastery near by pending the receipt of orders from Lhasa as to his disposal. Although the Tibetans are very incensed against him, both on account of his past actions, which include the destruction of the Chamdo monastery some years ago, and on account of his recent attitude which resulted in a resumption of hostilities, the Kalon Lama is treating him well and it is understood that his life is in no danger. Of the four Chinese battalion commanders in Chamdo during the siege, one has been removed to Lhasa as a prisoner, one was killed in action, one committed suicide by jumping into the river at the time of the surrender, and one is still detained here.

On the whole, the Chinese seem to have put up a good defence. We went over their fortifications behind the monastery, which were in places only a hundred yards or so distant from the nearest Tibetan barricades, and found them covered with bullet marks and littered up with empty cartridge cases.

The Tibetans have undoubtedly behaved very well at Chamdo, treating their Chinese military prisoners with humanity and kindness, judging by oriental standards, and leaving the civilian Chinese unharmed, except for a little mild looting when the victorious Tibetan soldiery first entered the town. This seems, on the face of it, all the more remarkable in view of the atrocities committed by both sides during Chao Erh-feng's campaigns and the subsequent fighting in 1912–13–14. The explanation lies in the fact that the Tibetan troops who are now operating on this frontier against the Chinese and who have just taken Chamdo are Lhasa regulars under comparatively good discipline, and not the local lamas and tribesmen who fought the Chinese so bitterly in former campaigns. Although many Chinese were shot during the actual siege, I have not heard of a single instance of a Chinese being killed since the surrender. The soldier prisoners were all properly fed, and even provided with a little rice and a few rupees apiece before being sent into Tibet. The civilian Chinese are at present moving freely about the town carrying on their usual business, each with a ticket on his arm, showing that he has been registered at the Tibetan headquarters.

The Chinese here blame four men for all their misfortunes,

General P'eng, two of his battalion commanders, and a renegade Tibetan named Gara Lama; they are alleged to have arranged to attack the Tibetans with the object of invading Tibet and looting the riches of the monasteries in the interior of the country.

The Kalon Lama states that he is anxious that the Chinese in his hands should be well treated in accordance with the precepts of his religion; he says the Tibetans have no quarrel with the Chinese as Chinese, or with the Chinese Government, but only with a certain class of Szechuanese, whom they accuse of having raided and laid waste their lands, burnt their holiest monasteries and temples, and killed laymen and priests alike. The Chinese *Ta Tsung T'ung* ("the Great President"), who, they understand, has taken the Emperor's place, must, they say, be ignorant of the proceedings on the frontier of recent years, and of the cruelties perpetrated on the Tibetan population by the Szechuanese military. The Tibetans say that they want nothing better than to live at peace with the Chinese and enjoy the benefits of Chinese trade; but after their experiences of the past few years, they refuse to submit to the direct rule of Chinese officials.

When one considers the state of law and order and comparative economic prosperity now prevailing in Autonomous Tibet and compares the same with the chaotic conditions reigning in Western China, where the people are groaning under the misrule of military satraps and being harried by countless brigands, one must admit that there is justification for the Tibetan contention that they should be left in peace to manage their own affairs. As regards the relative state of affairs in Tibetan and Chinese-controlled territory in Kam, as long ago as 1894 General Bower wrote (in *Across Tibet*) as follows:

> Towards the end of the march we crossed a bridge and entered a country under the Deva Zhung's[1] jurisdiction. The change in the attitude of the people was at once apparent: the identical people under the rule of China differ enormously from those under Lhasa. The Lhasa Government may not be a strong one; but compared to the Chinese it seems so; thieves instead of being the rule are the exception, and the people can certainly be restrained and kept in order by those in authority over them. A good deal of it may be owing to the fact that the Tibetan of high rank is superior to

[1] *Deba Shung* means the Lhasa Government.

the Chinese mandarin, in intellect his equal, in strength of character his superior; there is a more healthy tone about him than about the *literati* of the Celestial Empire.

The condition of the wounded here is very painful. In the absence of any kind of medical treatment, their wounds, now many weeks old, are all in an advanced state of putrefaction, and the stench from the houses where they are lodged poisons the air of the neighbouring streets. Both sides are largely armed with an ancient Mauser, which fires a soft lead bullet the size of one's finger; and the condition of a limb which receives one of these missiles and then remains without any sort of treatment for three or four weeks may be imagined. The wonder is that so many of them have survived these wounds; but both Chinese and Tibetans up here seem to be very hardy and tenacious of life[1]. I have visited the so-called hospitals, old temples where the men lie on the bare ground with their suppurating wounds oozing pus on to the mud floor, and have distributed all my small stock of drugs, bandages, and cigarettes amongst them. The Kalon Lama has agreed to my request that the American missionary doctor at Batang should be invited to tend them[2], if I can arrange for him to visit Chamdo, and has promised in reply to my representations to permit all who recover to return direct to Szechuan or Yunnan, instead of sending them into Tibet as prisoners-of-war; this assurance has done more to cheer up these wrecks of humanity than anything else I have done for them.

There is much military activity at Chamdo at present, caravans of supplies coming and going, troops drilling, and arms being repaired and overhauled, and it is evident that the Tibetans propose pressing their advantage and continuing their advance towards Szechuan. Troops are now being sent forward in two directions, south-east against Batang and east into De-ge. On the former road they have, I am told, already

[1] In this connection mention may be made of the Tibetan custom of punishing by mutilation. Except in actual warfare there is the usual Buddhist reluctance to taking life amongst the peoples of Eastern Tibet, and criminals are mutilated rather than executed, amputations of the hands and feet being common punishments for serious offences. These operations are carefully done at the joints, and friends stand by with pots of boiling butter into which the stumps are thrust to stop the bleeding.

[2] Dr Shelton, of the American Mission at Batang, visited Chamdo in due course, performed a number of major operations and saved a great many lives.

taken Markam Gartok (Chinese Chiangka), and expect to be in Batang shortly; on the latter road they have reached and occupied De-ge Gönchen, and are advancing thence towards Nyarong and Kanze.

There is really little to stop the Lhasa Tibetans from advancing up to Tachienlu, which many of them allege to be their objective. But the Chinese will never surrender their claim to the Batang-Litang stretch of country, which has been nominally a part of Szechuan for two centuries; and, unless we succeed in making peace immediately, before the Tibetans have advanced any further, years of bitter frontier warfare must result.

The Tibetan advance would best have been arrested on the old historical frontier line between Markam and Batang and between Chamdo and De-ge. Now it is probably too late to stop them even on the line of the Yangtze, if it is true that they have crossed that river and taken De-ge Gönchen (the capital of De-ge).

The Kalon Lama, after much argument, states his readiness to negotiate peace if a Chinese representative can be found with whom he can discuss terms; otherwise his forces must, he says, continue their victorious advance.

On the Tibetan side the position is simple enough; the Kalon Lama is Commander-in-Chief of all the Tibetan forces and all the various Tibetan leaders on the frontier will obey him without question. On the Chinese side, however, the situation is very different; Western China and the Szechuan Frontier Territory are controlled by several mutually independent military Chiefs, each of whom is probably hostile to and indifferent to the fate of the others; while the distant Peking Government has no control whatsoever over the Western Provinces, and is perhaps, for the moment, indifferent as to what may happen on the border.

Apart from the majestic figure of the Kalon Lama, we have met a number of interesting people amongst the Tibetan officers here, including no less than three *Dabön* (Generals or Colonels in the regular army of Tibet). One of these latter is a kodak enthusiast, and we had to submit to being photographed in various groups. The pictures were developed the same evening and turned out very well. The fact of the matter is that these Tibetan officers from Lhasa and Shigatse, whom the Chinese profess to regard as savages, are nowadays more civilised and better acquainted with foreign things than their equals in rank amongst the Chinese military of Western Szechuan. The reason for this state of affairs lies in the fact that it is much easier for the Tibetans of Central Tibet to come and go between Lhasa and India than it is for a native of Western Szechuan to visit Shanghai or Hankow.

Another interesting figure we met at Chamdo was an individual named the *Sobo Gegen* (meaning the Mongol Teacher), who combined the duties of instructor in Russian military drill and general factotum to the Kalon Lama. A native of the extreme west of Mongolia, on the Ili-Siberia border, he had spent a number of years in the service of a Russian officer, with whom he had travelled in Tibet, China, Russia and Japan, and had many interesting experiences to relate.

We leave to-morrow for Batang to see what can be done towards making peace, and shall take with us a number of Chinese civilian refugees whose release the Kalon Lama has sanctioned. I was at first afraid that it would be impossible to get through the opposing lines on the main road, and that it would be necessary to make a détour through the neutral territory of Yunnan as we had done through the neutral territory of Kokonor. The Tibetan Authorities, however, say that they can make the necessary arrangements and assure us that it will be all right. We have a short breathing space in which to see what can be done towards making peace, as the Chinese at Batang are said to be averse to fighting if they can possibly avoid doing so, while the Tibetan troops will not, for the moment, advance beyond the boundary of Markam, where they are awaiting reinforcements from Chamdo.

CHAPTER IV

FROM CHAMDO TO BATANG BY THE MAIN ROAD *VIA* DRAYA AND MARKAM GARTOK

A Tibetan army on the march—The Ipi La (15,300 feet)—Marmots—Ruined villages of Draya—Prayers for rain and fine weather—The Gam La (16,000 feet)—Draya Jyamdun—The Lama Ruler of Draya and the Chinese magistrate—Chinese refugees on their way out of Tibet—Encircling tactics of the Tibetans—The Shepu La (15,500 feet)—More refugees—The Gangso La (15,200 feet)—Markam Gartok—The Governor of Markam and a Chinese General—Conclusion of a month's truce—Crossing the frontier into Chinese territory—The boundary stone—Descent to the Yangtze and arrival in Batang—Protestant and Catholic Missions—Precarious position of Chinese at Batang—Difficulties of peace-making owing to destruction of telegraph lines—Lapse of month's truce and departure from Batang for peace negotiations at Chamdo.

May 28. At DRAYA.

After reforming our caravan by procuring some new ponies in exchange for those of our animals which were too exhausted to proceed, we left Chamdo on the 22nd. Most of the inhabitants seemed to have turned out to see us off, including a pitiful little deputation of Chinese wounded, hobbling along on sticks and crutches, who had struggled out to say good-bye and to remind us of our promise to procure them assistance and a speedy repatriation to Szechuan.

Our first day's march took us down the Mekong for three miles, and then up a side ravine, over a steep little pass called the Sodri La (14,200 feet), and down the other side to a hamlet called Mengpu.

We are now following a portion of the main road from Lhasa to China, on which the stages are short and well defined and provided with official rest-houses.

The next day we reached the hamlet of Bomde (Chinese Paotun), the trail leading down one ravine nearly to the Mekong, and then up another. Bomde, having been the scene of one of the earlier fights between Chinese and Tibetans at the beginning of the year, was mostly in ruins. By seizing it the Tibetans, who had crossed the Mekong by an ice bridge in the neighbourhood, had cut the main line of communications of the Chinese at Chamdo.

We found ourselves travelling this portion of the road in the company of the Tibetan reinforcements bound for Markam Gartok and the attack on Batang. This Tibetan army on the march resembled a migrating Tartar horde, and the way was often blocked by the trains of yak, laden with women, children, tents and household impedimenta. The soldiers, however, are well behaved, and are evidently on good terms with the local people, who seem to be willing enough to supply them with everything they want. The commanding General, the Ragashar Dabön, travels in some state, richly attired in silks and mounted on a fine mule, accompanied by a bodyguard of cavalry, and preceded by standard-bearers, trumpeters, and bagpipe-men[1]. This regiment and their commander come from Lhasa, but many of the men, having been on the frontier a long time, seem to have taken Kamba wives. At Bomde they were camped all around us in small family groups[2]. I exchanged visits with the Ragashar Dabön, an intelligent Tibetan gentleman and a scion of a well-known Lhasa family.

On May 24 we crossed a big pass, the Ipi La (in Chinese Kulung Shan, or "Hole Mountain," so named from the holes in the cliffs near by), height 15,300 feet, whence we dropped down into a ravine, and, passing round the shoulder of a grassy mountain dotted with pine trees, descended into a valley to reach Bagung, a hamlet perched up on the hillside with a rest-house in the valley below. This place lies in Draya State.

On this march we saw many partridges, hares and marmots. Two small yellow Tibetan dogs, resembling beagles, and said to be a special breed of hunting dog from Gongbo in South-east Tibet, have been presented to us. They chase every marmot they see into his hole; one they happened on

[1] The *Dabön* (General or Colonel in the Tibetan army, literally "Lord of the Arrow") nominally commands 500 men; on the frontier at present they seem to command a great many more, probably owing to the local levies attached to their forces; they are officers of the 4th rank. Below the *Dabön* in the military hierarchy are the *Rubön*, *Jyabön* and *Shingo* (majors, captains and lieutenants), holding 5th, 6th and 7th rank and commanding 250, 100 and 50 men respectively. The Tibetan military are very fond of the bagpipes, which appear to be the national instrument.

[2] See Plate XXVII.

TIBETAN TROOPS IN CAMP

SUMMIT OF THE GAM LA (16,100 FEET)

PLATE XXVIII

DRAYA JYAMDUN, LOOKING EAST

DRAYA JYAMDUN, LOOKING WEST

sufficiently far from his earth to catch him in the open; but to our surprise the marmot sat up, whistled and made faces, and the dogs did not dare to tackle him.

From Bagung, there is a good road down the level valley of the Me Chu, past a small monastery, to the village of Wangka, where we were met by a small Tibetan official belonging to Draya State. He had just returned to his post, on the withdrawal of the Chinese, after eight years of absence in Central Tibet, and will shortly be followed by the Chief Reincarnation of Draya and other lama officials.

The villages in this valley, as indeed throughout Draya, are in a very ruined condition, the result, not of the present hostilities, but of the fighting of 1912–13–14. These rebellions were suppressed with the severities and atrocities customary in this wild border warfare, and the natives have since suffered severely from the oppressive rule of the Chinese military. The Drayawa have the reputation of being, after the Chantrengwa[1], the most irreconcilable to Chinese rule of all the Kamba tribes.

Two or three miles below Wangka the trail leaves the Me Chu, which flows south, and turns up a ravine to the east to reach a steep little pass called the Dzo La (14,500 feet), from which it descends to another river flowing south, and then turns up a side ravine to a hamlet called Gam (Chinese Angti).

The country in this neighbourhood had been suffering from drought. The lamas prayed for rain and it rained. Then the Tibetan army protested, on the ground that their military operations, the object of which was the ejectment of the Chinese troops, were of more importance and of greater interest to the local people than the state of the crops. The natives endorsed this view, and asked the lamas to pray for the rain to stop. So the fine weather and the drought now continue.

On May 27th we crossed the big Gam La (Chinese Angti Shan) in fine weather, and descended down a long straight ravine to Draya. The Gam La is the biggest pass we have yet crossed. I made it over 16,000 feet high. The ascent from the Gam side is rather steep and difficult, with a good

[1] The people of Chantreng (Hsiang-ch'eng in Chinese) who occupy the country south of the Batang-Litang road.

deal of snow and ice at the present season; the descent is easy[1].

The road from Lhasa to Tachienlu is one of the most ancient and important of the highways of Asia, and at the same time one of the most arduous roads in the world. A big pass has to be crossed nearly every day.

Draya, or more properly Draya Jyamdun, i.e. the Jyamdun in Draya (in Chinese Chaya), is a desolate-looking place, the principal feature being, as at Chamdo, the gaunt ruins of the once splendid monastery. The destruction of these great religious institutions by the Chinese has done more than anything else to rouse the hostility of the Tibetans against the Szechuanese. The place lies in a kind of basin formed by the junction of three streams, which combine to flow south and west to the Mekong, and is surrounded by absolutely bare mountains of red and yellow sandstones and shales. The elevation is about 12,000 feet.

Draya Jyamdun is the capital of the lama-ruled Tibetan State of Draya, which covers a considerable area of country on both sides of the Mekong. Chao Erh-feng established a Chinese magistrate here in 1910, having expelled the lama officials, who fled to Lhasa. The Chinese occupation was, however, limited to that portion of the State lying east of the Mekong river, the latter serving as the frontier line in this neighbourhood from 1911 to 1917. A battalion of Chinese troops used to be stationed here. When General P'eng opened hostilities with the Tibetans at the end of 1917, he ordered this force to advance by a road leading west across the Mekong into the Tibetan district of Bashü in the Salween valley, in conjunction with his other two columns advancing from Enda and Riwoche. The Draya battalion duly advanced across the river, and were met and routed by the Tibetans, who then pursued them back to Draya and captured the whole battalion with scarcely a fight.

We were received here by the chief lama official (as at Chamdo, called the *Tsangdruba*)[2], who had just returned

[1] Rockhill (*Journey through Mongolia and Tibet*) makes the height of the Gam La 15,644 feet, and of Draya Jyamdun 11,700 feet; which I believe to be too low. Huc refers to this pass as one of the most formidable on the road from China to Lhasa, and says he was delayed for several days at Gam (Angti) because it was blocked with snow.

[2] See footnote on p. 115 and Plate XXXI.

from Central Tibet to resume his position at the head of the administration, and by the former Chinese battalion commander who had also been magistrate. The position of the latter is peculiar. He is actually a prisoner, having been permitted to remain here, instead of being marched off with his men to Lhasa, apparently as a favour for having surrendered so readily. Together with the Tsangdruba he came out to meet us, well mounted and followed by quite a retinue of Chinese, though the latter were unarmed. Subsequently he entertained us and the Tsangdruba with a dinner, in the course of which he expatiated at great length on his kindly feelings towards the Tibetans and on the reluctance with which he had taken up arms against them under the orders of his superior officer. The lama, a benevolent-looking old gentleman, treated him with every respect. But when he came to the point, which was that he wanted the Tsangdruba's permission to return with us to Szechuan, the latter refused to let him go, pleading the absence of the Kalon Lama's written authority to that effect.

Subsequently, after much argument and discussion, it was agreed that his Chinese wife and family, and the civil secretaries of his yamen, should be permitted to join our band of refugees, and they will therefore leave with us tomorrow[1].

All is peaceful here, and the local people are evidently overjoyed to be once more under their former lama rulers. We are well housed in a Tibetan building, which used to be the residence of the Chinese official. The Tsangdruba lives in a small monastery which survived the Chinese occupation. Apart from these buildings, and another large Tibetan house which is used as the official rest-house, the place is almost entirely in ruins.

June 4. At MARKAM GARTOK (Chiangka).

We left Draya on May 29, and marched up the river to the hamlet of Radzi (Chinese Lochiatsung). Here we found three more destitute Chinese in hiding from passing Tibetan troops, one being the former Chinese *Taishu* (the rest-house keeper in charge of the official mail and courier service).

[1] This Chinese battalion commander was later on, after the conclusion of peace, allowed to return to China by the Yunnan road.

They were living on doles of *tsamba* from the villagers. As no one seemed to object, we allowed them to attach themselves to our party.

Our progress was by now beginning to resemble the exodus from Egypt, and our party, swollen to large proportions, and encumbered with the wives, children and baggage of the refugees, covered on the march many miles of road. It is difficult to provide transport for so many people. All who are able to do so march on foot; the rest are provided with *ula* yak, whose rate of march is about two miles per hour or less. The local people are on the whole very complaisant about providing these animals, which we have no authority to requisition and for which they receive little or no payment, the refugees being mostly destitute or professing to be so. It appears that the natives are not sorry to see this exodus of Chinese, and are therefore ready to provide the necessary *ula* yak to further what they consider so worthy an undertaking. The refugees themselves are not very afraid of the natives; but are nervous when they meet the Lhasa soldiers.

Beyond Radzi the road crosses an easy pass, the Puchung La (13,700 feet), and then follows down a grassy valley and crosses a spur to reach a river called the Le Chu[1]. The valley of this stream is followed up south-east for the rest of the way to the hamlet of Atsur, where there are a few fields, though the elevation, close on 13,000 feet, is near the height limit for cultivation.

This place had been the scene of some fighting between a company of Chinese troops of the Batang command and the advancing Tibetans early in the year. The Chinese, who had been posted here to guard the main road against a Tibetan advance on Batang, awoke one morning to find themselves surrounded by the Tibetans, who, having pushed on after the fall of Draya, had seized the surrounding heights during the night. After a few days' fighting, over two hundred Chinese had surrendered.

The Tibetans displayed the same tactics here as at Chamdo,

[1] This river probably flows directly into the Mekong; but may possibly flow north-west to join the Me Chu just below Draya, where there is a valley trending in that direction. It is impossible to settle these points by enquiry amongst the natives, as they are always so vague about geographical details.

Draya, Toba and other places where they met the Chinese forces this year, that is to say, they made no attempt at a direct attack, but were content to occupy the commanding positions on the hills all round, and then snipe the Chinese camped in the village below until the latter surrendered.

At Atsur our party was again increased, this time by some Chinese secretaries and the native wife and family of the former Chinese magistrate of Gonjo (Chinese Kungchüeh, the district lying east of Draya), who have been in hiding near by. The magistrate himself appears to have escaped across the Yangtze before the Lhasa Tibetans arrived.

The refugees, who are mostly in a state of semi-collapse from the anxieties and hardships they have undergone, keep on coming to me for medicine, usually, *more sinico*, to cure some mysterious *huo* ("fire") in their insides. The habit of taking medicine is a national characteristic of the Chinese, who thus provide an excellent market for the vendors of patent pills of all kinds. Unfortunately, my small stock of drugs is almost exhausted.

From Atsur the trail leads south over another divide, the Shepu La (15,500 feet—according to Rockhill 15,000), a high but easy pass, and descends to the hamlet of Asenyewango (in Chinese Shihpankou), lying in the valley of another stream flowing west to the Mekong. This pass is the boundary between Draya and Markam.

The next stage, to Rusho, is rather a long one for Tibetan travel. The road continues south over a small pass, and descends, through a pleasant ravine amongst pine woods and grassy mountains of red sandstone, to a group of farms called Aratang lying on a sort of plateau. Here one turns east to cross another easy pass, and descends down a wooded gorge to a large valley which is followed up to Rusho (Chinese Lishu), a village and a small monastery.

Here we found a few hundred Tibetan troops, and twenty-odd destitute Chinese prisoners, who begged us to secure their release. The usual negotiations with the Tibetan commanders, two Rubön (Majors), followed, with the result that the Chinese were eventually permitted to attach themselves to our party.

Leaving Rusho the road follows up the stream to its source on the Gangso La (also called Nyimo La, 15,200 feet), a big pass with a double summit a mile or two apart[1]. This ridge is the Yangtze-Mekong divide. After a long descent down an uninhabited valley we came to a rest-house, which was, however, so small and dilapidated that we went on to a nomad camp near by.

The weather on this march was bad, rain, snow and cold, and one of the few of our original Tachienlu ponies still remaining, and also the baby of the Gonjo magistrate's wife, died on the Gangso La. The Chinese refugees spent a most miserable night in this camp, the tents being insufficient to provide shelter for more than a few. I bought two big sheep for ten rupees from the nomads, so that everyone at any rate got a good meal.

On June 3 we had only nine or ten miles left by a good road down the valley to reach Markam Gartok (Chinese Chiangka)[2], passing the trail which leads to Samba Druka on the Mekong, and thence to Drayü Gomba and the Salween valley, a mile or so before getting in.

Markam Gartok is a small place consisting of a Tibetan *Dzong* (official residence), a small monastery, and a few houses, now mostly burned. It lies in a flat grassy valley with very little cultivation at an elevation of about 12,500 feet (Rockhill, 12,240; Bower, 12,990; A. K. 11,900). The stream flows south into Yunnan. Previous travellers, such as Huc, Rockhill and Bower, refer to Draya Jyamdun and Markam Gartok as towns and considerable centres of population. There is very little left of these places nowadays, as the result of ten years of frontier fighting and unrest. Perhaps they will now revive, if peace is restored on the border.

The Catholic missionaries were established at Markam Gartok for a year or two round about 1860, but were forced to withdraw at the time of the Nyarong troubles in 1863–5. In 1861 Bishop Thomine and Fathers Renou and Desgodins even reached Chamdo, where they were turned back. Since those days, however, the Catholics have never been able to

[1] Rockhill makes this pass 15,095 feet high; Bower calls it the Khonsa La and makes it 15,020 feet high, the same as Shepu La, which I made 300 feet higher.

[2] The name means *Gartok* ("military camp") of Markam, and is to be distinguished from the Gartok in Western Tibet. Markam probably means "Lower Kam." The Chinese used to call Markam Gartok, Chiangka, and now call it Ningching.

penetrate beyond the old frontier line on the Ningching Shan near Batang.

Markam was formerly a province of Tibet Proper and was ruled by a Governor, called the Markam Teji, who was appointed by Lhasa[1]. The Chinese invaded the country in 1910, expelled the Tibetan officials, and established a Chinese district magistracy, which they called Ningching Hsien. The Chinese occupation was, however, limited, as in the case of Draya, to that portion of Markam lying to the east of the Mekong. When the Lhasa Tibetans recovered the province this year the Teji, who had been waiting on the other side of the Mekong, had only to cross the river to resume his old post as Governor at Markam Gartok.

After their victory at Atsur the Lhasa Tibetans advanced rapidly and captured Gartok, with its Chinese magistrate and small garrison of Chinese troops, by surrounding it in the usual way.

We were received here by the Teji, a tall dignified Tibetan official, after the Kalon Lama the most important personage in Kam, and also, much to our surprise, by General Liu Tsan-ting, the *Tungling* (Chinese Commandant) of Batang. The latter had come here with Dr Shelton, of the American Mission at Batang, to attempt to make peace and stop the Tibetan advance by negotiation. The Teji had received them as honoured guests, but had given them to understand that while there would be no further advance until the Tibetan reinforcements arrived, he could not talk peace, pleading the absence of the Kalon Lama's authority to do so. Dr Shelton had thereupon returned to Batang, but General Liu had remained at Markam Gartok in the hope of something turning up.

In view of the fact that the Kalon Lama had stated that he would be willing to negotiate peace if a Chinese representative could be produced with whom he might discuss terms, I have been able after lengthy discussions to induce the Teji to sign an agreement with General Liu, engaging to refrain from all hostilities for a period of one month, during which time I am to endeavour to get into touch by means of

[1] *Teji*, according to the Tibetan dictionary, is a Mongolian word, meaning "hereditary governor"; perhaps it represents, like the *Horba*, a relic of the Mongol invasion of Tibet two centuries ago. (See Plate XXXII.)

9—2

the Batang telegraph line with the Szechuan Authorities with a view to making a more permanent peace.

We leave to-morrow for Batang. General Liu will follow in a few days, as soon as the Teji has obtained the Kalon Lama's permission to let him go. It is recognised that he is an envoy, and not a prisoner; but the Teji, like all the other Tibetans on this border, will do nothing without the Kalon's instructions. The other Chinese here, the ex-magistrate, his secretaries, and a few civilians and wounded soldiers, are in a different position, as the Tibetans regard them as prisoners. However, by pointing to our large company of refugees, collected at different places on the road, I have been able to obtain the release of all of them, with the exception of the magistrate himself. The latter, an elderly gentleman, who appears to be dying from the effects of opium, or perhaps from the lack of it, is being detained pending an enquiry in connection with his alleged misdeeds and oppression of the local people.

June 15. At BATANG.

We left Markam Gartok on June 5, and turned up a ravine south-east to reach a pass called the Jyarong La (14,700 feet), whence we descended through pine forests and down a valley to the hamlet of Gusho (Chinese Kushu). As at Gartok, the barley was here just showing above ground.

This road across the Jyarong La is a short cut; the main road, followed by most travellers, runs down the Gartok river to the south, and then turns east across a low pass to reach Gusho.

The next stage is a short one, across a small pass covered with pine forests called the Lamar La to the village of Hlandun (Chinese Nantun), where we found the last Tibetan outposts. Arriving early, we pushed on across the old frontier line on the Bum La (in Chinese Ningching Shan), an easy pass over a bare grassy mountain ridge dividing the basins of the Gartok river and the Yangtze, and descended to the valley of Bum (Chinese Pamut'ang).

The Bum La, the frontier between Markam and Batang territory, was for two centuries the boundary between China and Tibet, from early in the eighteenth century until the

Chinese invasion of Tibet early in the twentieth, and is now again serving as the temporary frontier line between the Tibetan forces under the Markam Teji and the Chinese troops of General Liu's Batang command. From the Bum La the frontier line slants south-west over hills and streams, crosses the Mekong a short distance above Yenching, and continues in that direction until it reaches the meeting point of Burma, Yunnan and Tibet on the Salween-Irrawaddy divide south of Menkung.

A boundary stone is said to have been erected on the Bum La in the fourth year of the reign of Yung Cheng (1726–7), when the frontier was delimited by the Manchus; and the Imperial Ambans travelling to Lhasa are supposed to have made a practice of descending from their chairs when crossing the frontier and ceremoniously inspecting the boundary pillar. All that we could find in this respect was an irregular and apparently unhewn slab of sandstone, without any inscription on either side, propped up on end near the heap of stones marking the top of the pass. A local Tibetan who was with us pointed to this slab and referred to it as the *doring* (meaning in Tibetan an inscribed memorial tablet of stone, or literally "longevity stone") marking the frontier between China and Tibet. It is possible that the lettering may have been worn away by the natural effects of weather erosion during 200 years on the soft red sandstone of which the slab was composed; moreover it appeared to have been used as a target for shooting practice by the Tibetan levies guarding the pass. The local associations connected with this pass as the frontier between China and Tibet are very strong, and a permanent reversion to the boundary line of 1727 probably represents the fairest solution of the boundary problem which could be arrived at.

I made the height of the Bum La 13,500 feet; Rockhill gives it as 12,931, Bower as 14,420. Mr Rockhill refers to the boundary stone as "a large red sandstone slab half sunk in the ground": and adds that he was told that there was an inscription on it, but on the part below the surface of the ground. Twelve years later, in 1904, Sir A. Hosie, coming from the direction of Batang, was escorted to the spot, as being the frontier between China and Tibet, by Chinese officials; he found no inscription on the Chinese side; and was not permitted to step across the frontier to examine the other face[1].

Pamut'ang is the name of a valley, dotted with farms and hamlets (and for this reason its position varies on the traveller's map according to which farm he stops in). It lies at the junction of the Batang-Tibet and Batang-Yunnan roads, the latter crossing the Ningching ridge further south, and then following down the valley of the Gartok river into north-west Yunnan.

About half our refugees, learning that the Chinese troops stationed at the Yangtze ferry were pillaging all travellers crossing the river, left us here and took the Yunnan road, which was reported quiet. It turned out that they had been well advised to do so; for most of those who took the Batang road were actually plundered at the ferry, including the wife of the ex-magistrate of Draya, who lost a large quantity of opium and silver, which, unknown to us, she had concealed in her baggage. It was certainly very hard on these unfortunate people, who had made the long journey from Tibet, past the various posts of Tibetan troops, in perfect safety, only to be held up and pillaged by Chinese soldiers when they had crossed the frontier and reached their own country.

From Pamut'ang the road runs down the valley for nine miles to the hamlet of Kungtzeding, just before reaching which the stream turns suddenly away to the east, dropping down through a deep gorge towards the Yangtze. Beyond Kungtzeding a low ridge is crossed, and the road then descends a long ravine down to the Yangtze, the valley of which is followed up for a short distance to reach the hamlet of Gora (Chinese Kungla).

Descending from Kungtzeding to the Yangtze we passed suddenly from spring to midsummer; at the former place (12,000 feet) the barley was only a few inches above ground; down on the Yangtze level (8,500 feet) it was being harvested.

In this neighbourhood we met Dr Shelton, of the American Mission at Batang, pushing on for Chamdo with all speed in response to my appeal for medical assistance for the wounded there.

From Gora the road continues up the Yangtze for a few miles to the ferry, called Drubanang Druka in Tibetan, and

[1] See Plate XXX.

THE YANGTZE RIVER BELOW BATANG, LOOKING UP STREAM

THE YANGTZE RIVER BELOW BATANG, LOOKING DOWN STREAM:
THE MAIN ROAD TO YUNNAN AND TIBET ON THE LEFT BANK

PLATE XXX

THE BOUNDARY STONE ON THE BUM LA (NINGCHING SHAN), THE HISTORIC FRONTIER BETWEEN CHINA AND TIBET

BATANG, LOOKING NORTH

Chupalung in Chinese, where the traveller crosses from the right to the left bank of the river by means of a large ferry boat. Here we found the first Chinese outposts, it having been agreed that they should remain on the Batang side of the Yangtze as long as the Tibetans did not cross the Ning-ching Shan. These were the gentry who were holding up and plundering passing travellers, a common failing with Chinese soldiers in the distant interior of China (where ever since the Revolution of 1911 soldiers and brigands have but too often been synonymous terms). They had perhaps some excuse for doing so as they had not been properly paid for years.

A further half-stage up the Yangtze brought us to the hamlet of Lewa (Chinese Shuimokou). Another of our original Tachienlu ponies died on this march, when all the passes had been surmounted and we were almost within sight of the promised land of Batang.

The Yangtze in this neighbourhood flows in a colossal canyon between mountains rising six to seven thousand feet almost from the water's edge. So narrow is its valley that there is no room for cultivation except in the mouths of side ravines. The tributary streams come tumbling down the mountain wall from ice-formed "hanging valleys" high up and out of sight. The water is a thick yellow in the summer but clears to blue in the winter.

All along the Yangtze we received a series of appeals from the headmen of the hamlets begging that peace might be arranged. The corn being ripe for harvest, the people were in a state of panic and despair, expecting every day that the fighting would begin and that the troops of one side or the other would burn their houses and turn horses into their ripening crops. The Tibetans of the Batang neighbourhood, besides remembering very well how Chao Erh-feng chastised the countryside after the lama rebellion of 1905, have now been accustomed to the Chinese as their rulers for so long that, in contrast to the natives of other parts of Kam further west, they have no very keen desire to see the Lhasa Tibetans arrive. Above all they fear hostilities, in which, as they well know, they will be the chief sufferers no matter what the ultimate result may be.

On June 9 we covered the remaining eight miles or so to Batang. The road leaves the Yangtze a couple of miles beyond

Lewa, crosses a spur, and descends into the valley of the Batang river, which is followed for the rest of the way.

Batang[1] lies in a small valley plain, carefully irrigated and manured and heavily cropped, a rich little oasis in a desert of wild mountains. The elevation is about 9000 feet. The grain raised here on irrigated land, in this dry sunny climate, both wheat and barley, is equal in quality to the best produced in Canada. The town consists of a Tibetan village clustering round the two castles of the former native Chiefs; near by are the ruins of what was formerly one of the largest monasteries of Eastern Tibet.

The territory of Batang was formerly ruled by two native Chiefs (*Deba* in Tibetan, *Tussu* in Chinese), under the protection of the Szechuan Authorities, who were represented by a commissariat officer (*Liangtai*) and a small garrison of troops. The Chinese took over complete control of the administration and established a Chinese district magistrate after the suppression of the lama rebellion of 1905, when the Chiefs were beheaded and the monastery razed to the ground. Another smaller monastery has been rebuilt in the neighbourhood. Of the two castles of the former native Chiefs, one is occupied by the Chinese officials, and the other has been handed over to the Catholic Mission in part compensation for the destruction of their property in 1905. This may be good business for the mission, but it can hardly tend to promote good relations between the local Tibetans and the Catholic priest.

The Tibetans of Batang speak a very corrupt dialect, but Lhasa Tibetan is understood. In the same way that a knowledge of Pekingese will take one through China with the exception of a few of the southern coastal provinces, a knowledge of standard, or Lhasa, Tibetan will enable one to make oneself understood throughout Tibetan inhabited regions, as well as commanding a certain respect for the speaker in out-of-the-way parts.

An American Protestant Mission and a French Catholic Mission are established at Batang. The former, recognising perhaps that direct evangelisation amongst the Tibetans is

[1] Called Ba by the Tibetans; the Chinese have recently given it the new name of Paan Hsien; the Batang-Litang stretch of country is often referred to as Ba Lé by the Tibetans (Litang being called Letang in Tibetan).

at present hopeless, are engaged chiefly in medical and educational work, laying the foundations for possible evangelisation later on. They are surpassed by no mission in all China in respect of the amount of good they do and the sensible manner in which they do it.

Batang is the headquarters of the Chinese troops garrisoning the southern districts of the frontier, and their commander is to all intents and purposes Governor of all the country from Litang in the east to Yenching on the Mekong in the west. These troops belong to the old *Pien Chün* (Frontier Force), which has been on the border ever since the days of Chao Erh-feng, and are now so completely worn out, sodden with opium, and generally demoralised as to be nearly useless as a fighting force.

Food is the all important question here at the present time. Batang has for years served as a dumping ground for all the disabled, sick, and destitute Chinese in Eastern Tibet, who drift in here and somehow or other manage to get their names placed on the official rolls as entitled to public rations. This year's events have resulted in a further influx of destitute refugees, such as accompanied us from Tibet; and, in the continued absence of supplies from Szechuan, the crops of the valley are no longer sufficient to feed the local inhabitants, the soldiers and officials, and this parasitic population. Money too is very scarce. The soldiers have not been properly paid for years; and whenever a few thousand rupees arrive from Szechuan and are distributed amongst the troops, they vanish immediately to Yunnan in payment for opium. A few years ago it would have been easy to raise any reasonable amount of silver from the local Chinese or Tibetan merchants by means of drafts on Szechuan; now not a single rupee can be secured by any means. The foreign missionaries have to go a month's journey into North-west Yunnan to procure silver for their needs; and the local branch of the Chinese Post Office is reduced to going round periodically to the missions and begging them to buy stamps. The Chinese officials have raised and spent every rupee that was to be got out of the people by means of taxes, forced loans, and other exactions, and have already collected and consumed grain representing a year's land tax in advance. At the time of writing the foreign missionaries are going round, at the request of the Chinese Authorities, from house to house and farm to farm trying to borrow sufficient grain to feed the soldiers and keep them from looting during the next two or three weeks before the new crops are cut and threshed[1].

We ourselves fortunately have ample supplies of food, as we happen to have brought several sacks of wheat and barley with us out of Tibet, where conditions are quite normal.

Tachienlu, the seat of the Frontier Commissioner, lies in China Proper, and is separated from Batang and the actual frontier by three weeks' journey over wild, mountainous, and purely Tibetan country. It is difficult for the Chinese to administer the frontier districts satisfactorily from so distant a centre. Chao Erh-feng intended moving the seat of the administration to Batang, and built a large yamen down by the river near the ruins of the monastery. But since the establishment of the Republic in China successive Frontier Commissioners, always deeply involved in the politics of Western China, have declined to move from so safe a base as Tachienlu, where they are in close touch with Szechuan, and bury themselves in the interior of Eastern Tibet. At present Batang is in much closer touch with Yunnan than with Szechuan; indeed communication with the latter has for the time being ceased to exist.

We had hoped to be able on arriving at Batang to get into telegraphic communication with Szechuan, with a view to discovering whether and on what terms the Szechuan Authorities would make peace with the Tibetans. It was,

[1] The extraordinary state of distress prevailing in the summer of 1918 at Batang, the result of continued disturbances in Western China and the consequent neglect of these frontier garrisons by the Szechuanese authorities, is well illustrated by the following extract from an open letter (published in the foreign press of Shanghai at the time) which was addressed to the public by an American missionary of Batang; this gentleman had worked unceasingly to help the Chinese authorities to tide over and avert a catastrophe:

"In the interests of Chinese, Tibetans and foreigners, I write these words. Owing to the fighting between Tibetans and Chinese in the West and North, and the complete collapse of the Chinese Government, the situation is most distressing. The officials and foreigners of Batang have worked night and day in the interests of peace, and the British Consul is now at Chamdo with General Liu working for a peaceful settlement. All the available money of the Tibetans, the Chinese and the foreigners has been used up by the Chinese officials as loans or taken by force directly or indirectly. Even in the case of immediate peace, unless money is sent into Batang to pay the soldiers and return borrowed money, unspeakable distress is upon us all. I therefore beg you to do what you can to relieve this distressing situation. The situation is very dangerous for all, and many are dead and dying of starvation. I again in the interests of all beg you to bring the matter to the notice of any official who is in a position to help."

PLATE XXXI

Tibetan photo

THE KALON LAMA, TIBETAN COMMANDER-IN-CHIEF

Chinese photo

THE TSANGDRUBA OF DRAYA

PLATE XXXII

THE TEJI OF MARKAM, AND DR SHELTON OF THE AMERICAN MISSION AT BATANG

therefore, a great disappointment to find that no means of communication with Szechuan and Tachienlu existed, the telegraph line having been destroyed, and the road between Litang and Batang rendered almost impassable by bands of Tibetan *Chagba* (mounted brigands), who have taken advantage of the general situation to rise in every direction.

The prospects of making peace and of stopping a further Tibetan advance are, therefore, not very bright. The Markam Teji, commanding the Tibetan southern column, is under an obligation to stay his hand for a month from the day we left Gartok. But in the meanwhile, the Tibetan northern column is reported to be driving on through De-ge towards Nyarong and Kanze, where the main body of the Chinese troops from Tachienlu is said to be stationed. Moreover, a regiment detached from this northern column is advancing on Batang from the direction of De-ge, has surrounded a battalion of troops belonging to the Batang command in the usual way at a place called Gaji (Chinese Kaiyü), a few marches to the north, and will doubtless arrive here as soon as the Chinese they have surrounded have surrendered. We have sent off letters in all directions to the local leaders of both sides exhorting them to stop fighting pending the result of our efforts to open peace negotiations, and hope for the best while we wait for news from Szechuan, whither couriers have been despatched.

June 29. At Batang.

News is now to hand that the Markam Teji, the month's truce which we concluded at Gartok having nearly elapsed, is about to resume his advance on Batang and Yenching, that the Chinese force surrounded at Gaji is *in extremis*, and that large Tibetan forces are heavily engaged with the Chinese near Kanze on the North Road. The Chinese Authorities here are in despair, and talk about a general evacuation and an attempt to cut their way through the brigand-infested country to Litang and Tachienlu; and it is evident that we cannot afford to wait any longer if peace is to be concluded at all. We have accordingly sent urgent letters to the Markam Teji and the Kalon Lama, informing them that General Liu and I are leaving for Chamdo at once in order to open peace negotiations there, and calling upon the Kalon to stop the advance of his troops on all fronts pending our arrival. Having once got to Chamdo and started talking, we hope that something may turn up in the meantime; while even if we fail to get into communication with Szechuan, it may be possible to conclude peace separately between the Tibetans and the various Chinese military leaders on the frontier. Moreover, our arrival at Chamdo, whether we are able to negotiate immediately or not, will at any rate be a guarantee to the various local leaders on both sides, scattered over a vast area of the frontier, that peace negotiations are genuinely intended, and will help to stabilise the situation, which tends otherwise to change from day to day. Every mile the Tibetans advance now makes it more difficult to arrange peace; since it will probably be equally impossible to persuade them to withdraw from territory which they have once occupied as to induce the Chinese to acquiesce in their remaining there. This applies especially to Batang, Litang, Yenching, Nyarong and Hor Kanze, none of which the Chinese are likely to agree to surrender.

We leave for Chamdo to-morrow, having arranged, in order to save time, to travel by a short cut, a little used trail leading directly to Draya, thus avoiding the détour to the south made by the main road *via* Markam Gartok. It is said that we can save six or seven days on the journey by this road.

Great difficulty has been experienced in raising sufficient funds to transport General Liu and his staff of secretaries, interpreters, and attendants to Chamdo. As usual, the American missionaries have come to the rescue by persuading the local people to provide the necessary funds, mostly in the form of bales of tea, on the grounds that the latter are as much interested as anyone else in the success of the peace-making mission.

CHAPTER V

FROM BATANG TO CHAMDO BY THE SHORT ROAD *VIA* JYASE GOMBA AND THE ONG CHU VALLEY

View from Shisongong above the Yangtze—Sangen and its robber tribes—Passage of the To La (15,200 feet) and the Dru La (15,100 feet) and descent into the Ong Chu valley—Jyase Gomba and Tibetan troops under the Ragashar Dabön—The Hlato plateau in Gonjo—Arrival at Draya—Reception at Chamdo—A Tibetan banquet—Chinese Tibetan interpreters—The Kalon Lama's A.D.C.—Tibetan culture—Peace negotiations—Chinese prisoners from De-ge—News from Kanze—Panic amongst the Chinese at Batang—Tibetan theatricals—Conclusion of provisional treaty of peace between Chinese and Tibetans—Arrival of Chala Chief from Kanze—Departure for Kanze to arrange further truce at Rongbatsa.

July 7. At DRAYA.

We left Batang on June 30, after a stay of exactly three weeks. Following down the valley of the Batang river to its confluence with the Yangtze, we crossed the latter by ferry at the hamlet of Nyugu, and climbed up the opposite mountain side by a steep zigzag footpath for three hours, rising three to four thousand feet, to reach a small monastery and group of farms called Shisongong[1] (Chinese Hsisungkung), lying on a cultivated slope overlooking the canyon of the Yangtze. The barley, already harvested on the Yangtze level, was here not yet in ear.

The situation of Shisongong would be difficult to match anywhere in the world. In front the ground falls away almost sheer to the Yangtze, thousands of feet below, while behind the pine-clad slopes rise almost as far again to the top of the range. Looking north, the canyon of the Yangtze appears as a great fissure in the mountains; to the north-east Batang and its fertile little plain, only a few miles distant as the crow flies, are in full view; while behind Batang, further east, towers a huge snow-clad mass, which must be twenty to twenty-five thousand feet in height. The main Batang-Litang road runs to the south of these snow mountains, to the north

[1] The name termination *gong*, which is frequently met with in Eastern Tibet, appears to mean a cultivated slope above a river valley.

of which lies the country of the wild Lengkashi Tibetans, in the unknown upper valley of the Batang river, the latter making a complete turn on itself and flowing first north and then south past Batang to join the Yangtze.

What with my own men and General Liu's numerous secretaries, interpreters, attendants and soldiers, we are far too big a party for comfortable travel.

On July 1 we continued to ascend the mountain side in a westerly direction through patches of pine forest, until, the latter giving out round about 14,000 feet, we found ourselves in a flat, bare, ice-formed valley, which led by easy gradients to the pass, the To La (15,200 feet, being about 7000 feet above the Yangtze level). After scrambling down a very steep descent the other side, we followed down a ravine through dense pine forests to a grassy clearing at the junction of two streams, called Rishisumdo, where we camped at an elevation of about 12,000 feet.

This spot is still in Batang district, and the stream flows north-east to join the Yangtze. Near by, to the north-west, is a peak called by the Chinese "Three boundary Mountain," because it is the meeting point of Batang, Markam and Sangen territory. The main trail into the latter country branches off here from the road we were following. Sangen (meaning in Tibetan "Bad Lands," transliterated by the Chinese as Sangai) comprises the country along the Yangtze north-west of Batang, and is inhabited by a congeries of robber clans with no proper ruler, who have from time immemorial been in the habit of raiding the more peaceful Tibetans of the surrounding country, more especially those of Batang. It was conquered by Chao Erh-feng and given by him the name of Wuch'eng district, but is now again in the hands of the Tibetans, the magistrate and all the other Chinese in the country having fled east across the Yangtze after the fall of Draya and Gonjo. Sangen is a most difficult country to enter or traverse, as it consists of deep narrow valleys draining into the Yangtze, divided off by very high and steep mountains. The only foreigner who has ever been there is, I believe, Dr Shelton of the American mission at Batang, who visited the headmen of the country on a peace-making mission at the request of the Chinese authorities a year or two ago.

Great changes have come over the grass country during the three weeks we were resting at Batang, and we found the grass at Rishisumdo already up and wild flowers in bloom, as well as flowering shrubs, such as the alpine rose, the rhododendron, and a purple gorse.

On the To La I shot a sort of pheasant grouse, perhaps a blood pheasant, a slatey-brown bird with red eyes. These birds perch in the pine trees, have a peculiar whistling call, and frequent the higher mountain slopes near and above the tree limit.

The next stage, from Rishisumdo camp to Ukagang, is another arduous march resembling the preceding one, an ascent up a pine-clad ravine obstructed by rocks and fallen trees, then a steep climb up the mountain side, and finally an easy approach through a flat valley to the pass, the Dru La (15,100 feet); whence there is a similar descent down the other side to the hamlet of Ukagang (11,400 feet) in the cultivated valley of the Ong Chu in Markam.

The ascents and descents to and from the To La and Dru La (as in the case of most other passes in these parts of Kam) are markedly divided up into two stages, narrow, densely wooded, water-eroded gorges below, and flat, bare, ice-formed valleys above.

The Dru La is the boundary between Markam and Batang territory, and therefore for the time being the frontier between China and Tibet. We were met on the further side by emissaries of the Markam Teji, Gartok being only a day or two's journey away.

The Ong Chu, an important tributary of the Yangtze, takes its rise on the grass-lands of Gonjo, and flows through Eastern Markam to join the Yangtze just below Drubanang Druka. The country lying between the Ong Chu and the Yangtze, crossed on these two marches, is an uninhabited wilderness of steep mountains densely forested on their lower slopes.

The road for the next stage, from Ukagang to Tara, is a good trail up the valley of the Ong Chu, which is picturesque and thickly wooded. Six miles out an important *Nyimaba* monastery called Jyase Gomba is passed. Here we found our former acquaintance, the Ragashar Dabön, and his column of Tibetan troops, all prepared for the advance on Batang.

The Tibetans evidently mean to attack the latter from three directions, that is to say, from here, from Hlandun on the main road, and from Gaji and De-ge on the North Road. The Dabön received our mixed party very amicably, and assured us that he would not advance until he received the Kalon Lama's orders to do so. General Liu endeavoured to induce him to send a letter to Gaji, ordering the Tibetan Commander there to cease from hostilities; but this he refused to do, on the grounds that the Tibetan force at Gaji belonged to the command of the Shigatse General operating in De-ge, whom he, as a Lhasa General, could not approach on such a matter except through the Supreme Commander, the Kalon Lama.

The hamlet of Tara, lying at an elevation of about 12,500 feet, marks the limit of cultivation in the Ong Chu valley.

On July 4 we made a very long march of twenty-five to thirty miles, travelling fast across grass country all the way. After following up the headwaters of the Ong Chu valley to an easy pass, the Podo Latse Ka, where a trail to Gonjo Dzong branches off to the north[1], we descended a long flat valley to the north-west and debouched on to a marshy plain of great extent, on the further side of which the nomads had prepared a camp for our reception. Thousands of yak, cows and calves were being pastured in the neighbourhood.

This basin-like plateau, on which we were encamped at an elevation of nearly 14,000 feet, is called Hlato and belongs to Gonjo. It appears to drain west into the Draya river; but the headwaters of streams flowing west to Draya, south to Markam, east to Sangen, and north to Gonjo, are all near by.

These grassy prairies abound in marmots and tailless field rats. We also saw the young ducklings of the orange-coloured sheldrake, the marshy pools of the plateau being evidently the breeding grounds of the latter.

The next day was cold and rainy. Travelling on the highlands of Kam in wet weather is a cold and miserable business even in July. Leaving our camp we crossed a small pass and descended through a ravine into the valley of the Draya river, halting at a wretched hamlet called Dotse.

Leaving this place, the main branch of the Draya river had

[1] The route taken by M. Bonvalot (*De Paris à Tonquin à travers le Tibet inconnu*) and Mr Coales (*Geographical Journal* for April, 1919).

HALT IN THE PINE FORESTS AT RISHISUMDO, NEAR THE MEETING-POINT OF BATANG, MARKAM AND SANGEN TERRITORIES

A VILLAGE IN DRAYA

PLATE XXXIV

OFFICIAL'S HOUSE AT DRAYA JYAMDUN

LOCAL TIBETAN HEADMEN AND THE TSANGDRUBA OF DRAYA

to be crossed. This was rather a difficult business, as it was in flood and running like a rapid; the baggage yak were almost submerged, but floundered through somehow. The trail then leaves the river, which makes a bend to the north, and crosses a small pass to reach Radzi, one stage out of Draya Jyamdun on the main road. Pushing on after a short rest, we reached Draya yesterday evening, and received a cordial welcome from the Tsangdruba and his distinguished prisoner, the ex-Chinese magistrate and commandant.

Here we received, much to our relief, a letter from the Kalon Lama stating that, in response to our urgent representations, he had issued orders to all his Commanders to cease from hostilities everywhere, and that he would hold his hand at any rate until we had arrived in Chamdo. General Liu immediately sent copies of this letter to all the various Chinese leaders on the frontier. This gives us a breathing space in which to see what can be done, and relieves us of all immediate anxiety. The Chinese are apparently ready to stop fighting for the moment at any rate; while the word of a high Tibetan official can be implicitly trusted, and the Kalon's authority is such that his orders are unquestionably obeyed by all classes of Tibetans[1].

July 15. At CHAMDO.

We left Draya on July 9 and returned to Chamdo by the main road along which we had travelled a month before.

We crossed the big pass, the Gam La, in fine weather, and found it almost free of snow. On the Ipi La, however, we encountered a snowstorm, and, though the season of the year was midsummer, the pass was covered with several inches of snow.

We eventually reached Chamdo yesterday, and were met outside the town by Tibetan officials and a guard of honour. After drinking tea and exchanging civilities in the tents pitched for our reception, we rode on across the Szechuan bridge into the town. Our entry was quite an imposing affair. First came the mounted escort of Tibetan soldiers followed by the Tibetan officials on their gaily caparisoned mules; then myself with my followers ranged fore and aft in

[1] It subsequently turned out that the issue of these orders marked the end of the campaign which had opened eight or nine months before.

the usual Asiatic way; and then General Liu in the midst of his retinue of secretaries and soldiers. All Chamdo had turned out to meet us, including a number of the Chinese wounded, legless, armless, and otherwise mutilated; these latter represented the handiwork of, and owed their lives to, Dr Shelton, who had come and gone during our absence in Batang.

July 21. At CHAMDO.

We are now waiting to hear from Szechuan whether the Chinese Authorities there desire to make peace, and if so, the terms on which they would be willing to do so. In the meantime, however, fighting has everywhere ceased, and we have arranged for the Chinese garrison which has been besieged at Gaji to withdraw unmolested to Batang.

General Liu is quartered in the rat-infested yamen haunted by the ghost of the decapitated General Nieh, in which we were lodged on our previous visit, while we have settled down in a large Chinese temple.

Chamdo, after a lapse of ten years, has become once again a purely Tibetan centre. Work has been begun on the reconstruction of the great monastery[1]. Tibetan money, silver *trangka* (value three to the rupee), and Lhasa printed paper notes for small amounts, have already ousted the Chinese copper cents, which had been introduced of recent years at the larger centres on the frontier, such as Batang and Chamdo[2].

The weather here is pleasant, much like that of an English summer; the Tibetans say the climate resembles that of Lhasa.

On the 19th and 20th the Kalon Lama entertained General Liu and myself, and our respective followers, with two days' continuous feasting, which is, it appears, the Lhasa fashion of welcoming honoured guests. The entertainment started about nine in the morning with a banquet, continued through the day with conversation and light refreshments, and closed in the evening with another feast. On the following day the

[1] See Plate XLVIII.

[2] Apart from the *trangka*, rupees are universally current in Tibet and its border lands from Ladak to Tachienlu. These rupees are both Indian and Chinese; the Chinese rupees, which were originally produced in imitation of the Indian coins, are minted at Chengtu in Szechuan, and bear the head of the former Chinese Emperor, Kuang Hsü. (See also note on p. 186.)

proceedings were repeated. The whole entertainment was very hospitable, but rather exhausting. The food served consisted of the best Chinese dishes with a few special Tibetan delicacies. The wines were Tibetan *arra* (a strong spirit) and *chang* (a light kind of beer brewed from barley). The Kalon Lama, who, presumably for religious reasons, eats and drinks nothing but *tsamba* and buttered tea, partook of none of the delicacies provided, but encouraged his guests to enjoy themselves[1].

General Liu, though (like most Chinese on this border) he has a native consort, speaks very little Tibetan, and what he does know is in the Batang dialect, which is largely unintelligible to people from Lhasa. Our conversations with the Kalon Lama and other Tibetan officials here are therefore usually carried on by means of Chinese-Tibetan interpreters. As very few Chinese officials ever speak Tibetan, or Tibetan officials Chinese, these interpreters, who are often half-castes, play an important part in life on this border. The Tibetans call them *lotsawa*, or *abula*, or *tungsi*—the latter being the Chinese word *t'ungshih*. One or two are attached to every Chinese yamen; they have a bad reputation and are supposed to be responsible for many of the abuses of Chinese rule. Unlike the British official in India or elsewhere in the East, it scarcely ever enters the head of a Chinese official that he ought to learn Tibetan because he happens to be serving in Tibet. To the average educated Chinese the Tibetans (and indeed all non-Chinese peoples, including those of Europe and America) have always appeared as uncouth and uncivilised barbarians by the very fact of their inability to speak the language of the Middle Kingdom[2].

[1] Wine is never drunk by monks of the *gelugba*, or reformed, sect, who are also strictly celibate; those of the old unreformed red sects, on the other hand, appear both to drink wine and take wives.

[2] In connection with the somewhat high-handed attitude of the average Chinese official towards peoples of non-Chinese race with whom he has relations, compare the following extract from Chapter XIX of Sir Francis Younghusband's *India and Tibet*:

"Of the attitude of the Chinese to the Tibetans I took particular note, for I was myself a Resident in an Indian Native State....One point which immediately struck me about it was its tone of high-handedness....Every British Resident gives a chair to an Indian gentleman who comes to visit him, but I found that the Chinese Resident (at Lhasa) did not give a chair even to the Regent (of Tibet). He, Councillors, Members of the National Assembly, Abbots of the great monasteries—all had to sit on cushions on the ground, while the Resident and his Chinese staff sat on chairs. In his reception and dismissal of them he preserved an equally high tone

The Chinese are handicapped when first learning to speak Tibetan by their national inability to pronounce the letter *r*; thus for "it is not good" a Chinese will say *yabo male* instead of *yabo mare*: in the same way that he will talk of "rice" as "lice" in English.

One cannot converse with the Kalon Lama without being impressed with his intelligence and force of character, and nearly every remark he makes shows his shrewdness, sound common sense, and understanding of men and things. Yet as a lama he presumably believes in the Tibetan theory of a flat world bounded by mountains at the four corners. But after all there have perhaps been distinguished European statesmen in the past similarly imbued with religious superstitions of their own. Men of character and ability are to be found in Tibet, as in China, Europe and America.

One of the Kalon Lama's secretaries helps to pass the time by giving me lessons in Tibetan. He is called the *Kadrung* (Henderson's *Tibetan Manual* gives the meaning of this word very correctly as "A.D.C. to Kalon," which is exactly what he is). He wears his hair fastened up in an elaborate knot on the top of his head[1] and carries a long turquoise ear-ring in his left ear, and uses an ordinary Tibetan pen, consisting simply of a pointed piece of wood, with which he writes with great ease and rapidity. A Tibetan writer prefers to do his work seated cross-legged on a rug on the ground, while a Chinese writer usually sits on a chair at a table[2]. In many other respects, however, Tibetan civilisation resembles the Aryan rather than the Chinese. Their alphabet, for instance, is an adaptation of the Sanscrit, and their numerals resemble the Arabic. Their calendar is a lunar one, like the Chinese; with which, however, it often fails to correspond, apparently owing to the irregular omission of unlucky days. But they use the seven-day week in the Aryan way, and name

of superiority. He did not rise from his chair to receive them, as any British Resident would rise to welcome Indian gentlemen or high officials; he merely acknowledged their salutation on entrance with a barely noticeable inclination of his head. And in dismissing them, he simply said over his shoulder to his interpreter, 'Tell them to go.'"

[1] All the Lhasa officials here wear their hair in this way; the Shigatse officials, on the other hand, wear their hair in a sort of queue wound round the head; lamas are always close-cropped.

[2] In this the Tibetans show their kinship with the Malays, Burmese and Japanese, rather than with the Chinese. Their language, also, has no apparent connection with Chinese, but is perhaps akin to Burmese.

the days after the sun, moon and planets, e.g. Sunday *za-nyima*, Monday *za-dawa*, Tuesday *za-migmar*, Wednesday *za-hlagba*, Thursday *za-purba*, Friday *za-pasang*, Saturday *za-penba*, meaning respectively, Sun day, Moon day, Mars day, Mercury day, Jupiter day, Venus day, Saturn day. It would be interesting to know when they adopted this system. The Chinese have only recently begun to use the seven-day week, as the result of contact with Western Christianity, and call the days *li-pai i*, *li-pai erh*, *li-pai san*, and so on (i.e. Sabbath one, Sabbath two, Sabbath three).

August 10. At CHAMDO.

Towards the end of July we at last received the long awaited replies from Szechuan and Tachienlu. The Governor of Szechuan stated that he was agreeable to peace negotiations, and engaged not to move troops towards Tibet pending their conclusion. The Szechuan Frontier Commissioner likewise agreed to make peace, and tentatively suggested the river Yangtze as a temporary frontier pending a definite settlement of the boundary question.

The Yangtze had from the start appeared to me as likely to make the best provisional frontier once the Lhasa troops had advanced across the old eighteenth century boundary; but unfortunately the Tibetans, having occupied the whole of De-ge and parts of Nyarong almost up to the Yalung river, are not of the same opinion.

Having at last received these messages, General Liu went to the Kalon Lama and demanded that negotiations be opened forthwith. The Kalon, however, appeared inclined to delay before committing himself definitely to making peace. He said it would be necessary to choose an auspicious day for the opening of the negotiations; and, on consulting his calendar, announced that no suitable date occurred before the 5th day of the 7th moon[1].

Towards the end of July a number of Chinese prisoners arrived from De-ge, mostly secretaries and minor officials belonging to the former Chinese magistrate's staff. They were being comparatively well treated, but were very miserable,

[1] According to Tibetan ideas all the days of the month are lucky or unlucky in varying degrees; thus the 1st, 2nd and 4th are usually bad, the 3rd good, and so on.

as the Tibetans had apparently given them to understand that they were to be sent into Central Tibet. General Liu did everything he could for them, and between us we managed to persuade the Kalon Lama to permit them to remain in Chamdo with a view to their being released and allowed to return to China if our peace negotiations prove successful. They were extremely grateful; for the one thing all these Chinese stand in dread of is deportation into Central Tibet, where, apart from other hardships and discomforts, they understand there is nothing but *tsamba* to eat and no opium to smoke.

On July 30 we received letters from Kanze, where, though fighting has ceased, the situation seems very uncertain, owing to the large bodies of Chinese and Tibetan troops facing one another at close quarters. These letters announced that the Chala Chief of Tachienlu[1] proposed coming to Chamdo as a peace emissary on behalf of the Szechuan Frontier Commissioner. It appears that the latter had despatched him, together with the Chinese magistrate of Tachienlu, to Kanze to make peace with the Tibetan forces on the North Road for fear lest the Tibetan advance should continue in that direction during General Liu's negotiations here. As the Dabön commanding the Tibetan forces near Kanze had refused to enter into any negotiations with these peace envoys, the Chala Chief had been urged by his colleague (who preferred to remain at Kanze on the safe side of the Chinese lines) to come on here.

On August 1 a message was received from the Chinese Authorities at Batang, who seem to be completely panic-stricken and to have little hope of the success of the negotiations here, offering to evacuate Batang and retire to Litang and Tachienlu, if the Tibetans would let them do so unmolested. It seems that the local Tibetans on the Markam border have been talking of an imminent Tibetan advance and that the Batang Chinese have lost their heads on that account. General Liu knew nothing of this message until after it had reached the Kalon Lama's ears and his position has been badly weakened by this unwise move; and it may

[1] The former Rajah of the old Tibetan State of Chala (now a Chinese district), of which Tachienlu was the capital; *Mingcheng T'ussu* in Chinese, *Chala Jyelbo* in Tibetan.

PLATE XXXV

TIBETAN THEATRICALS AT CHAMDO

PLATE XXXVI

TIBETAN BANQUETING TENTS PITCHED ON THE BANKS OF THE MEKONG AT CHAMDO

TRAVELLING LAMAS ENCAMPED AT CHAMDO; TEA AND BUTTER CHURN IN THE FOREGROUND

now be much more difficult to induce the Tibetans to make a reasonable peace.

On August 8 and 9 we had another two days' feasting in celebration of the 1st day of the 7th Moon, a festival all over Tibet and Mongolia. On the first day a theatrical performance was held, starting at eight in the morning and finishing at dusk. The stage was an open piece of ground in front of the Kalon Lama's house and the players were Tibetan soldiers. We watched the play from the windows of the Kalon Lama's apartment, conversing and consuming light refreshments between the morning and evening banquets. The players refreshed themselves at frequent intervals with copious draughts of *chang* provided by the Kalon's stewards; so that their acting became more and more energetic as the day wore on.

Tibetan plays are either religious or lay. Of the former, which are performed by lamas and are often called Devil Dances by foreigners, the commonest is the "Dance of the Black Hat," illustrating the killing of the notorious persecutor of Buddhism, King Langdarma, by the monk Palgidarje in the ninth century. The present play, being performed by soldiers, was a lay one; it was a sort of musical comedy and was accompanied by singing and dancing and clown-like antics. The plot centred round the love affairs of a Tibetan King, named Kalawonga, who got into difficulties over his two wives. The principal comedians represented semi-savage Tibetans from the extreme west of Tibet and swashbuckling braves from Kam; these being the characters assigned to the people of Western and Eastern Tibet respectively by the more refined and civilised inhabitants of the central Brahmaputra basin[1]. The piece is one of the best known of Tibetan plays and the acting was loudly applauded by the audience, who, apart from ourselves, consisted of most of the popula-

[1] The Kambawa are considered rather wild and lawless by the more highly civilised Tibetans of Central Tibet. Yet the people of De-ge, for instance, are widely known for their skill in metal working and other handicrafts and for their literary attainments. The number of people in De-ge who can read and write (all monastery taught, of course) is surprising. Probably the Kambawa owe their reputation for turbulence to their distance from Lhasa, the metropolis of Tibet, which renders their manners uncouth in the eyes of the latter. The real wild men of Tibet are the nomads of the North; while everywhere the house-dwellers in the agricultural valleys, of which Kam has a liberal share, are much more civilised and have a much higher standard of living than the tent-dwellers of the grass country.

tion of Chamdo, as well as many Tibetans from the neighbourhood. The Sobo Gegen (the Kalon Lama's Mongolian major-domo mentioned in a previous chapter) was stage manager and master of ceremonies, a part which he filled to the satisfaction of everyone.

Towards the end the house was brought down by the appearance of five actors representing the "Tribute Nations" (i.e. tributary to the Manchu Emperor), dressed respectively as a Chinese, a Tibetan, a Mahomedan, a Mongol and a Bhutanese[1]. The actor dressed as a Chinese elicited further roars of applause by saluting the Kalon Lama in the old-fashioned Peking way by bending down and touching his boot. The grand finale, as darkness was falling, consisted in presentations of parcels of tea, sacks of barley meal and packets of rupees to the actors. The rupees were thrown down by the members of our party from the windows of the Kalon's house and the players, festooned with complimentary *katas*, then came and expressed their thanks. The scene finally closed with a bonfire of green juniper bushes and clouds of *tsamba* cast into the air; everything being done, said the Kalon, strictly according to *Lhasa lugso* (Lhasa fashion). Everyone seemed very happy and not a few were considerably inebriated by the end of the day. A popular beanfeast is indeed much the same thing all the world over, whether it be August bank-holiday on Hampstead Heath or Chislehurst Common, or the 7th Moon festival at Chamdo.

September 1. At CHAMDO.

The negotiations between General Liu and the Kalon Lama have at last been satisfactorily concluded on the basis of each side remaining in possession of the regions occupied by their respective forces at the time hostilities ceased, pending a reference to Peking and Lhasa and the settlement of the boundary question between the Chinese and Tibetan Governments.

On August 29 the Chala Chief arrived, accompanied by his son, his secretary and a De-ge Reincarnation, who acts

[1] The Tibetans maintain that their *status* in the past was the same as that of the Chinese themselves, that is to say, that both were equally tributaries of the Manchu Throne; from this the nationalists argue that on the abdication of the Manchu Dynasty the Tibetans ceased to owe any allegiance to anyone and became, like the Chinese themselves, independent.

as a sort of chaplain to him; the secretary, a capable Chinese gentleman of the old school named Chou, speaks excellent standard Tibetan (a rare accomplishment for a Chinese), having served for several years on the staff of the Manchu Amban at Lhasa.

The Chala Chief brought letters from the Chinese officers at Kanze, from which it is evident that further measures will have to be taken to stabilise the situation in that neighbourhood and to avert a renewed outbreak of hostilities. It appears that at Rongbatsa near Kanze some three thousand comparatively good Chinese troops from Tachienlu are faced and partly surrounded by as many Tibetans, the two sides being barricaded almost within a stone's throw of one another. Though no fighting has taken place since the armistice became effective in July, the situation appears to be very strained and to be getting worse, so that a clash may occur at any moment. We have already tried, unsuccessfully, by correspondence to induce the two leaders on each side to get together and arrange for both parties to withdraw one day's march; but the only result was to increase the tension. The Chinese will insist on treating the Tibetans as naughty children; while the Tibetans, who consider that they have taken the measure of the Chinese, at any rate for the time being, are itching to renew the conflict.

It has, therefore, been decided that we are to proceed at once to Rongbatsa, together with the Chala Chief and his party, and endeavour to arrange for a mutual withdrawal of troops by both sides. General Liu will remain here until he learns that we have arranged matters at Kanze. He probably feels that if he returns to Batang and we fail in our object, the Tibetans will take advantage of any resumption of hostilities at Rongbatsa to advance on Batang; whereas if he remains here he may still, even if the worst comes to the worst, be able to stave off an attack by means of more talk. We are therefore leaving to-morrow by the main North Road for De-ge Gönchen and Rongbatsa, after a stay here of about a month and a half. We shall be glad to be on the move again; for Chamdo is not altogether an entertaining place for a prolonged visit.

CHAPTER VI

FROM CHAMDO TO DE-GE GÖNCHEN, AND THENCE THROUGH CENTRAL DE-GE TO RONGBATSA ON THE YALUNG

Crossing the Ja-pe La (15,800 feet)—Toba and the grass country of the Yangtze-Mekong divide in summer—The Native State of Hlato—T'ungp'u in De-ge—Release of a Chinese magistrate—The Yangtze—De-ge Gönchen—More Chinese released—The lama of Dordra Gomba—Through Central De-ge *via* Bagung, Mesho, and Dehlung—Dzenko and the Dzin Chu—Crossing the Yangtze-Yalung divide by the Tsengu La (15,800 feet)—Descent to Rongbatsa on the Yalung—Chinese and Tibetan lines at Rongbatsa—A Conference between the two sides—Comparison of the Chinese and Tibetan forces on the Rongbatsa plain—Hardships of life at Rongbatsa—Conclusion of supplementary truce—Withdrawal of Chinese and Tibetan troops from Rongbatsa.

September 8. At KARGUNG.

We left Chamdo on September 2. Our party is again a large one, myself, a Tibetan official deputed by the Kalon Lama to accompany us, the Chala Chief, his son and secretary, and the De-ge Reincarnation, and our respective followers. But this time, with the exception of my three Chinese servants, the party is entirely Tibetan in composition, which renders the question of accommodation and supplies a much simpler one.

After crossing the Szechuan bridge the trail ascends the mountain side in an easterly direction, reaching the pass, the Tamar La (14,900 feet), after three or four hours' march. The views from this pass are very fine; S.S.E. over the snow peaks beyond the Mekong, N.N.W. to a rocky snow-sprinkled peak overlooking the upper Dza Chu, and east towards the big range to be crossed on the next day's march. The Tamar La lies on the same ridge which is crossed at the Sodri La on the Batang road. After following along the top of the spur for a mile or two, the path descends to the hamlet of Reya (12,200 feet), consisting of two or three farms in the valley of the Le Chu.

From Reya the trail leads straight up the opposite mountain

side again, at first through a long ravine and then across easy grass country; finally, there is a steep scramble up a bare slope of disintegrating rock to reach the pass, the Ja-pe La (15,800 feet). This is a formidable pass; but fortunately the weather was fine, and there were only a few patches of snow. This range consists of huge crags of limestone thrust upward through the underlying red sandstone, and is a continuation of the same ridge crossed at the Ipi La on the Batang road. From the pass we descended a long winding valley in the grass country to the junction of the stream with another flowing north-west, and soon after reached a ruined Chinese rest-house and camping ground called Toba. Here we camped, at an elevation of about 13,000 feet, on the banks of a clear stream flowing through a grassy flat surrounded by pine woods and limestone crags.

These grass-lands are now very different to what they were when we struggled across them with starving animals in April and May, and are covered with abundance of good grass and carpeted in places with a pretty blue flower. As usual there are innumerable marmots, which sit up on their hind legs whistling in front of their earths, only diving in at the last moment as the dogs rush up to them.

On the way down from the pass to Toba the valley contracts at one place to a narrow gorge, hemmed in by perpendicular cliffs of rock hundreds of feet high. This was one of the points held by the Tibetans against any possible Chinese force advancing to the relief of Chamdo. By the erection of a few stone barricades the position had been rendered so strong, that a few riflemen could have held it against a company. Such narrows, which lend themselves admirably to purposes of defence, are often met with on the roads of Eastern Tibet, owing to the existence of numerous limestone gorges breaking up the open grass country.

A mile or two south-east of Toba the stream branches, half of it coming down from the south and half from the south-east. Up the former branch lies a road to Gonjo[1], past a monastery where the Chinese relief force, under orders to cut its way through to Chamdo early this year, took refuge, was surrounded, and surrendered to the Tibetans[2].

[1] Probably the road taken by Bonvalot (see p. 177).
[2] Once the Chinese were safely in the monastery, the usual result followed,

On September 4 we found the trail across the grass country so good that, travelling fast, we pushed on and covered what the Tibetans consider two stages. Following up the south-eastern branch of the Toba river, we arrived before midday at the pass, the Lazhi La (14,600 feet), an easy grass-covered ridge, though it is the Yangtze-Mekong divide[1], and descended down a similar valley to another ruined Chinese rest-house called Chorzhung. The trail lay all day across the open grass country, where not a tree or shrub is to be seen.

Crossing the Lazhi La we passed from Chamdo territory into Hlato (Chinese Nato), a small native State constituting a narrow wedge between De-ge and Chamdo. The *Podrang* (castle) of the Chief, who has the rank of *Jyelbo* or King, lies a march or two to the north of the pass. It would have been interesting to have visited it, but we could not spare the time[2].

From Chorzhung we made an easy march to a camping ground called Dorka, where we pitched our tents alongside the ruins of another Chinese rest-house. The trail lay across a small pass called the Gara La, the boundary between Hlato and De-ge, and down into and across another similar valley on the other side. All the streams in this neighbourhood flow south to join the Mar Chu, a large but little known tributary of the Yangtze draining Gonjo. We saw some gazelle on this march, which lay across the same treeless grass country. Dorka, like Chorzhung, is over 13,000 feet high.

From Dorka to Kargung is another easy stage. After crossing a small pass, the trail descends a ravine, which brings one down to a lower valley where houses and cultivation are again met with at the *Sajya* monastery of Tretso Gomba. Kargung consists of a small *Podrang* and a few scattered farms lying just round the corner above the confluence of two streams flowing from the south-west and north-west

the Tibetans seizing the heights all round and compelling them to surrender after a short fight. An account of this incident, written by the Commandant of the Chinese force, is given on p. 55.

[1] South of Jyekundo the Yangtze-Mekong divide is a big snow range; this range, however, crosses the Yangtze below Dengko, and in De-ge and Gonjo the Yangtze-Mekong divide consists of rolling grass country and elevated plateaux.

[2] There are said to be only some 550 families in Hlato, mostly nomads. There are five *Jyelbo*, or Kings, in Eastern Tibet, namely, Chala, De-ge, Lintsung, Hlato and Nangchen; the other states being ruled by hereditary officials (*Bön* or *Deba*).

PLATE XXXVII

CAMP AT DORKA, NEAR CHAMDO-DE-GE BOUNDARY

NOMADS ON THE GRASS COUNTRY OF THE MEKONG-YANGTZE DIVIDE, MAIN ROAD FROM CHAMDO TO DE-GE

PLATE XXXVIII

SKIN CORACLES AT GANGTO FERRY ACROSS THE YANGTZE, MAIN ROAD FROM CHAMDO TO DE-GE

CROSSING THE YANGTZE BY SKIN CORACLE AT GANGTO FERRY, MAIN ROAD FROM CHAMDO TO DE-GE

which join to flow east towards the Yangtze. It is considered an important point owing to its position at the junction of several roads.

September 11. At DE-GE GÖNCHEN.

Leaving Kargung on September 7, we made a very long march down the valley of the river, here called the Dzin Chu. For the first half of the journey the valley is open and the road good; but for the second half the river flows through narrow forested gorges, and the trail, a rough footpath obstructed by rocks and fallen trees, is as bad as it can be. The river has to be crossed and recrossed several times by rotten wooden bridges, the destruction of which would render the road impassable in summer. To compensate for the badness of the road, the scenery, made up of foaming torrent, pine forests, and rocky limestone mountains, is unsurpassed even in this country. At length the gorges open out and T'ungp'u (also called Rangsum by the Tibetans) is reached. It consists of a big Tibetan building, which serves as the official residence, and a few farms lying on a cultivated slope above the junction of two branches of the Dzin Chu.

The former Chinese magistrate of T'ungp'u, a Szechuanese gentleman, who had been captured by the advancing Tibetans but had managed to avoid deportation into Tibet, was living here as a *détenu*, subsisting on doles of *tsamba* provided by the charity of a neighbouring monastery. Fortunately we had already heard from the Chala Chief of his presence here, and I had taken the precaution of securing a sealed paper from the Kalon Lama authorising his release. So that when he applied for permission for himself and his secretaries to accompany us into the Chinese lines, we had no difficulty in obtaining the consent of the local Tibetan headman to his release. None of these Chinese frontier officials who were caught by the advancing wave of Tibetans was killed or even seriously maltreated. But in most cases they lost all their effects, and suffered considerable hardships before being released and finding their way back to China after the conclusion of peace.

At T'ungp'u the Dzin Chu flows south, and the road turns up its northerly branch through a densely wooded gorge for a few miles to a small *Sajya* monastery called Wara Gomba.

Here the De-ge trail turns east up a side ravine, and leads through an open valley and across a steep little pass, the Nge La (14,600 feet), and down the other side to the hamlet of Ngenang.

On September 9 we descended to the Yangtze through one of the typical limestone chasms, which in Eastern Tibet so often lead down from the highlands to the deeply eroded valleys of the big rivers, and arrived at Gangto Druka (Gangto Ferry). This is a well-known spot, one of the three principal Yangtze crossings in Kam, the other two being Drenda Druka on the Jyekundo road and Drubanang Druka on the Batang road. The elevation of the Yangtze is here a little over 10,000 feet. The river flows, as elsewhere in Eastern Tibet, at the bottom of an immense canyon with its valley no wider than the river bed. Crossing by coracle ferry, we found a reception camp pitched in the mouth of the opposite ravine, where we drank tea and exchanged civilities with the De-ge officials sent to meet us; after which we continued for a few miles up the picturesque valley of the stream, a tributary of the Yangtze called the Zi Chu, to reach Changra Podrang (Chinese Kungya), a fine Tibetan residence, which used to be the summer palace of the De-ge Kings. A monastery of the same name is passed just before getting in. On the following day we covered the remaining eight miles or so up the valley to De-ge Gönchen.

De-ge Gönchen (meaning literally "The Big Monastery of De-ge") is the capital of the old Kingdom of De-ge[1], the largest and most important of the former independent States of Kam, and consists of a large *Sajya* monastery and two Tibetan castles, residences of the King, packed together in the mouth of a narrow ravine. The Chinese, who occupied De-ge in 1909 and were driven out this spring, made it the centre of a district which they called at various times Teko, Tehua and Kengching. The principal building in the monastery is the printing establishment, where an edition of the lamaist scriptures, well known throughout Tibet, and other religious and historical works are published[2].

[1] De-ge is the correct spelling: it often appears as Derge or Darge on foreign maps; the *e* is pronounced short and the *g* hard. The meaning of the Tibetan words seems to be "Happy Land."

[2] The lamaist scriptures are, it appears, only printed at De-ge Gönchen in Kam and at Trashilumpo in Central Tibet. There used also to be a Peking

PLATE XXXIX

CASTLE OF THE RAJAH OF DE-GE AT DE-GE GÖNCHEN

A CORNER OF THE MONASTIC PRINTING ESTABLISHMENT AT DE-GE GÖNCHEN: PART OF THE MONASTERY IN THE BACKGROUND

PLATE XL

BAGUNG GOMBA IN DE-GE

THE CHALA CHIEF (LEFT) AND THE LAMA OF DORDRA GOMBA LUNCHING ON THE ROAD FROM CHAMDO TO RONGBATSA

We were received at De-ge Gönchen by the former Rajah, Dorje Senge[1], and a Tibetan General called the Drentong Dabön, the latter a well-educated Tibetan of aristocratic family from the Shigatse neighbourhood, who had visited India and was well acquainted with foreign customs and ideas. The Tibetans are at present administering De-ge through the ex-Chief and his officials; but the former seems to have no power of his own, and nothing can be done without the authority of the Dabön.

The Chinese magistrate made good his escape from De-ge Gönchen before the Tibetans arrived. The staff of the yamen, however, and some other civilians were captured, and fifteen of them are still here. In response to our representations the Dabön has agreed to release them, and they will accompany us when we leave to-morrow. We shall thus again be encumbered with a large train of Chinese refugees.

The main road between De-ge Gönchen and Kanze, usually followed by the Chinese, runs up the gorges of the Zi Chu to Kolondo, crosses a big pass called the Tro La (Chinese Chiu-erh Shan), and descends thence across the Yilung grass-lands to Rongbatsa and Kanze. The Dabön has, however, arranged for us to travel by another route, which is, it appears, the road usually taken by Tibetan travellers. As this trail seems to lead through a part of central De-ge unknown to European geography, it should be more interesting than the main road.

September 16. At Dzenko.

We left De-ge Gönchen on September 12, retracing our way down the valley past Changra to a *chöten*[2] at the confluence of two streams. Here we turned up a side ravine and then climbed up the mountain side to reach a group of farms called

edition, the blocks of which were, however, destroyed during the Boxer troubles in 1900. The Tibetan scriptures consist of the Kanjyur (The Commandments) and the Tanjyur (The Commentaries); the former is contained in over 100 volumes (the De-ge edition 108, the Trashilumpo edition 100), and the latter in over 200; a complete set requires a large caravan of yak to transport it from place to place. (See Plate XXXIX.)

[1] For history of De-ge and the story of the feud between the two brothers, rival claimants to the Throne, see p. 7.

[2] The *chöten* is the onion-shaped monument built by lamaists in honour of Buddha; they are often built at the confluence of two streams; the word means "religious receptacle," and they were originally receptacles for relics of Buddha; there are some fine specimens to be seen in and around Peking.

Shigargarba. The next day we crossed a pass, the Götse La (14,700 feet), and descended to a celebrated De-ge monastery called Bagung Gomba, lying in a pleasant region of grassy vales and pine woods draining south into the Yangtze.

A small *Nyimaba* monastery called Dordra Gomba lies on the mountain side a little way off to the south-west. This is the home of the Reincarnation who accompanies the Chala Chief, partly as religious adviser and partly as associate peace envoy. Nearly all the monasteries of Kam, of which there must be many hundreds, have one or more of these Reincarnations attached to them, though not always in residence[1]. This lama is a learned and intelligent individual, and a mine of information on such subjects as the history of De-ge. He was anxious that we should go and stop in his monastery; but the visit would have entailed a détour and a climb up and down the mountain; and as we have now reached the stage when we avoid all excursions which will take us off our direct line of march, we declined the invitation and kept to the main road.

From Bagung Gomba the trail runs up a long wooded valley to a pass and descends the other side through a pine-clad ravine which suddenly debouches on to a cultivated valley at a big *Sajya* monastery called Dzongsar Gomba. Another two miles or so down this valley, which is called Mesho, brought us to Somo Podrang, a castle belonging to the King of De-ge. The stream, the Me Chu, flows south towards the Yangtze.

We found the barley harvest here in full swing, the elevation being about 11,500 feet. The valley is one of the chief agricultural centres of De-ge.

The next march took us over another small pass and down into a similar valley called Dehlung. This river also runs south; I was unable to establish for certain whether it joins the Mesho river before flowing into the Yangtze. All these streams come off the big Dzogchen range of snow mountains.

We are using *ula* transport on this journey, which I am always averse to doing; but we are in a hurry and travelling

[1] The doctrine of incarnation applied in this way is a Tibetan development of Buddhism. The Dalai Lama is an incarnation of Chenrezi, the Buddha Redeemer of the Northern Buddhists; the ordinary *trülgu* (incarnation) one meets, however, is usually an incarnation, not of a god but of a famous lama or saint.

too fast to use our own mules. The animals, mostly yak, are provided by the local people on the strength of our *lam-yig* (road-bill) sealed by the De-ge Chief and counter-sealed by the Dabön.

From Dehlung another small pass is crossed giving access to a ravine which debouches on to an open basin in the mountains, such as is rarely met with in Eastern Tibet, formed by the junction of several streams. The main river, the Dzin Chu, a big tributary of the Yangtze, flows in a gorge below the open slopes of the valley, which are partly cultivated and dotted with farms and monasteries. This valley is called Dzenko ("Vale of the Dzin"), and is considered an important centre owing to its position at the junction of trails leading to De-ge Gönchen (the road by which we arrived), to Rongbatsa and Kanze (the road by which we are leaving), down the river to Beyü, Gonjo and Batang, and south to Litang and Nyarong. The latter would be an interesting road to follow from a geographical point of view; it runs across a large plateau on the borders of De-ge, Litang and Nyarong territory *via* a place called Hlakundo.

Dzenko being the base immediately behind the Tibetan front at Rongbatsa, there is considerable activity here in the way of caravans coming and going and loading and unloading. The provisioning of the Tibetan army is, however, a simple matter owing to the few needs of the Tibetan soldier, and consists in the forwarding of an endless stream of sacks of barley from all parts of Eastern Tibet to the front[1].

So far this road has been an easy one; but we are told that there is a formidable pass ahead over the Yangtze-Yalung watershed range, which takes two days to cross.

September 19. At RONGBATSA.

Leaving Dzenko we descended for nearly a thousand feet, past two monasteries, Dagmo Gomba and Bamdzor Gomba, to the Dzin Chu, here flowing in a narrow gorge. We were surprised at the size of this river, supposing it to come, like the Mesho and Dehlung streams, straight off the watershed range. As a matter of fact it takes its rise a long way to the south, probably somewhere near the Nyarong-Litang border,

[1] See Plate XLI.

and is here already as big as the She Chu at Drango. Our trail lay up the valley of the Dzin Chu, hemmed in by forest-clad mountains, for a few miles to a group of farms called Darando. Here the path leaves the river, turns up a gully to the north, and ascends the mountain side through pine forests. Eventually one emerges on to the usual waste of rock and snow leading to the pass, the Tsengu La (15,800 feet), the divide between the Yangtze and the Yalung rivers and the boundary between De-ge and Nyarong. Descending a few miles, we camped after a long and tiring march in a boulder-strewn valley at an elevation but little below 14,000 feet. The Tsengu La is a formidable pass, but we had good weather, and found it nearly free of snow[1].

After a cold night in our tents we awoke to find snow on the ground and the temperature down to below freezing. Breaking camp in falling snow is always a miserable business. A long descent down swampy rock-strewn valleys brought us to a *chöten* at the junction of two streams, where a few trees make their appearance and the landscape becomes less dreary. The valleys we had been descending are known as Aser, a nomad region belonging to Nyarong. From the *chöten* a trail leads up the opposite stream in a southerly direction and over a pass *via* Norlo Gomba to Middle Nyarong. This road and that from Dzenko *via* Hlakundo to Nyarong were much used in the days when Nyarong belonged to the Dalai Lama and De-ge was a Lhasa protectorate, but have now fallen into disuse. Continuing down the valley in a north-easterly direction, we passed the Nyarong-Kanze border at a narrow place where the cliffs close in on the river, and eventually debouched after a long day's march on to the sloping plain of Rongbatsa, a westerly continuation of the Yalung valley plain.

At the mouth of the gorge we were met by the Tibetan General, the Chungrang Dabön, rather a startling figure in these out-of-the-way parts, as he was dressed exactly like an Indian sportsman in riding breeches, tweed coat and sun hat. He was accompanied by a Lhasa official called the Kenchung

[1] See Plate XLI. Crossing this pass again four or five months later, we found its northern face covered with a sheet of frozen ice and snow, and had literally to slide down; on this occasion we halted for a night at Darando, thus dividing up the distance between Dzenko and Rongbatsa into three marches, which makes the passage of the big range much easier.

VIEW OF THE DZENKO BASIN, SHOWING YAK CARAVAN CONVEYING SUPPLIES OF BARLEY FOR THE TIBETAN TROOPS AT RONGBATSA

ON THE SUMMIT OF THE TSENGU LA (15,800 FEET), THE PASS ACROSS THE YANGTZE-YALUNG DIVIDE ON THE ROAD FROM DZENKO TO RONGBATSA

PLATE XLII

TIBETAN GENERAL (ON LEFT), WITH ATTENDANTS AND BAGPIPE-MEN, ON THE RONGBATSA PLAIN

TIBETAN GENERAL (WITH SWORD, IN CENTRE) AT RONGBATSA WITH MONKS OF A MONASTERY IN TEMPORARY TIBETAN OCCUPATION

Lama, who seemed to occupy the position of Chief Political Officer to the Tibetan force.

After a cup of tea and a talk we rode on across the cultivated plain, accompanied by the Lama and the Dabön and the latter's mounted escort, standard-bearers and bagpipe-men, to the hamlet constituting the Tibetan headquarters, where we found accommodation prepared for us[1].

To-day, together with the Chala Chief and his retinue, and taking all our Chinese refugees in tow, we rode over the plain, across the stream, and into the Chinese lines to visit the Chinese headquarters established in the village of Rongbatsa. Here we received a cordial welcome from Colonel Chu, commanding the Chinese troops, and the Tachienlu magistrate, Mr Han, the latter being associated with the Chala Chief as one of the Szechuan Frontier Commissioner's peace envoys. The Chinese professed to be anxious to negotiate an arrangement under which each side might withdraw out of contact with the other, but complained that the Tibetan leaders had been so overbearing and hostile at the two conferences which had been held that it had been impossible to come to terms. The Tibetans said much the same of the attitude of the Chinese. The Szechuanese will insist on regarding the Tibetans as "Barbarians," and they always use the term *Fan Kuan* ("Barbarian Official") in referring to a Tibetan officer, the underlying idea being much the same as that which led the Chinese to dub all foreigners "Barbarians" in the days of the old Canton Factories. The said *Fan Kuan* are, as a matter of fact, usually more civilised than the Szechuanese. The Daböns, for instance, have in most cases visited India, carry Kodaks and field-glasses, sleep on camp beds, and often wear foreign clothes, whereas the Szechuanese leaders know nothing of the world beyond the confines of their own province away in the back blocks of Western China, and have for the most part never seen a railway train or a steamer.

It has been arranged that we open our conference to-morrow, both sides engaging to do their best to be more accommodating.

The position here is a peculiar one. When the Szechuan Frontier Commissioner, who appeared quite indifferent to the fighting as long as it was going on to the west of the

[1] See Plate XLII.

Yangtze, realised that if he did not bestir himself the Tibetans would soon be bombarding Tachienlu, he sent out his forces along the North Road with orders to stop the Tibetan advance on the line of the Yangtze. The main body of his troops duly reached Rongbatsa, a long day's march west of Kanze, and halted there because they could not get transport to convey them across the grass-lands of De-ge ahead.

While they were sitting in Rongbatsa, comfortably billeted in the houses of the village, and contemplating the inhospitable wastes ahead, they awoke one morning to find the Lhasa Tibetans, who had advanced rapidly after the fall of Chamdo, streaming down the two valleys along the roads from Dzenko and Yilung. Some sharp skirmishing ensued, which ended in the Chinese retiring to the main village of Rongbatsa and leaving all the farms and hamlets on the plain to be seized by the Tibetans.

Following these events, the Tibetans, while masking the main Chinese force at Rongbatsa, began moving eastwards down the Yalung plain with the object of cutting the Chinese off from their base at Kanze. They were in fact applying their usual encircling tactics, which had proved so successful at Chamdo, Draya and other places. At the time when orders arrived to cease fighting the object of the Tibetan General had nearly been attained. Two roads connect Kanze with the Rongbatsa plain, one on each side of the Yalung, which can be crossed at various points by coracle ferry. The road south of the river had been cut by the Tibetans seizing Darjye Gomba and the village of Lingtso (Chinese Lintsung), the Chinese force stationed there having been driven back to the stronghold of Beri; and the Chinese were on the point of losing control of the other road also when fighting stopped. Since the commencement of the truce both sides have remained in occupation of the positions they held when the orders came to cease fire, and have since been busying themselves with building stone barricades and strengthening their defences.

The local Tibetan leaders say that had they been permitted to continue hostilities they would have captured the whole Chinese force at Rongbatsa, and then advanced on Kanze. The Chinese profess to hold that they would have had no difficulty in maintaining themselves until the arrival of rein-

MAP 7

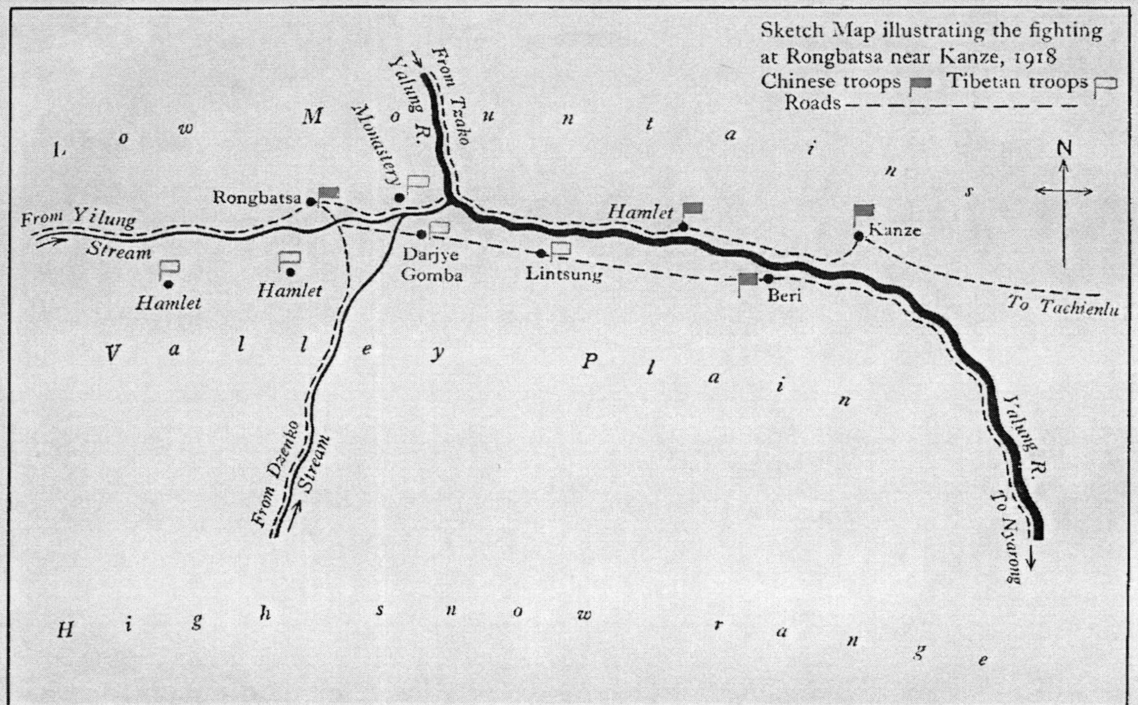
Sketch Map illustrating the fighting
at Rongbatsa near Kanze, 1918
Chinese troops
Tibetan troops
Roads
N
Low Mountains
Valley Plain
High snow range
From Tzako
Yalung R.
Monastery
Rongbatsa
From Yilung
Stream
Hamlet
Hamlet
Darjye
Gomba
Lintsung
Hamlet
Kanze
Beri
To Tachienlu
Yalung R.
To Nyarong
From Dzenko
Stream

forcements from Tachienlu, when they would have annihilated the Tibetan force between two fires and driven the remnants back across the Yangtze.

Local opinion is all in favour of the Tibetan contention. The truth, however, probably is that both sides, in spite of their bellicose talk, were getting uneasy; the Tibetans because they were involved in serious hostilities with a comparatively large Chinese force so far from their base; the Chinese because they knew that the Tibetans were working round into Nyarong and that, in the event of the latter region falling into Tibetan hands, there was grave danger of the Tibetans securing control of all the country along the main road in their rear.

About half a mile distant from the group of farms constituting the Tibetan headquarters lie the Chinese headquarters in the village of Rongbatsa, the two main forces being separated only by a small and easily fordable stream. One big shell would blow the headquarters of either side to smithereens; fortunately neither party have anything larger than small mountain guns of Chinese origin, of which they do not appear to have made very effective use.

October 26. At Rongbatsa.

On September 20 a conference between the leaders on both sides was held in a large tent pitched in the open between the opposing lines. After interminable discussions an agreement was reached providing for the adherence of the Tachienlu Chinese to the truce concluded at Chamdo and for the mutual withdrawal of the troops of both sides out of contact with one another. It was the second point which gave rise to all the difficulties. Both sides talked round and round the point for hours on end. The Chinese position was generally based on the argument, which was quite true as far as the Tachienlu Chinese were concerned, that as they were not the aggressors, it was not for them but for the Tibetans to withdraw; while they kept on explaining that they were making peace, not because they were afraid of the Tibetans, but because they were reluctant to chastise them. To this the Tibetans would reply with references to General P'eng's action in starting all the trouble at Chamdo, demonstrate that they were the victorious party, and offer to resume hostilities if the Chinese doubted it. The understanding eventually arrived at was to the effect that each side should withdraw approximately one long day's journey, the Chinese to Kanze and the Tibetans to within the De-ge border, and the agreement was then referred by express couriers despatched the same evening to Chamdo and Tachienlu, for the approval of the Kalon Lama and the Szechuan Frontier Authorities respectively. Various other small matters were attended to at this meeting, including an arrangement permitting the unfortunate local Tibetans inhabiting the plain to harvest their crops; for though the corn was now ripe, they had so far been unable to proceed to the harvest owing to the tension prevailing between the opposing forces. After the conference had adjourned, each side returned to their respective quarters to await the replies from their superiors, which were to be expected in about three weeks' time.

On September 23 I spent the day on horseback making a tour of inspection of the rival positions in the valley. The Rongbatsa plain, which is almost entirely under cultivation, is a glacier-formed continuation of the Yalung valley plain. On the south side rises the rocky snow-clad range which serves as the Yangtze-Yalung divide from the neighbourhood of Kanze to Dzogchen Gomba, while on the north are low grassy downs. To the west the valley ends and the ground rises towards the Jambe Latse La on the De-ge border and the grass-lands of Yilung. To the east one looks down the open valley plain of the Yalung bounded in the distance by the snow-clad masses of the Kawalori mountains. We rode down the plain past Darjye Gomba[1] and Lingtso, both in Tibetan hands, nearly as far as Beri castle, which was strongly held by Chinese troops guarding the road to Kanze. Beri is an important strategic point, as the mountains here close in on the river and bring the valley to an end, the narrow passage being completely dominated by the castle.

The Chinese here are under the disadvantage of being far less mobile than the Tibetans. Also their hearts are not in

[1] There are thirteen big monasteries in the Horba States, and of these Darjye Gomba is the oldest and most important foundation. The others are Beri, Kanze, Tongkor, Joro, Drango, Dawu, Sangdru, Gonsar, and four more in the Tzachuka grass country.

the fight, they are dissatisfied with their rations of *tsamba* and with the hardships of life in these highlands, and are generally inferior to the Lhasa Tibetans in this kind of warfare. A Chinese soldier is content to discharge his piece into the air, often from the hip, in the direction of the enemy, whom he prefers not to see; and the battles of the civil wars of recent years in Western China have for the most part consisted in long range rifle fire until one side or the other chose to retire. The Tibetan, on the other hand, seldom discharges his rifle unless he has covered his enemy at comparatively short range. In the fighting at Lingtso the Tibetans had got in amongst the Chinese with their swords; and the Tibetan broad sword wielded by a native is a very ugly weapon capable of beheading a man at a blow.

By the end of September the harvest was over and the crops neatly stacked on the flat roofs of the houses. We have received many expressions of gratitude from the local people for having arranged matters so that they could gather in their corn in peace. For the past few days they have been busy with flails threshing out the barley on the flat house-tops, a proceeding which is often accompanied by showers of earth in the room below. The crops consist almost entirely of barley. A little wheat is grown, but the elevation of the plain, about 11,600 feet, is near the height limit for the latter. Oats grow amongst the barley, apparently as weeds, producing no ears to speak of.

As October wore on the weather became wet and cold, and the snow line crept down the slopes of the big range to the south. Life was very dull, with nothing to do but ride about the plain, which was entirely bare of game, and exchange visits with the Chinese and Tibetan officials.

The principal hardships of life at Rongbatsa are connected with the absence of fuel, vegetables and fruit. The only thing available in the latter line is a species of dried apricot from the Indian border. These apricots, sewn up in bags of yak skin, form a regular article of commerce in Eastern Tibet; they are so hard and dry that one can cut a sackful in half with a sword, and yet leave them a congealed mass. When soaked and stewed they are quite good, or at any rate seemed so to us who had not tasted fresh fruit of any kind for so long.

On October 10 the replies from Chamdo and Tachienlu having at length arrived, the conference tent was again pitched between the opposing lines. Both the Kalon Lama and the Szechuan Frontier Authorities had accepted the agreement, which was thereupon duly signed and sealed.

The Chinese were greatly indebted to the Chala Chief for the successful conclusion of these negotiations. Being a Tibetan himself, and understanding the Tibetan mentality and the Tibetan point of view, while at the same time representing the Chinese case, he was able to smooth away many difficulties. The remaining Chinese negotiator, on the other hand, seemed obsessed with the idea that the only way to deal with the Tibetans was to browbeat and patronise them alternately; an attitude which, however suitable in the days of the Emperor Ch'ien Lung, was here out of place and out of date.

After the negotiations had been satisfactorily concluded the Chala Chief gave a fraternising banquet to all concerned in a big tent pitched by the stream. In spite of all the angry talk which had gone before, the entertainment was a great success, and the whole party spent some three hours or so in eating and drinking on the friendliest terms. Now that the main issues have been settled both Chinese and Tibetans have become very accommodating over smaller matters such as the exchange of prisoners and the re-opening of the main road to Chinese and Tibetan traders.

As middleman and guarantor, it has been my duty to remain here until both sides have withdrawn their troops in accordance with the arrangement, and I have spent a considerable portion of my time during the last few days sitting on the flat roof of my house watching through field-glasses the movements of the retiring troops. As was to be expected, there were delays and procrastinations, each side waiting for the other to begin the withdrawal on a large scale. But at last it is all over; and yesterday I rode over the plain of Rongbatsa, and found it completely deserted by both Tibetan and Chinese troops. The local Tibetan inhabitants are naturally immensely relieved to be left to follow their own pursuits in peace.

We leave to-morrow on our return journey to Chamdo, in order to fix up a few matters of detail, and more especially to arrange with the Kalon Lama for the release of all the Chinese, wounded soldiers and civil officials, left there in the hands of the Tibetans. We have arranged to travel through Draya and Gonjo, partly to see how matters stand in those centres, and also with a view to taking advantage of the opportunity of travelling through country hitherto unknown to European geography.

CHAPTER VII

FROM RONGBATSA ON THE YALUNG THROUGH GONJO TO DRAYA, AND THENCE *VIA* YEMDO TO CHAMDO

Passage of the Yangtze-Yalung divide by the Hön La (15,800 feet)—Down the gorges of the Dzin Chu to Horbo—Gato Gomba—The Mizo La (16,300 feet)—Beyü Gomba in Southern De-ge—The Lungdri La (15,800 feet)—The bends of the Yangtze at Polo Gomba—A mule over the precipice—A salt caravan from the Kokonor—The Nadzong La (16,000 feet), the boundary between De-ge and Gonjo—Mapping the rivers of Gonjo—Gonjo Dzong—Crossing the Yangtze-Mekong divide and the Gonjo-Draya boundary—Arrival at Draya Jyamdun—Yemdo and its ruined monastery—Return to Chamdo *via* the Ipi La—Release of remaining Chinese prisoners at Chamdo—A long lost Chinese exile in Tibet—Departure from Chamdo by the Yunnan road.

October 28. At DZENKO.

We left Rongbatsa yesterday after a stay of nearly six weeks. Everyone was glad to see the last of this somewhat dreary neighbourhood. Our first day's march took us back up the Dza Chu to our former camp under the Yangtze-Yalung divide.

To-day we crossed the big range; but as the Tsengu La was said to be deep under snow, owing to the bad weather during the past month, our guides took us over another pass further north, called the Hön La, equally high (about 15,800 feet), but said to be easier in snowy weather. Starting very early in the morning, we followed up the main branch of the Dza Chu north-west nearly to its source and then turned west for a mile or two, struggling up through deep snow, to reach the pass. Fortunately the weather was fine. From the pass we dropped down to Dzenko through the valley of a stream which joins the Dzin Chu from the north.

November 3. At BEYÜ.

Leaving Dzenko on October 29 we retraced our road of two months ago nearly as far as the pass, the Baya La, and then turned up the mountain side to the left to reach the top of the spur dividing the Dzenko and Dehlung rivers. From

A PECULIAR TYPE OF TIBETAN FARM-HOUSE COMMON IN THE DZIN CHU VALLEY NEAR HORBO, SOUTHERN DE-GE

A VILLAGE NEAR HORBO, DZIN CHU VALLEY, SOUTHERN DE-GE

PLATE XLIV

GATO GOMBA, A BIG MONASTERY IN SOUTHERN DE-GE

BEYÜ GOMBA, ANOTHER BIG MONASTERY IN SOUTHERN DE-GE

this point there are wonderful views over this wild country of high mountains and deep valleys, including the snow giants behind Dzogchen to the north. The trail then kept near the top of the ridge for a few miles, passing a picturesque little monastery clinging to the mountain side amongst limestone crags and pine trees; and crossing over another small pass, dropped down steeply through a ravine, past a group of farms called Racha Hlaba half-way down, to debouch on to the Dzin Chu, the latter flowing in a tremendous pine-clad canyon, thousands of feet deep. Continuing for a few miles down the river we reached the village of Racha Nachi, where accommodation had been prepared for us. The top of the mountain on the opposite side of the river is crowned by a monastery, Racha Gomba. This day's march, like the preceding two, was a very long one.

On the following day we had an easy march down the gorges of the Dzin Chu to Horbo, where we were well housed in a small *Podrang*, the seat of a subordinate De-ge official. Horbo, one of the twenty-five *Dzongka* (Tibetan districts) of De-ge, is said to be one of the chief centres of the De-ge metal industry, that is to say, the manufacture of knives, swords and especially tea-pots, which are used all over Kam. The work is done in the homes of the people.

The Dzin Chu joins the Yangtze a few miles below Horbo. Our road, however, here left the valley and turned south up a ravine, blocked at the end by the snow range which has to be crossed on the next march. After ascending this ravine for a few miles the path climbs up the mountain side by steep zigzags for 2000 feet or so to reach the large and well-known monastery of Gato Gomba, which is strikingly situated at an elevation of over 13,000 feet just below the top of the range, with steep pine-clad slopes falling away in front down to the valley thousands of feet below.

Near the Gomba is the dissecting ground, where deceased lamas are cut up and fed to the vultures with a view to securing an early reincarnation. An operation of this kind, which is a very unpleasant proceeding, had just been concluded as we rode up[1].

From Gato Gomba to Beyü Gomba is not far in actual distance, but the march is a hard one owing to the formidable

[1] See p. 84.

pass called the Mizo La, over 16,000 feet high, which has to be crossed *en route*. The trail leads over the ridge immediately behind Gato Gomba, and then runs along the mountain side for a few miles with the ground on one's right hand falling away down to the Yangtze, 5000 feet below. After passing round the head of a ravine we reached the foot of the big pass, and climbed up to the top through deep snow. From the summit of the Mizo La we looked south across a tremendous canyon, the valley of the Ngü Chu, to a similar range beyond, which we were informed had to be crossed on the next stage on the road to Gonjo. To get from the one pass to the other one has to descend some 6000 feet into the valley and ascend the other side almost as far again, a long hard day's journey; but an aeroplane could have flown across in a few minutes. From the Mizo La we marched down a long straight ravine through large pine forests for hour after hour; until finally, after passing a small monastery situated on a spur, we dropped down by zigzags for the last 2000 feet to reach Beyü in the valley of the Ngü Chu.

Beyü consists of a large monastery (like Gato, of the *Nyimaba* sect) and a few farms lying on a cultivated slope a few hundred feet above the Ngü Chu, backed by forests of pine and juniper. The Ngü Chu is a replica of the Dzin Chu, a dark green stream flowing at the bottom of a narrow canyon, the pine-clad slopes of which rise for 5000 or 6000 feet directly from the water's edge. It joins the Yangtze a few miles lower down.

The general situation of Beyü is precisely similar to that of Horbo, and the elevation of the valley, about 10,300 feet, is in each case much the same. In both cases the Yangtze is only a few miles off; but the main road, instead of making the slight détour *via* the gorges of the latter, leads straight over the big Mizo La ridge, over 16,000 feet in height. In Tibet, as in China, the main roads always seem to run if possible straight to their objective over the intervening obstacles instead of following, like European roads, the line of least resistance round the corner.

Southern De-ge is a remarkable country of deep narrow valleys, dense pine forests and huge mountains. It is a very beautiful region to look upon, but a very arduous one to travel across. A more difficult country to campaign in it would be hard to find. The Chinese established a district magistracy at Beyü, which they called Paiyü Hsien. The Chinese officials and troops stationed here, belonging to the Batang command, evacuated the place when the Tibetans advanced after the fall of Chamdo, but managed to get themselves trapped and surrounded in a precisely similar valley called Gaji (Chinese Kaiyü) two marches further south; whence they were eventually permitted to withdraw to Batang as a result of the peace negotiations.

The accommodation being good, and the valley warm and sunny, we have been resting here for a couple of days after our tiring marches from Dzenko.

November 5. At Polo Gomba.

Leaving Beyü yesterday we marched up the left bank of the river for a few miles and then turned up the mountain side to the west. A long pull up hill followed, through the usual three stages of pine forest, open grassy slopes and bare rock. The pass is called the Lungdri La (15,800 feet). The view looking back across the valley of the Ngü Chu to the Mizo La is very fine; further back again, bearing a little east of north, towers a huge snow mass. I am uncertain whether these mountains are connected with the big peaks behind Dzogchen or whether they belong to another unlocated snow massif; the same or similar peaks bear due north from the Gato Gomba ridge. From the pass we descended through more pine forests to a group of farms called Karnagong, lying on a cultivated slope 2000 to 3000 feet above the Yangtze. Beyond the latter, bearing south-west, is a steep rocky range, behind which, we were informed, lay Sangen.

November is a good month for travel in Kam; day after day a brilliant sun shines out of a cloudless sky, and the big passes are almost free of snow.

To-day we descended by steep zigzags to the Yangtze, which we found flowing as usual in a gigantic canyon. Crossing by coracle at a ferry called Rushi Drango Druka, we were met on the further bank by the local *Bön* of the *Dzongka* of Polo, one of the sub-districts of De-ge. Resuming our march after the customary talk and tea-drinking we followed up the right bank of the Yangtze for the rest of the way to Polo Gomba, a small monastery of the *Sajya* sect situated at the point where the big river making a right angle bend from north-east to south-east is joined by the stream from T'ungp'u.

The big bends made by the Yangtze in this neighbourhood were unknown to European geography before Mr Coales placed them on the map[1] as the result of a recent journey. From near De-ge Gönchen the river flows south-east; from its junction with the Dzin Chu below Horbo it flows south-west; and from Polo Gomba it flows south-east again towards Sangen and Batang.

Marching along the Yangtze to-day by a narrow foot-path a couple of hundred feet above the river, one of the pack animals slipped over the edge and rolled down the precipice to the stony beach below. The pony was not seriously hurt; but this sort of treatment was too much even for the yak-skin boxes, which exploded on hitting the rocks by the water, scattering our small remaining stocks of candles and sugar amongst the sand and stones. We shall now have to go short until we get back to Chamdo. It is impracticable to carry any large quantity of foreign stores on such long journeys in these remote parts, and we have been living entirely on the country for some time past. A few luxuries, however, such as sugar from Yunnan, candles and cigarettes from India, and soy and vermicelli from Sining, can be purchased locally in the larger centres like Chamdo.

The last time we crossed the Yangtze, at Gangto ferry some two months ago, it was a thick yellow in colour; here it is now again a beautiful blue. The French call the Upper Yangtze "le Fleuve Bleu." This is a very appropriate name for it in the winter, when it is a most wonderful blue in colour, due presumably to the clear Tibetan sky reflected in its deep waters. But for half the year the name "Blue River" is absurdly inappropriate, as its waters are the colour of thick pea soup throughout the summer. This discolouration is due to the open plateau country of red sandstone contained in its basin in De-ge and further north. In winter, the streams draining this elevated sandstone region freeze, and the river is then fed only by the perennially clear streams issuing from the limestone gorges at a lower elevation.

At Polo Gomba the road from De-ge to Gonjo (which we

[1] See *Geographical Journal* for April, 1919.

THE FORESTED CANYON OF THE NGÜ CHU, THE RIVER OF BEYÜ

APPROACH TO THE LUNGDRI LA, A HIGH PASS ON THE BEYÜ-GONJO ROAD

PLATE XLVI

CORACLE FERRY ACROSS THE YANGTZE AT RUSHI DRANGO DRUKA, BEYÜ-GONJO ROAD

THE YANGTZE RIVER NEAR POLO GOMBA, BEYÜ-GONJO ROAD

are following) is joined by trails from the north *via* T'ungp'u and Kargung. It is therefore quite an important centre of communication for these roadless regions. A large yak caravan arrived this evening, carrying Kokonor salt southwards. This is one of the staple trades of Kam. The salt is brought down by the northern nomads and exchanged for the barley of the agricultural valleys along the Yangtze. Still further south the Tibetans get their supplies of salt from the brine wells on the banks of the Mekong at Tsakalo (Yenching); which, however, supply a comparatively small area of country compared to that covered by the Kokonor and Nagchuka salt.

November 11. At Gonjo Dzong.

From Polo Gomba we made a short march of only a few miles up a branch valley to a group of farms called Shutzashi, and on the following day turned south-west across a small pass to reach a valley named Nyashi; the stream here flows south-east to its junction with the Yangtze, though whether or not it joins the Re Chu on the way we are unable to determine.

The next day's march took us over a high pass, called the Nadzong La (16,000 feet), the boundary between De-ge and Gonjo. The view from this pass, looking west over a deep valley, was extensive and interesting, as it explained much of the drainage system of the province of Gonjo, which consists apparently of the basin of one river. This stream has two main branches, the Re Chu and the Mar Chu, which, flowing from the Chorzhung country in the north and from Gonjo Dzong in the south respectively, meet and then flow east and south-east to join the Yangtze near Gaji. A desire to place this river on the map had been one of the reasons which had impelled us to take this route; and it was therefore a satisfaction to find that from the Nadzong La we were looking down on the confluence of the northern and southern branches some distance away. Descending from the pass we halted at some farms called Norba, lying in Gonjo.

From Norba we descended a ravine for a short distance to reach the Re Chu, which we found a stream of considerable size, flowing at an elevation of about 11,800 feet in the usual narrow canyon between pine-clad slopes. It was just fordable at a broad shallow spot, the water being up to the ponies' bellies. After crossing the Re Chu our path ascended the mountain side through pine forests and then trended away from the river, climbing in and out of side ravines. After a few miles of very bad going through these forests we emerged suddenly into an absolutely bare region of red sandstones and shales, the formation characteristic of the Chamdo and Draya portions of the Upper Mekong basin. Ana, where we halted, consisted of a few farms and a large Tibetan fort, Karto Podrang, the seat of a Gonjo *Bön*. The elevation was about 13,000 feet. It is a curious fact that cultivation appears to be carried on at greater heights in the bare sandstone country than anywhere else in Eastern Tibet. To the N.N.W. one looked up the long straight valley of the Re Chu towards Chorzhung. The confluence of the Mar Chu and the Re Chu, at a place called Sharundo, was out of sight a thousand feet below, and I was too lazy to go down and examine it; but from local information I gather that a third stream from the west also joins the Re Chu in this neighbourhood.

On November 10 we made a long march in order to reach Gonjo Dzong. The trail lay through a dreary region of red sandstone, up and down small valleys just off the Mar Chu. In some places the ground was covered with a white alkaline efflorescence, as in the "Bad Lands" of Kansu in North-west China. At last we descended into the valley of the Mar Chu itself, here quite a small and easily fordable stream at the present low water season, and, following it up, shortly reached Gonjo Dzong.

This place consists of a Tibetan *Dzong* (fort and official residence), a small monastery, and a dilapidated sort of rest-house which served as the Chinese magistrate's yamen during the Chinese occupation. The elevation is about 12,400 feet, and we found it miserably cold and bleak at this time of the year. It is the capital of the Tibetan province of Gonjo, which was formerly ruled by a *Deba* appointed by the Markam Teji and twelve native headmen (*Bön*). It must be a very poor and sparsely populated region even for Eastern Tibet. The Chinese occupied it in the time of Chao Erh-feng and turned it into a district, which they called Kung Hsien, or Kungchüeh. It is now being administered by a *Dzongbön* appointed by the Kalon Lama; he turned out to be an old acquaintance, a young Lhasa monk, whom we had met in Chamdo.

To-day we rested at Gonjo Dzong, where we were presented with the usual courtesy gifts of grain and sheep. In summer sheep are presented alive; in winter dead and skinned, but complete with head, horns and feet, and frozen stiff in the attitude of a galloping racehorse.

There is a road from here to Chamdo *via* Toba, which is said to be six marches distant. I should like to have followed this road in order to place more of Gonjo on the map. But the Dzongbön, who had come that way from Chamdo, said that one had to march for two or three days across an elevated and uninhabited plateau on the Gonjo-Chamdo boundary, where the cold would now be very severe. We have, therefore, decided to return *via* Draya.

Sangen can easily be reached from Gonjo by a road leading south-east up the Mar Chu; another road leads south to the Hlato plateau and so to Markam.

I believe the French traveller, M. Bonvalot, must have come this way, though I have not seen a proper map of his route. He appears to have been deflected north of Chamdo, to have been guided south, perhaps from Toba, to Gonjo Dzong, and to have proceeded thence south *via* Hlato to Markam.

November 13. At Draya.

We left Gonjo yesterday in cold windy weather, after a snow-storm during the night. This was our first taste of the approaching winter; as in North China, the wind makes all the difference in the cold weather. The trail lay up a defile away from the Mar Chu to an easy pass, and then down the other side into a grassy valley dotted with the black tents of nomads looking cold and miserable in the snow. These nomads belonged to Draya, the pass just crossed being the Mekong-Yangtze divide and Draya-Gonjo boundary. They were in their autumn quarters and preparing to move lower down. The nomads of Kam appear generally to make three moves a year. After a rest in one of the tents we continued over another and rather higher pass, whence we followed down a long uninhabited valley to a group of farms and a

Chinese rest-house called Ranjur, lying a few hundred feet above the main branch of the Draya river.

From Ranjur we followed down the Draya river until we joined the main Batang road at the *chöten* seven or eight miles from Draya Jyamdun, where we arrived to-day for the third time on our travels. As a result of the Tibetan occupation the place is looking much improved, and the houses and temples are being repaired and white-washed.

We leave to-morrow for Chamdo by a trail down the Me Chu valley, which is said to be easier and no longer than the main road. It is only used in the winter because it entails fording the Me Chu, which is impassable at high water.

November 27. At CHAMDO.

The first stage out of Draya took us over a steep pass, the Ge La, nearly 15,000 feet high, and down the other side to the village of Rangdru in the valley of the Me Chu, which makes a big bend to the south below Draya Jyamdun. The scenery in this neighbourhood is typical of the Draya region, and consists of dreary-looking mountains of red, yellow and green sandstones and shales, absolutely bare of all vegetation, with the strata most curiously twisted, often from the horizontal to the perpendicular.

The descent from the Ge La we found rather dangerous, the path, often less than a foot wide, being ledged in a precipice of disintegrating rock. On such roads it is better to be mounted on a mule than on a pony.

On the following day we continued down the Me Chu valley to Yemdo. The road is good, except for two bad places where it is carried round the corners of cliffs on rotten wooden stagings. Yemdo (Chinese Yent'ait'ang) is a desolate-looking place, a few hovels below the gaunt ruins of the big monastery with a background of bare sandstone mountains. The Chief Reincarnation of Draya used to reside part of the year here and part of the year at Jyamdun. The destruction of the monastery by the Chinese in 1913 or 1914 marked the end of one of the Draya rebellions. Several hundred Tibetans were penned up in the monastery and perished in the flames. No Tibetan can view the ruins of the great monasteries at Chamdo, Draya, Yemdo and other places without feeling deeply incensed against the Chinese for what he regards as

VIEW FROM THE GE LA, LOOKING SOUTH-WEST ACROSS THE ME CHU VALLEY AND THE BARE SANDSTONE MOUNTAINS OF DRAYA

FORDING THE ME CHU BELOW THE GE LA, DRAYA-YEMDO ROAD

PLATE XLVIII

A PORTION OF THE RUINS OF THE GREAT CHAMDO MONASTERY DESTROYED BY CHINESE TROOPS IN 1912

COMMENCEMENT OF RECONSTRUCTION WORK ON THE CHAMDO MONASTERY AFTER THE TIBETAN OCCUPATION SIX YEARS LATER

the most terrible of outrages against his religion and his fellow countrymen.

Yemdo is only about 10,400 feet high, and we found the weather quite warm again. Autumn ploughing was even still in progress. The plough is drawn by yak from a yoke attached to their horns.

The Me Chu joins the Mekong a few miles below Yemdo There is a coracle ferry here, and a road leads thence westwards to the Tibetan district of Bashü and the Salween valley. This was the route followed by the Chinese troops from Draya who crossed the Mekong in an attempt to invade Tibet, with disastrous results to themselves, as narrated elsewhere[1]. The trail we were following led down the Me Chu as far as the hamlet of Dowa, about half-way to the Mekong, and then turned up a side ravine to the north. A long march up this valley brought us to a group of farms called Jyaragong.

On the following day we continued up the same ravine to emerge eventually at the Ipi La, the big pass on the main road. This is a curious mountain knot, from which streams flow north-west to Bomde, south-east to Bagung, south-west to Jyaragong, and west to the Mekong. The last time we crossed this pass was in July, when we found it covered with soft snow; on this occasion it was almost free of snow and the weather was fine and sunny. The big passes are usually easier to cross in the early winter than at any other time of the year.

From the Ipi La we descended to Bomde, and followed the main road *via* Mengpu to Chamdo, where we arrived on November 18 and were given a warm welcome by the Tibetan officials and General Liu and his staff of Chinese. Everyone seems greatly relieved at the definite cessation of hostilities.

In accordance with the understanding previously arrived at, the first thing to be done now that peace had been definitely concluded was to obtain the Kalon Lama's formal assent to the release of all the Chinese, civilians and wounded soldiers, left in Chamdo, and his permission for them to return with General Liu to Batang. This was finally agreed to, the Kalon Lama only stipulating that the men's native wives should remain behind[2], and also that *ula* transport should only be

[1] See p. 53.

[2] In the days of the Manchus there was a strict rule that no Chinese woman was permitted to cross the passes (*k'ou wai*) from China into Tibet, and a similar custom has been generally observed since the advent of the

granted to those incapacitated by wounds or able to pay the regular charges; this latter decision gave rise to a great deal of grumbling, as no Chinese ever walks a mile in Eastern Tibet if *ula* animals can possibly be obtained from the natives.

There was one other matter which had to be arranged before leaving Chamdo. I had received a communication from the Governor-General of Szechuan asking me to endeavour to trace and obtain the repatriation of a friend of his student days, who had entered Tibet with General Chung Ying's expeditionary force in 1910, and had never been heard of since; at the same time he enclosed his friend's photograph, taken some ten years ago, before he left Szechuan for Tibet.

I brought the matter to the notice of the Kalon Lama, showed him the photograph, and asked him to do his best to trace the lost exile. To my surprise he recognised the photograph at once, and said that the original was a learned Chinese, living as a sort of hermit in a state of extreme poverty at Shuopando, a place a few marches distant on the Lhasa road.

Further enquiries elicited the whole story. Mr Wang, the individual in question, found himself stationed in Bomi, or that neighbourhood, in the capacity of a sort of military governor when the Chinese troops in Tibet mutinied at the time of the revolution in China in 1911. Though looted of all his effects he managed to escape with his life. But instead of making his way to Lhasa, whence he would in due course have been repatriated with all the other Chinese in Central Tibet *via* India to Shanghai, he fled north through the mountains to Shuopando, where he arrived in a destitute condition and threw himself on the mercy of the Kalon Lama. He has been living there ever since, subsisting on the charity of the local Tibetans. Why he had not come out through Eastern Tibet was not quite clear; either he had been afraid

republic. As a consequence Chinese soldiers and officials always take Tibetan women for their consorts. Such women are much despised by the Tibetans, though their progeny grow up as Tibetans and become merged in the Tibetan population. In some cases these marriages turn out well; but more usually the women become merely the slaves of their Chinese husbands, and their lot is particularly painful when their Chinese masters take them back to Tachienlu and even further into Szechuan to Yachou, where they usually end their days in Chinese brothels. The Chinese call these women *yatou* (slave girls); owing to the numbers of these unfortunate native women left stranded in Tachienlu and other border cities, such places are very immoral.

to leave the place for fear of falling into the hands of hostile Tibetans *en route*, or else the local Tibetans had kept him there as a sort of curio or mascot.

The Kalon Lama has now promised to send immediate instructions to Shuopando to have Mr Wang forwarded to Batang, whence he will be able to return with us to Szechuan. As I have learned by experience that a high Tibetan official never fails to carry out his promises, I regard Mr Wang's repatriation as good as accomplished.

On the 24th the Kalon Lama entertained us and the Chinese mission to a farewell feast, at which everyone was in high spirits at the successful termination of our peace negotiations. On the 25th General Liu and his staff departed for Batang, an event which seemed to occupy most of the day.

We are leaving by what is known as the Yunnan road, which runs south from Chamdo, in order to assist, at the request of the Chinese and Tibetan officials, in settling a small dispute about the boundary near Yenching. This will give us further opportunity of mapping unknown country.

The weather here is now very pleasant, cold frosty nights followed by sunny and absolutely cloudless days. The only trouble, as elsewhere in Eastern Tibet, is the question of artificial heating, charcoal being only found in Chinese centres. The problem is best solved by remaining in one's fur sleeping bag until the sun tops the mountains.

CHAPTER VIII

FROM CHAMDO, THROUGH TSAWARONG, TO YENCHING ON THE YUNNAN BORDER, AND THENCE BACK TO BATANG

Marching down the Mekong—The Riwoche river and Jyedam—Crossing the Mekong-Salween divide on the Bashü plateau—On the headwaters of the Yu Chu—Tsawa Dzogang—Drayü Gomba—Travelling down the Yu Chu through Tsawarong—Yunnan tea entering Tibet—Tibetan troops at Di—The Chamdo-Yunnan road—Back across the Salween-Mekong divide by the Di La (15,000 feet)—Yenching and its salt wells—The Mekong—Moso tribesmen—A Catholic Mission—The deeply-eroded country of South-eastern Tibet—Tranquillity in Tibet and disturbed conditions in China—Previous foreign travellers on the borders of S.E. Tibet—Settlement of dispute about the Tsando valley—Through Markam to Batang.

November 29. At Wayo.

We left Chamdo yesterday by the Yunnan bridge, and have been marching down the right bank of the Mekong for two days. The river flows all the way in a deep narrow canyon between scrub-covered mountains of red sandstone, with occasional farms, hamlets and patches of cultivation in the mouths of side ravines. The water is again a clear blue, though not so deep a blue as the Yangtze. The river freezes later on in its quieter reaches, and can be crossed on the ice bridges which form in this way; already blocks of ice are swirling down stream.

We are again accompanied, somewhat against our wishes, by a few Chinese refugees, who, desiring to go to Yunnan instead of Szechuan, did not therefore accompany General Liu when the latter left with most of the Chinese for Batang a few days ago.

Mr Rockhill crossed the river in this neighbourhood on his return journey from Tibet to China; he was deflected by the Tibetans to the south of Chamdo, and rejoined the main Batang road at Bomde.

December 1. At Yushi.

From the hamlet of Wayo we continued down the Mekong for a few miles, and then ascended the mountain ridge on

GORGES OF THE MEKONG BELOW CHAMDO ON THE YUNNAN ROAD

PLATE L

LOOKING WEST ACROSS THE BASHÜ PLATEAU FROM THE MEKONG-SALWEEN DIVIDE (14,800 FEET) ON THE CHAMDO-YUNNAN ROAD

HEADWATERS OF THE YU CHU RIVER ON THE BASHÜ PLATEAU, CHAMDO-YUNNAN ROAD

our right hand. Here the journey began to get interesting; for, on reaching the top of the spur, which was only about a thousand feet above the valley, we found ourselves, to my great surprise, looking down on to another river, flowing in a precisely similar gorge, parallel to and only a mile or so distant from the Mekong. This turned out to be the river of Riwoche (here called the She Chu), which is shown on British maps of Tibet as flowing south-west from Enda to join the Salween. Chinese maps rightly make it a tributary of the Mekong, which it joins below Drentsa Druka, at a place called Tsunpo. Descending into the valley of the She Chu, which is eroded down to within a few hundred feet of the level of the Mekong, we crossed over by a bridge, and marched down its right bank to a place called Jyedam, consisting of a number of farms in an open cultivated valley together with the *Podrang* of the local Tibetan official, in which we were lodged.

Jyedam is the chief centre of trans-Mekong Draya. It lies at the junction of the Chamdo-Yunnan road, which we are following, with an east to west trail connecting Draya with Bashü and the Salween valley. From this point the Riwoche river flows south-east to its confluence with the Mekong, said to be a short day's march distant. Due south are some big snow peaks.

To-day we left the She Chu valley, and made a short march up a side ravine to the south-west to reach this place, a group of farms called Yushi. We have at last left the dreary sandstone country of Draya and Chamdo, and the hills here are well wooded with pine trees.

So far this road has proved an easy one; but we are warned to expect some hard travelling during the next few days, as it appears that an uninhabited plateau, the Mekong-Salween divide, several marches in extent, has to be crossed before we reach houses again. In order to avoid having to camp more than necessary in such country, which is always exceedingly cold at this time of the year, we have arranged to make three or four very long marches.

December 3. At Bomda Gomba.

Yesterday we were travelling nearly from dawn till dusk. Following up a ravine, and winding round the corner of a mountain, we reached the top of the Mekong-Salween watershed at a height of about 14,800 feet. The summit of the divide is so flat that we had marched some distance before we noticed a frozen streamlet trending west, and realised that we had crossed the pass. We then found ourselves marching westwards across a vast plateau, stretching away as far as one could see, at an elevation of over 14,000 feet. At midday we reached some nomads' tents, where we rested and took refuge for a while from the bitter wind blowing directly in our faces. Continuing in the afternoon, we followed a trail trending west, south-west and south, across rolling downs, and eventually descended a few hundred feet into the valley of a stream flowing south-east, down which we marched for a few miles to another nomad encampment. We were here in the Tibetan province of Bashü, having left Draya shortly after crossing the pass.

The stream on the banks of which we were camped was frozen so that one could only guess its size; probably its sources are not far distant. It is called the Yu Chu[1] and we are to follow down its valley for two or three weeks' march, to the neighbourhood of its confluence with the Salween near Menkung, just north of the meeting point of the Burma, Yunnan and Tibet frontiers.

From the point where we turned south-west on this day's march another trail continues west to Sha-yi Zamka (in Chinese Chiayü Ch'iao), the bridge over the Salween (in Tibetan Jyemoho Chu, in Chinese Nu Chiang), on the main Lhasa road. According to Chinese accounts the formidable Waho Shan, crossed on the main road between Enda and Sha-yi Zamka, consists of a similar plateau to the one we traversed on this march, and it is probably a continuation of the same tableland.

To-day we made another long march down the flat valley of the Yu Chu and reached Bomda Gomba, a typical grass-country monastery like Dzogchen, Nangchen, Seshü, and others, surrounded by a few mud hovels lit by holes in the

[1] *Chu*, meaning literally "water," is the common word for "river" in Eastern Tibet; *Tsangpo* also means river, but is confined to big rivers; thus the upper Brahmaputra flowing through Central Tibet is known as the Tsangpo (hence the European name Sanpo), meaning "the River"; compare the Chinese words *shui* (literally "water") for a small stream, *Ho* for a river, and *Chiang* for the big river, e.g. Yangtze Chiang.

roofs instead of windows, and distinguished by a particularly large heap of *mani* stones. The elevation is gradually falling, and we are now down to 13,400 feet.

The cold has been severe during the past two days, the thermometer standing near zero Fahrenheit in the mornings. Like Tzachuka, this is a hard country in winter, especially when the wind blows. Not a tree or shrub is to be seen, and the only fuel, yak dung (*chowa*), is not always easily obtained.

December 6. At Dzogang.

Another long march down the uninhabited valley brought us to Tento Gomba, like Bomda, a *Gelugba* establishment housing seventy to eighty lamas. A little cultivation makes its appearance here. On the following day we continued down the valley, here partly under cultivation, to Dzogang (also pronounced Dzogung or Dzogong). This place consists of a *Gelugba* monastery, a small village, and an official residence, all built on a spur overlooking the river and facing a pine-clad mountain slope opposite. The fall in the valley is very gradual, the elevation here being still over 13,000 feet, and the weather remaining bitterly cold.

Dzogang, also called Tsawa Dzogang, is the capital of the Tibetan province of Tsawa, which embraces the basin of the Yu Chu from the vicinity of Bomda to that of Menkung (the latter being under the jurisdiction of the Tibetan official at Sangachu Dzong beyond the Salween). The lower portion of the Yu Chu valley is called Tsawarong (i.e. the *rong*, or "agricultural valley," of Tsawa). This name is sometimes shortened to Tsarong, in which form it appears on modern maps of Tibet.

We are stopping a day here, as everyone is in need of a rest after our long marches across the grass country. Our wants are being well provided for by the local official, a *Drungkor* from Lhasa[1]. This region has always been in Tibetan hands (except for Chinese raids in 1910 and 1911), and contrasts favourably, in regard to absence of ruins and like signs of devastation, with Draya and other territories which have for so long been in dispute between Chinese and Tibetans.

[1] A *Dzongbön* (Tibetan district magistrate) is, if a layman, also known as *Drungkor*, and if a monk as *Tsedrung* (*drung* meaning "associate").

Markam Gartok can be reached from Dzogang in two or three days by a trail up a side valley and over the divide to Samba Druka, the ferry across the Mekong.

December 11. At DRAYÜ GOMBA.

For the past five days we have been marching down the Yu Chu valley, descending gradually until now we have got down to about 11,300 feet. The travelling has been easy, as there have been comparatively good houses to stop in, with abundance of supplies and firewood, and even occasionally a little charcoal. Most of the way the valley is densely wooded and sparsely populated. In places glimpses can be caught through the pine forests of big snow ranges which run parallel to the river on either side. Between Uya and Moku one passes through some very fine limestone gorges which probably indicate that the river here breaks through a cross range. The people in the farms and hamlets where we stopped seemed happy and contented, and often entertained us with dancing, for which they were glad to be rewarded with a few *trangka*[1].

Drayü Gomba is a large but dilapidated *Gelugba* monastery lying on a slope above the river backed by pine forests and a snow range. It is an important centre, and lies at the junction of the Chamdo-Yunnan road which we are following with a trail from Markam Gartok *via* Samba Druka to Sangachu Dzong in South-eastern Tibet. This was the road followed by the Indian traveller A. K. (Krishna) who was here in 1882. He calls the place Dayül Gomba; thus omitting the *r* which is subjoined but pronounced, and including the *l*, which is a silent affix, as in Seshü(l), Beyü(l), Zayü(l). A. K. omits this subjoined *r* in all his Tibetan words, and talks of *Daba* for *Draba* (monks) and *Dokba* for *Drokba* (nomads).

The Yu Chu is here quite a fair size, comparable to the She Chu at Dawu; it is frozen only in its quieter reaches, where useful ice bridges form, enabling the traveller to cross from one bank to the other at will.

[1] The *trangka* is a Lhasa minted silver coin, exchanging three to a rupee; with the exception of those recently minted they are for the most part thin, battered, defaced and irregular in circumference; but in Tibetan territory we always carried a good stock of them as they form a useful subdivision of the rupee; where they are not available one has to make use of rupees cut in half.

MONASTERY AT TSAWA DZOGANG, THE CAPITAL OF TSAWARONG

WINTER SCENE IN THE VALLEY OF THE YU CHU, THE RIVER OF TSAWARONG, JUST BELOW THE LEVEL OF THE TREELESS GRASS COUNTRY

PLATE LII

AN ICE BRIDGE ACROSS THE YU CHU ABOVE DRAYÜ GOMBA, CHAMDO-YUNNAN ROAD

GORGES OF THE YU CHU, SHOWING CANTILEVER BRIDGE ON THE CHAMDO-YUNNAN ROAD

In 1910 or 1911, after the Chinese expedition had successfully occupied Lhasa, Chao Erh-feng sent a column of troops into Tsawarong. They looted but did not destroy Drayü Gomba, and then passed on to Sangachu Dzong beyond the Salween, where the Chinese proposed to establish a district, to be called Sangang or Komai Hsien. Almost immediately afterwards the revolution in China occurred, and all Tibet west of the Mekong relapsed automatically into Tibetan hands.

The Tibetans in this valley (as elsewhere, I suppose) have no idea of exact distances; indeed there do not appear to be any words in their language properly denoting measures of distance. If one asks a Tibetan how far it is to a place, he will reply *taringbo* ("a long way"), or *tanyebo* ("a short way"); or if he wishes to be more explicit he may say it is *shagsa* ("a day's journey," say six hours' march), or *tsasa* or *tsapo* ("half a day's journey," say three hours' march).

December 15. At Di.

We are now getting down into the deeply-eroded country of South-eastern Tibet, the river flowing in a narrow gorge between two snow-clad ranges with peaks probably over 20,000 feet in height. For the first day's march we followed down the valley to another monastery called Changmar Gomba, lying on a wooded spur above the river. On the next day the trail ascended the mountain side, the river appearing as a silver thread at the bottom of the immense canyon in which it flows, and then worked away from the main valley through pine forests and over a spur into a side ravine. Yesterday we again rejoined the river, meeting it at a point where it emerges from a cleft in the limestone mountains, and immediately afterwards turned up a side ravine to reach a pass called the Do La across a great buttress of limestone, which here forces the Yu Chu to bend to the south-west. This pass, though only about 14,000 feet high, is very steep on both sides, and we had some difficulty in getting up as the northern face was covered with frozen snow and ice between the pine trees.

The scenery in this part of Tsawarong is exceedingly beautiful. From the summit of the Do La there is a good view down the Yu Chu, which flows in a pine-clad valley between two snow-capped ranges on either side. An enormous snow massif is visible, bearing S.S.E.; these are probably the snow mountains lying north-west of Atuntze in Yunnan, which force the Yu Chu west to join the Salween.

On this march we met a large caravan of yak carrying Yunnanese tea into Tibet. It is made up into packets, similar to those containing the Szechuan teas, two of which make one load for a yak. From the appearance of the men accompanying this caravan, who were not real Tibetans, but of some kind of Moso or other mixed race, we realised that we were getting out of Tibet Proper and were approaching the Chinese border country, which is populated by a mixture of aboriginal tribes.

From the Do La we descended to some farms in a side ravine off the Yu Chu, and to-day followed down the main valley to this place, a group of farms called Di. All around are dense pine forests, through which can be caught glimpses of the snow-fields on the big mountains behind.

Here we found some hundreds of Tibetan soldiers drawn up to meet us, while on all sides blinding bonfires of juniper bushes were burning in celebration of the occasion. These troops are merely local levies, and are not to be compared in appearance with the well-equipped and organised Lhasa and Shigatse regiments who have been doing the fighting further north. They have been collected from Markam, Tsawa, Menkung and Sangachu Dzong, and appear to have been waiting here ever since the truce became effective five or six months ago with the intention of attacking Yenching if hostilities are resumed. The latter place has long been coveted by the Tibetans of Tsawarong on account of its salt wells and the revenues derived from the taxation of the salt produced. The presence of these levies at Di has for months past been a sort of sword of Damocles hanging over the heads of the Chinese troops at Yenching on the Mekong just across the divide, the latter realising full well that the Tibetans are waiting here, and not knowing when to expect their attack. We talked to the Tibetan officials in charge of these levies, told them that peace had been concluded and that hostilities would certainly not be resumed, and advised them to disband their men. They said they would do so after we had spoken in a similar sense to the Chinese commander at Yenching.

It is pleasantly warm down here, the elevation being only about 10,500 feet. The meeting point of Burma, Yunnan and Tibet lies a few marches to the south. The road to Atuntze in Yunnan continues down the river for two or three short stages and then turns east across the divide to the Mekong. Another trail leads south-west to Menkung, and thence to Rima and Assam; we are, in fact, here at the back of beyond of Burma and Assam. It is noticeable that the Tibetans of these parts are of much poorer physique than those on the northern uplands.

To-morrow we leave the Yu Chu, which we have been following for the past fortnight, in order to cross the watershed to Yenching on the Mekong. It is to the valley of this river, the Yu Chu, trending in exactly the required direction, that the so-called "Yunnan Road" from Chamdo to Atuntze owes its existence. It is one of the main trade arteries of Eastern Tibet, and is quite a good trail for these parts. As well as linking Atuntze with Chamdo, it connects Yunnan with the main Lhasa road by a branch running across from the Bashü uplands to Sha-yi Zamka (Chinese Chiayü Ch'iao, the bridge over the Salween), and is the route generally followed by Yunnanese merchants bound to Lhasa and Central Tibet. It is also much frequented by pilgrims from all parts of Kam bound to and from a sacred mountain in North-western Yunnan, which they circumambulate. We often met these pilgrims on the road, always on foot, and usually accompanied by sheep carrying their baggage[1].

December 18. At YENCHING.

Leaving Di and the Yu Chu valley, there is a long steep climb uphill through pine forests, which gradually thin out in the usual manner, giving way first to grassy slopes and then to bare rock and snow. The pass, called the Di La, about 15,000 feet high, is the Salween-Mekong watershed. A short way off on the same ridge is another pass, called the

[1] Since the closing of the high road *via* Batang and Chamdo owing to the hostilities between the Szechuanese and the Tibetans during the past ten years, all the Sino-Tibetan trade has been carried on by this Yunnan road and the Jyekundo route to the south and north of Chamdo respectively. I do not know whether the Yunnan road has ever been travelled by a foreigner before our journey; probably part of it was known to the Abbé Desgodins. A. K. crossed it, going from east to west.

Beda La, whence a trail leads down to Beto Gomba in the Yu Chu valley and so to Menkung; this was the road followed by Colonel Bailey in 1911, from Batang *via* Yenching, Menkung and Rima, to Sadiya in Assam. We found the Di La covered with frozen snow and ice, while a bitter wind made it almost too cold to breathe. From the pass we descended for several hours, dropping 5000 to 6000 feet, through a long forested ravine to a group of farms called Trongtse.

The Di La and Beda La are sometimes closed by snow in the spring. Probably the snowfall is heavier down here than in the more northern parts of Kam.

At Trongtse the stream which we had followed down from the pass turns off to the east to join the Mekong, while our trail continues north-east up a long straight valley to reach Lagön, the ruins of a once celebrated monastery, destroyed by the Chinese some years ago, lying on the top of a narrow ridge immediately overlooking the Mekong. The view over Yenching from this point is a remarkable one. The Mekong flows at the bottom of a deep narrow canyon, 3000 feet below, but almost directly under one's feet, and on both sides of the river along its banks are the brine wells and salt evaporating pans; Yenching itself, consisting of some farms and a hamlet, lies on a cultivated slope a few hundred feet above the river; immediately beyond rises the mountain range constituting the Mekong-Yangtze watershed, which is crossed by the main road to Batang at the Chia La, the latter being almost within view.

Descending from the Lagön ridge by a steep zigzag path we crossed the Mekong by coracle ferry (there is also a single rope bridge near by) and ascended the cliff the other side to reach Yenching.

The Di La range is here the boundary between the Chinese district of Yenching and the Tibetan province of Tsawarong, and we are therefore now again in Chinese-controlled territory.

Yenching (in Tibetan Tsakalo[1]) was formerly a part of the

[1] Yenching, or Tsakalo, appears on many maps of Tibet as Yakalo, or Yerkalo, which is the name of one of the hamlets near by; this name, Yakalo meaning "the high ground" (above the brine wells) is unknown to the Tibetans of Kam excepting the local people: the place is well known, however, all over South-eastern Tibet as Tsaka, or Tsakalo (meaning "the Southern Brine Wells"). The Chinese name Yenching also means Brine Wells.

ON THE DO LA, A PASS NEAR DI ON THE CHAMDO-YUNNAN ROAD

LOCAL TIBETAN LEVIES AT DI IN LOWER TSAWARONG

PLATE LIV

LOOKING WEST OVER THE MEKONG-SALWEEN DIVIDE FROM NEAR DI IN LOWER TSAWARONG

SUMMIT OF THE DI LA (15,000 FEET) IN WINTER, THE PASS ACROSS THE YU CHU-MEKONG DIVIDE NEAR YENCHING

territory of the Batang Deba, and was made into a district by Chao Erh-feng. The district really consists of nothing beyond the bottom of the canyon of the Mekong for a few miles above and below the salt wells, to which the place owes its existence as an official centre. The wells are on both sides of, and almost on a level with, the river, and become flooded every summer when the water rises. The brine is drawn up out of the wells, which are quite shallow, and is evaporated in the usual flat pans. The salt produced supplies North-western Yunnan, Batang, Markam and Tsawarong. The Chinese troops and officials are mainly dependent on the revenues they derive from taxing it as it leaves the wells to the extent of two rupees per mule load. As a result of this income they are much better off here than anywhere else in Chinese Tibet. The foreign-controlled Chinese Salt Administration get their share of the revenue derived from the Yenching brine wells by taxing the salt that goes to Yunnan when it reaches Atuntze.

On a cultivated slope nearly a thousand feet above the river and the salt wells are two villages, called Puding and Yakalo, which are separated by a ravine many hundreds of feet deep; so that what appears to be a ten minutes' walk from the one to the other takes in reality nearly an hour. Puding is the seat of the Chinese magistrate, and is therefore entitled to be called Yenching. Yakalo is a Catholic settlement grouped round the Mission.

The water of the Mekong is now (in midwinter) a clear blue in colour. The river is here called the La Chu and also the Da Chu by the Tibetans; at Chamdo it is known as the Dza Chu. Discontinuity of river names is one of the difficulties which face the map-maker in Eastern Tibet. Other instances of this are the names Tza Chu and Nya Chu for the Yalung, Dje Chu and Ngom Chu for the western branch of the upper Mekong, and Dzi Chu and She Chu for the Riwoche river. The Chinese call the Mekong the Lantsang Chiang from Chamdo down, being for the most part unacquainted with its course above the latter place.

Our reputation as successful peace-makers being now well established, we received a warm welcome at Yenching from the native population as well as from the Chinese troops and officials. The former are for the greater part Mosos; they have long become accustomed to their Chinese masters, and, being of a non-Tibetan race, they regard the Lhasa Tibetans more or less as strangers, and fear them as an unknown quantity.

The Moso race is one of the aboriginal tribes of North-western Yunnan, where their former Kingdom occupied a considerable extent of territory between China and Tibet with its capital at Lichiang. The Tibetans call them *Jyong* and their former king *Sadang Jyelbo*. Yenching appears to be the most northerly point at which they are found. Their religion, composed of magic, sorcery and nature worship, is probably, like that of the Lolos of Szechuan and the Abors of Northern Assam, a relic of the original Shamanism of Eastern Asia, which in China and Tibet became overlaid with the invading Buddhism. It is not unlikely that a comparative study of the religions of the Mosos, Lolos and Abors with the practices of the Lama sorcerers (especially those of the *Bön* sect) in Tibet and of the Taoist priests in China would show many points of similarity[1].

There is a Catholic Mission at Yenching, in charge of an able and open-minded priest, who has many converts amongst the Moso tribesmen but few or none amongst the Tibetans.

Yenching lies in the Szechuan Frontier Territory, but the Yunnan border is only about ten miles distant to the south. Both the Yunnanese and Tibetans covet the place because of its revenue-producing salt wells. The Tibetans could probably have taken Yenching without difficulty last June, but their doing so would have seriously compromised the prospect of peace; as, apart from the Szechuanese, who would scarcely have consented to surrender it even provisionally for any length of time, the Yunnanese, whose salt supplies would have been interfered with, would in all probability have taken the opportunity to seize it themselves. As it is, the Yunnanese, like the Kansu Mahomedans, have so far remained neutral in this quarrel between Szechuan and Tibet.

The elevation of the Mekong at Yenching is only about 8000 feet, the village itself being a thousand feet higher. We find it quite warm down here, a pleasant change from the climate of the bleak uplands from which we have come.

[1] See note on p. 79.

Winter-sown barley is even beginning to sprout, whereas higher up there is not a sign of green from October to May.

This is the country of the great parallel rivers and the land of deep erosions, where east to west travel is extraordinarily arduous. In a few marches one can cross the basins of the Yangtze, Mekong, Yu Chu and Salween, all flowing in deep narrow canyons 7,000 to 10,000 feet below the level of the intervening ranges. The main road from Yenching to Batang runs east up a ravine and across the Mekong-Yangtze divide by a pass called the Chia La to Tsongen (Chinese Chungai), and thence *via* Pamut'ang to the Yangtze. We are going to follow another trail leading north up the Mekong into Markam in order to enquire into a frontier dispute in that neighbourhood.

Travelling down the Yunnan road from Chamdo through Tsawarong, we could not fail to be impressed by the general state of tranquillity and absence of brigandage in the regions traversed, which have been uninterruptedly under Tibetan control since 1911, when compared with the conditions prevailing in the Chinese-controlled districts further east. Indeed, in the course of the past year we have travelled all over the Tibetan-controlled parts of Eastern Tibet, usually without any armed guard except for the few rifles carried by my own servants, and accompanied only by a small Tibetan official to represent the authority of his Government and provide for accommodation and transport; nor did it ever appear to enter the minds of anyone that a military escort was necessary. Now that we are back once more in Chinese-controlled territory, all the talk is again of brigands and rebels and the dangers of the roads. Many wild rumours are current, including an alarming report that the turbulent natives of Hsiangch'eng have revolted and are marching on Batang.

Yenching has been visited by many competent foreign travellers, missionaries and others, notably General Davies and Mr Kingdon Ward, coming from Yunnan, and M. Bacot and Colonel Bailey, coming from Szechuan. The last named travelled through to Assam *via* Menkung and Rima. Amongst the missionaries who have explored these parts must be mentioned the names of the Abbé Desgodins, and, a generation later, those of Messrs Muir and Edgar of the China Inland Mission. The reason why Colonel Bailey succeeded where others failed is probably to be found in the fact that he travelled without any Chinese and accompanied only by a Tibetan servant. From the days of Gill and Cooper up to the present time most travellers attempting to enter Tibet from the Chinese side have been accompanied by a Chinese personnel, and have thus unconsciously increased their difficulties tenfold. The successful travellers in Eastern Tibet have been those, like Bower, Rockhill, Bonvalot and others, who travelled with Tibetans. The ordinary Chinese has, not unnaturally, an intense dislike of Tibet and of the hardships of life in Tibetan country, and fears the Tibetan, whose customs and language he does not understand. In fact most Chinese are as much strangers and foreigners in Tibet as the foreign traveller they accompany. The Kansu Mahomedans of the Kokonor border country are, however, an exception to this rule.

December 25. At BATANG.

Leaving Yenching we marched up the gorges of the Mekong for twelve or thirteen miles, and then, leaving the river, which here flows down from the north-west, we turned north across a small pass, which serves at present as the frontier between the Chinese and Tibetan forces in this neighbourhood. Here we found ourselves marching up a wooded ravine, which opened out higher up into a cultivated valley called Tsando (in Chinese Hsiao Ch'angtu), now occupied by Tibetan troops from Markam. From Tsando the trail ascends through thick juniper woods to the pass, the Hlung La (14,000 feet), the Mekong-Yangtze divide and the true Markam boundary. From the pass, whence there are fine views over the snow peaks of the Mekong-Salween watershed range to the west, we descended through pine forests to a group of farms called Getoding[1], lying in the valley of the Gartok river just below its confluence with the river of Gusho[2]. The road which we had followed so far was the main route between Yenching and Markam Gartok, the latter being reached from Getoding in a couple of short marches up the river *via* Pulo. We were here again in the middle of winter; the elevation is about 12,000 feet.

[1] The name termination *ding*, common in this neighbourhood, means the "bottom" of a river valley, i.e. a cultivated flat.

[2] The course of the Gartok river and its tributaries is very incorrectly shown on most maps of these parts; especially so before the journeys of Mr Kingdon Ward.

The reason for our coming to Yenching was to assist in settling a dispute about the Tibetan occupation of the Tsando valley, which the Chinese claimed to be part of Batang, i.e. Yenching territory. The Tibetans on their side had put in a counterclaim to certain hamlets now in Chinese hands on the right bank of the Mekong opposite Yenching itself. An examination of the ground showed that Tsando, lying to the south of the Hlung La, was undoubtedly in Batang, and therefore in Chinese territory. On the other hand, local investigations also proved that the hamlet of Nguchuka and some other farms lying on the right bank of the Mekong opposite Yenching had originally belonged, not to the Deba of Batang like the rest of the neighbourhood, but to the Deba of Tsawa Dzogang; the arrangement being typical of boundary conditions in Eastern Tibet, where the jurisdiction of the Chiefs and Kings is often over families rather than territories. The matter was eventually amicably settled by both sides agreeing to the other remaining provisionally in occupation of the ground already in their hands.

From Getoding we followed down the Gartok river for a few miles and then turned north-east through pine woods and across grassy downs, descending eventually into the valley of the Hlandun river and following up its course to Hlandun. Here for a time we were marching almost along the Markam-Batang boundary, the road from Pamut'ang to Yunnan, which lies in China while we were in Tibet, running parallel to our route a short distance off.

Markam is a pleasant region of forests and park-like grasslands, most of it being too elevated for cultivation. It is a pleasant country in the summer, but too cold to be agreeable in the winter.

Near Hlandun we joined the main road, which we had followed half a year before, and returned *via* the Bum La and Pamut'ang to Batang, where we arrived yesterday. Our march was quite a triumphal progress, the local people everywhere overwhelming us with gifts and attentions in their gratitude and relief at the conclusion of peace. Batang itself, however, we found in a similar state of panic to that in which we had left it in June last; then the place was in imminent danger of being captured by the Lhasa Tibetans; now it is threatened by an irruption of the wild tribesmen of Hsiangch'eng.

CHAPTER IX

THE RETURN JOURNEY FROM BATANG TO TACHIENLU

Batang threatened by Hsiangch'eng insurgents—Return of a Chinese exile from Tibet—Precarious position of Batang—Departure from Batang by the South Road—The caravan ambushed by *Chagba*—Return to Batang and departure by the North Road—Further skirmishes with *Chagba*—A dangerous march through the forest—Arrival in Gaji in De-ge—An unexplored route to Nyarong—Beyü, Rongbatsa, and Kanze—Return to Tachienlu.

January 11. At BATANG.

Hsiangch'eng (in Tibetan Chantreng) is the name of the stretch of country lying south of the Litang-Batang road and north of the Yunnan border. It is a comparatively low-lying region of agricultural valleys, drained by streams flowing south into the Yangtze, and has of recent years been divided up into two Chinese districts called Hsiangch'eng, or Ting-hsiang, and Taoch'eng. The Tibetans of Hsiangch'eng, before the days of Chao Erh-feng controlled by the Litang Deba, have always been very restless under Chinese rule, and have been for the past twelve years the chief obstacle to the subjugation by the Chinese of the Southern Circuit of the Szechuan Frontier Territory. In 1906 Chao Erh-feng spent the best part of a year in besieging and destroying their principal monastery; in 1910 the local Chinese garrison made common cause with the natives in a bloody revolt against Chinese rule; in 1912, at the time of the revolution in China, the lamas and people rose again and expelled the Chinese; in 1913 the Chinese spent most of the year in re-subjugating the country; in 1914 the natives joined some revolted Chinese troops, and drove the Frontier Commissioner's forces back to Tachienlu and beyond; while in the intervals between the various revolts, when nominally at peace, bands of Hsiangch'engwa were in the habit of raiding the Chinese and Tibetans of the surrounding districts, notably a year or two ago, when they penetrated as far as Rongbatsa and Kanze, pillaging and burning.

Hsiangch'eng falls within the area nominally controlled by the Chinese Authorities of Batang, who have remained on fairly good terms with the natives during the past year or two by the simple expedient of leaving them alone; that is to say, there was an understanding that no Chinese troops would be stationed in Hsiangch'eng territory as long as the natives kept the peace. This arrangement was successful for a time, and the Hsiangch'engwa remained quiescent all through the recent hostilities between Szechuan and Tibet. Probably they were busy with their agricultural pursuits; now, having harvested and threshed out their grain, they are at leisure to go on the war path.

The trouble started a month or two ago, when the Chinese garrison stationed at a place called Dzungdza, south of Batang on the Hsiangch'eng road, surrendered, apparently without a fight, to the advancing Hsiangch'engwa. It is said the latter bought their rifles from the Chinese in return for opium and silver, which they promptly made them disgorge as soon as they were disarmed. Now the Hsiangch'engwa have written to the Chinese officials here announcing their intention to advance on Batang immediately, and alleging that they have received the orders of the Tibetan Government to expel all the Chinese left in Eastern Tibet.

The peace negotiations have left the Chinese Authorities at Batang full liberty of action in suppressing disturbances amongst the Tibetans in Chinese-controlled territory. But, unfortunately, they are in no condition to do so. If the Hsiengch'engwa come to Batang, burn the villages and massacre the Chinese, under the pretext of having received the orders of the Lhasa Tibetans to do so, the fat will be once more in the fire, and all our peace-making efforts will have been in vain; for the Chinese in Szechuan and Yunnan, unable to distinguish one kind of Tibetan from another, will not unnaturally accuse the Tibetans of a gross breach of faith and a general resumption of hostilities will ensue. The situation is also one of some danger for the missionaries, and more especially for the Catholics, seeing that the Hsiangch'engwa are, unlike the Lhasa Tibetans, no respecters of persons, foreign or Chinese.

On our first arrival in Batang the Chinese here, who rather regard me as the God-out-of-the-Machine specially provided to extricate them from all their difficulties, intimated that they would be very grateful if I would go to Hsiangch'eng and pacify the rebels. This I refused to consider, on the grounds that such a mission would have been difficult and doubtful of success owing to the absence of any recognised leaders amongst the Hsiangch'engwa, and that my work as peace-maker was limited to mediation between the Chinese and the Lhasa Tibetans; whereas the Hsiangch'engwa are rebels in Chinese territory in revolt against Chinese rule. But, in view of the allegation of the Hsiangch'engwa that they are revolting under orders from Lhasa, I have done all in my power, by writing to the Markam Teji and the Kalon Lama, to induce the Lhasa Authorities to use all their influence with the rebels to persuade them to return to their homes. As I expected, they responded immediately, and the Markam Teji has sent two emissaries direct to Hsiangch'eng and two more to Batang. The two latter arrived here a day or two ago, in order to proceed to Hsiangch'eng together with Chinese representatives from Batang. Their presence has had a calming effect on the people here, though they themselves do not seem very sanguine of success, nor anxious to venture their lives amongst the Hsiangch'engwa.

The Lhasa Tibetans indignantly deny the truth of the charge that they have incited the Hsiangch'engwa to revolt; and there is no doubt that their denials are true, seeing that they have nothing to gain by such a rebellion at the present time[1].

The local populace of Batang, both Chinese and Tibetan, would like the Chinese Authorities here to invite the Lhasa Tibetans down from Markam to take charge of Batang, and protect them from the Hsiangch'engwa. But such action would be sure to be misrepresented by the Szechuanese later on as a violation of the truce; while once the Tibetans had occupied Batang, it might be very difficult to get them to withdraw. If the worst happens, the foreign missionaries and Chinese officials will probably be able to escape across the Yangtze and take refuge with the Markam Teji. In the meantime there is nothing to be done but hope that the Teji's emissaries will be successful in inducing the Hsiangch'engwa

[1] It subsequently transpired that the Hsiangch'engwa had similarly alleged that they had received orders from the Yunnan Authorities (then at war with Szechuan) to expel all the Szechuanese from Eastern Tibet. This statement was of course equally untrue.

to abandon their projected attack on Batang[1]. It is said they intend taking Latang first, which would give Batang a week or two's respite.

In the meantime we cannot afford the time to wait here to see what is going to happen, and we are leaving for Tachienlu to-morrow by the main south road. It seems probable that we shall meet raiding bands of Hsiangch'engwa at Litang or *en route*. But we hope to be able to get through peaceably; while, if we do meet them, it will at any rate give us an opportunity to do our best to exhort them not to attack Batang.

After we had been in Batang a few days Mr Wang, the long-lost Chinese exile whose repatriation the Governor-General of Szechuan had requested me to obtain, arrived from Tibet, having been duly forwarded under the Kalon Lama's orders from Shuopando to Chamdo and thence on to meet us here. The Tibetans had looked after him well enough *en route*, but he arrived in an absolutely destitute condition, with nothing but the Tibetan gown in which he was dressed. Having lived for six or seven years on a diet of *tsamba* as a Tibetan hermit at Shuopando, he was quite unrecognisable as a Chinese, and even seemed to speak his own language in a slow and halting fashion. After a few days, however, washed and shaved and dressed in Chinese clothes, he was again a cultured Chinese gentleman. Having received no news of what had been going on in China and the outer world during his long years of exile in Tibet, he knew little or nothing of the history of events in the far East since the establishment of the Chinese Republic in 1912, nor of the long struggle between north and south in China, nor of Yuan Shih-k'ai's imperial dream and subsequent fall and death. During the first few days he talked so much that he completely lost his voice, and had perforce to relapse for a time into silence again.

Of the other Chinese refugees who came out with us and General Liu's party from Chamdo, some have departed by the Yunnan road, while another large batch left for Tachienlu by the Litang road a few days ago. They had to be practically

[1] These Tibetan emissaries did in the end proceed to Hsiangch'eng, together with Chinese representatives from Batang, and were successful in their mission.

driven out of the town, where there was simply not enough grain left to feed them. Each man was given a ration of *tsamba* calculated to keep him alive until he reached Litang. Considering their lack of food and clothing, the cold on the big passes, and the probability of their meeting *chagba* and raiding Hsiangch'engwa *en route*, their prospects of getting back to China alive are not too bright.

The remaining refugees, mostly of the better class, all insist on accompanying us on our return to Tachienlu. I am only too ready to take them, but there are great difficulties in connection with transport. We have our own animals but none to spare. The country between here and Litang, several days' journey in extent, is uninhabited at present except by roving bands of *chagba*, and the people of Batang naturally refuse to supply *ula* animals to go to Litang, seeing that they could hardly expect ever to see them again if they did so. However, the refugees insist on going, some on foot, and others on yak which they have secured somehow or other.

The state of affairs at Batang at present is very painful, and if anything worse than it was when we were here in June. Not a rupee or a bushel of rice has come in from Szechuan in the meantime, and the soldiers are still living from day to day on what they can beg, borrow or steal from the local people. Had it not been for the exertions of Mr Ogden, Dr Shelton, and the other American and Canadian missionaries here, who have again and again assisted in various ways, even borrowing grain on their personal security, the soldiers would long since have looted the place and then been killed off by the local Tibetans. Chinese and foreigners here cannot but feel very bitter against the Szechuanese, who, secure in their fat rice-growing lowlands, have done nothing during the past year to help their compatriots in this outlying frontier post, reduced to the verge of starvation and at the mercy of a few hundred Tibetan brigands.

January 16. At BATANG.

After almost endless delays and much confusion connected with the refugees and their transport animals, we at last got off before midday on January 12. Our route, the main South Road, lay up a narrow rocky ravine to the east, passing a few miles out a memorial stone which marks the spot where the

Amban Feng was killed with all his followers in 1905; this event marked the beginning of the long drawn-out struggle between Chinese and Tibetans in Kam which has lasted until to-day[1]. Further on the ravine opens out and there are some farms and cultivated fields, called Hsiaopachung by the Chinese. Beyond this place there follows a long pull up through thick pine forests until at last a ruined Chinese rest-house called Pangchamu is reached, lying in a clearing in the forest four to five thousand feet above Batang.

Our progress was slow on this march because we found the trail obstructed by barriers of felled trees and other obstacles, which had probably been placed there by the Tibetans of the Lengkashi valley last summer at a time when, just before peace was made, Batang was practically invested and threatened with an attack from all sides. Some of the barricades, however, looked suspiciously new, and their unexpected presence, as well as the sight of occasional strands of wire hanging in festoons amongst the pine trees, the only visible remains of the telegraph line which used to connect Batang with the outer world, had a very depressing effect on our party and caused the more fainthearted of the refugees to doubt the wisdom of ever having left Batang.

On the following day we made an early start to cross the big pass, said to be nearly 17,000 feet high, on the way to Taso. For the first two hours or so we climbed up hill through dense forest, emerging at last on to the usual waste of rock and snow above the tree limit. Shortly afterwards, when we had reached a height of 15,000 feet or more, we heard a prolonged fusillade down in the forest below. As all our rifles were with us, it was evident that the caravan, which was some way behind with most of the refugees, was being attacked by *chagba*. No one had expected to meet with these brigands so near to Batang, and we had unwisely taken none of the necessary precautions against an ambush. The more active of our men hurried back down the mountain, while the rest of the party followed behind as rapidly as the bad trail and the rarefied air permitted; for it is almost impossible for anyone but a Tibetan to move quickly at 15,000 feet above the sea. Some distance down we met one of our mule drivers on foot with the news that the caravan had been ambushed

[1] See p. 20.

by Tibetan raiders, several of the Chinese refugees shot dead, and all the mules driven off with their loads. At this stage matters looked rather serious, as apart from the men killed, we had lost all our baggage, tents, silver and ammunition, not to mention fifteen good mules. As we hurried on down through the forest, our men in front reached the scene of the ambush and a renewed burst of rifle fire broke out. A few minutes later we ourselves reached the scene, and found a dead Chinese lying on the grass in a clearing, a confused mob of mules and ponies wandering about amongst the pine trees further up with their loads strewn on the ground, and our own men emptying their rifles into the forest at the retreating *chagba*.

What had happened was that the brigands had ambushed the caravan from amongst the trees, fired a few ill-directed volleys, which killed one of the Chinese refugees and wounded a few more, and were proceeding to adjust the loads preparatory to driving the mules off up hill through the forest when our men suddenly arrived and opened fire. Whereupon the *chagba*, doubtless misjudging our armed strength, had considerately bolted and left us in possession of the field.

There was nothing to be done for the principal victim, who was quite dead, shot through the body in two places. He was a man named Li, one of the refugees who had come with us all the way from Chamdo, a good honest fellow, always talking of his home in far-off Szechuan, to which he was returning after an absence of many years in Tibet. After counting the animals and the baggage and finding that all had been recovered, with the exception of two ponies belonging to the refugees, we discussed the situation and decided that it was too late to attempt to cross the big pass that day.

It was a very depressed procession which filed back to Pangchamu that afternoon. We marched with half our rifles in front, the baggage and refugees in the middle, and the rest of the rifles and myself in the rear. Arrived at Pangchamu we held a further council, and decided to make another attempt to cross the pass the next day. Mr Wang and most of the refugees said that now their faces were turned towards home they would not go back to Batang for all the *chagba* in Tibet; others were more faint-hearted, and decided to return. My reasons for thinking that we ought to be able to get through if we marched with greater precautions were that I felt certain that the caravan had been attacked by mistake for a Chinese transport column. Our assailants, who were said to be Lengkashi Tibetans[1], and the builders of the barricades of felled trees we had met on the way, had allowed my own party to pass unscathed at point blank range. They probably knew quite well who we were. We also propose to take the precaution, after crossing the big pass, of travelling, not by the main road, but by another trail known to one of the refugees. This route is said to keep further north above the eroded valleys, and to pass through open grass country all the way to Litang, thus avoiding the pine forests, where one is always at the mercy of *chagba* in ambush.

In the evening some local Tibetans went out and brought back the body of the dead man, in order that his friends might cremate him and take his ashes back to Szechuan. The cremation was rapidly and efficiently carried out by means of a huge bonfire, the pine woods providing ample fuel as dry as tinder.

Late that night we were awakened by the arrival of a panic-stricken Chinese soldier, who professed to be the sole survivor of the Chinese garrison of Litang. According to his story the Hsiangch'engwa had reached Litang a few days before, had overwhelmed the Chinese there, and were now roaming in bands all over the country between here and Tachienlu. To make matters worse, some men who had been sent out after dark to see whether any of the lost loads had been left on the scene of the ambush, returned and reported newly-built barricades of felled trees blocking the road; from which it appeared that the Lengkashiwa, whatever their intention towards us, did not intend to let any Chinese pass. There are, however, some amongst our Chinese refugees whom I am determined to see safely back to Szechuan if it can possibly be done; and so, after further consideration, we changed our minds and decided to return to Batang and try another road.

The whole party marched back to Batang on the 14th in

[1] Lengkashi is the name of the valley of the upper Batang river, which makes a complete bend on itself; so that the Lengkashiwa have only to cross a pass to descend on the main road to Litang; they have always been turbulent and unruly, and have the advantage of living in a valley which is almost inaccessible to the Chinese.

a very depressed frame of mind, Batang being regarded as a sort of trap from which they thought they had escaped. Misfortunes never come singly, and on the way down one of our animals went over a precipice, and a box containing papers and rupees was burst open in the ravine below.

We have been busy during the past two days in arranging for our return journey to Szechuan by another route.

The main South Road *via* Litang being blocked, we have two other routes to choose from, namely (1) through North-west Yunnan *via* Atuntze to Chungtien, and thence through Mili to Tachienlu, or (2) *via* Beyü and De-ge to Kanze and thence by the main North Road to Tachienlu. The Yunnan road is long, entailing some fifty to sixty marches, while we may have difficulty in getting through the Mili[1] country. By the North Road, on the other hand, we should be able to reach Tachienlu in a month. But the Yunnan road is probably fairly safe; whereas the North Road is considered by the Chinese to be as impassable as the Litang route owing to the *chagba* from Sangen and Lengkashi infesting the forested valleys through which it passes for the first few marches out of Batang.

In the end we decided to try the North Road, in order to save time. Once we get through the dangerous country, only a few marches in extent, between here and the De-ge border, we are sure to find law and order and efficient protection in De-ge territory now under Tibetan rule.

In spite of my warnings and against the advice of nearly everyone, more than half of our former Chinese refugees insist on accompanying us again. They say they prefer to take the chance of being shot in my company by *chagba* on the North Road to the certainty of being at least held up and pillaged if they travel alone by the Yunnan route. No *ula* transport being obtainable, those who have not got their own animals will have to walk.

January 21. At DE-NE.

We started at last on the afternoon of the 17th on our second attempt to get out of Batang, and marched ten miles

[1] Mili, known to the Chinese as the country of the Huang Lama ("Yellow Monk"), is a Tibetan native state under the suzerainty of the Yunnanese Government; it is ruled by a lama, who permits Yunnanese traders to pass through his territory on payment of presents.

TIBETANS OF GAJI IN SOUTHERN DE-GE

A TIBETAN FARM-HOUSE ON THE DE-GE-GONJO BORDER

PLATE LVI

CROPS STACKED ON THE FLAT ROOF OF A FARM-HOUSE IN SOUTHERN DE-GE

SCENE IN ONE OF THE LOWER AGRICULTURAL VALLEYS OF SOUTHERN KAM

up the valley of the Bar Chu to a hamlet called Dam (in Chinese Tangts'un). Here we were well received, the local people even providing a few *ula* yak to carry the baggage of the refugees and some of our grain. This was a pleasant surprise; for Chinese authority was practically non-existent even this short distance out of Batang, and the natives of the valley (known to the Chinese as Ch'its'un Kou, "The Vale of the Seven Villages") have the reputation of being very hostile to the Chinese, owing to the severe chastisement they had received at the hands of Chao Erh-feng after the rebellion of 1905.

On the 18th we continued up the valley, passing another hamlet where the headman met us with presents of walnuts, which seemed a reassuring sign. About seven miles out we left the valley, ascended through thick juniper woods to a small pass, and descended the other side to rejoin the river, which here flows north before bending right round to flow south to Batang. Up the valley to the south-east lay the trail to the notorious Lengkashi country, overlooked by huge snow mountains. We were, therefore, here again in dangerous country.

On this march I took the precaution of travelling in the company of all my men and our own mule caravan. The yak, however, carrying some of our grain and the effects of the refugees, had been allowed to lag behind owing to their aggravatingly slow rate of march and to the assurances of the *ula* men from Dam that they would be all right in that vicinity. Having crossed the pass and reached a pleasant spot by the river soon after midday, we halted to refresh ourselves with tea and an excellent Yunnanese ham which had been given to us in Batang. I had just finished my meal, and was thinking of starting again, when the ominous popping of rifle fire broke out from half-way up the wooded pass, down which the *ula* yak were slowly wending their way.

We realised at once that the yak were being attacked by *chagba* again; but this time we were not so anxious, as we had all our own mules and baggage with us. However, feeling that we had to do something to try and save the effects of the refugees, I despatched five of our men back up the hill to see whether anything could be saved out of the wreck, telling them to start firing into the trees as soon as they got near the scene of the hold-up, and generally to make as much noise as possible.

Shortly afterwards a renewed burst of rifle fire showed that our men had reached the spot. As on the previous occasion, they came up with the *chagba* just as the latter were making off with their booty. Some of the yak had already been driven away; others were standing about with their loads undone; while the ground was strewn with bags and boxes slashed open to ascertain the contents. Our men pursued the brigands, firing away at random, and managed to recover about half of the loads. All the *ula* men from Dam disappeared; they were evidently in collusion with the *chagba*.

Our men, consisting of Tachienlu and Nyarong Tibetans, headed by the half-caste interpreter, behaved very well on this occasion as on the former one. Tibetan *chagba*, like Chinese robbers, are easily bluffed by a determined show of force; the great thing is to start shooting into the trees as soon as possible, as it is the noise of firing which frightens them more than anything else.

By the time we had got the loads down the hill night was falling and it was too late to go on. Fortunately for the refugees, who had no tents, there happened to be a ruined village near by called Sudong, where, though the people were rather sullen, we managed to find accommodation of sorts in the house of an old lama. Everyone was uneasy and depressed. The hamlet where we were camped lay at the very mouth of the Lengkashi gorge, and it was impossible to say whether we should be attacked during the night or not; the natives were anything but friendly; and the most dangerous part of the road was still ahead.

After an anxious night we started at sunrise on the following day and marched down the Batang river, here flowing north, to the village of Hlamdo, which we should have reached on the preceding day. Here to our great relief we received a friendly welcome.

At Hlamdo we left the Batang river, which makes its southerly bend in this neighbourhood, and marched up a side ravine to a group of farms called Baongshi (Maohsi in Chinese). Here again we were received in a friendly manner, and in response to my request the local people agreed to provide some *ula* yak for the refugees for the long march ahead.

The next day's march, from Baongshi to Sama, was supposed to be the most dangerous on the whole journey, as the trail lay up a long densely wooded valley between two districts notorious for robbers, Sangen on the west, and Lengkashi on the east. Forests are our bugbear. We always feel safe enough in the open; but in the forest, where one cannot see thirty yards through the pines, one never knows where a band of *chagba* may not be waiting in ambush to greet the traveller with a volley from the trees. The march was a very long one, as we did not dare camp in the forest *en route*; and we were on the road from daybreak till nightfall without a break. The Baongshi people, who seemed quite honest, were not very optimistic, and opined that we should probably meet with *chagba* watching this road for Chinese; but they thought we should not be attacked if we kept well together with some of our armed Tibetans in the rear. We placed the yak in front to set the pace, the refugees on foot in the middle, and our own mule caravan in the rear; two of our rifles rode in front, while the rest with myself formed the tail of the procession.

Soon after starting we came suddenly on two armed Tibetans round a corner, who behaved very strangely. At first they seemed friendly, and told us that there were *chagba* ahead waiting below the pass, and then, after marching with us for ten minutes, suddenly bolted through the trees. Shortly afterwards some shots were fired from the forest, whether as a signal or at us we never discovered, but nothing untoward happened. It was a most unpleasant march, stumbling along in falling snow for hour after hour along a bad trail impeded by rocks and fallen trees, with rifles loaded and ready for instant use, and expecting a burst of fire from the trees at any moment. The pace of the yak was exasperatingly slow, and every now and then we came on places where the trail was covered with sheets of ice, the great obstacle to winter travel in Kam, each of which meant a laborious détour through the pine trees, entailing delays in unloading and loading up the animals.

About midday we passed a clearing, said to be the Batang De-ge boundary; and at last towards evening we emerged from the forest and soon after reached the pass, the Ngupa La (14,000 feet), whence we descended in the dark to a group of farms called Sama in De-ge. The people seemed to expect us here, and had made preparations of a kind for our reception.

On the following morning, after a good night's rest at Sama, we followed down a winding gorge and emerged after a while into a more open but thickly wooded valley. Here we were met by the *Bön* (official headman) of Gaji, and realised with feelings of great relief that our troubles were at an end, as we were now under the protection of the Tibetan officials of De-ge. Continuing down the valley, still through thick forest, which no longer had any terrors for us, we reached De-ne, a group of farms surrounded by cultivated fields, where a good house had been prepared for our accommodation.

Gaji (Chinese Kaiyü) was in ancient days a part of Litang, and subsequently became a portion of De-ge, of which it formed the southern-most *dzongka*, or district. When the Chinese occupied De-ge in 1909 they incorporated Gaji in the Chinese district of Paiyü. Before Chao Erh-feng's time it was ruled by two brothers, one a lay official (*Bön*), the other a reincarnation and head lama of the local monastery; these offices were hereditary, and have been, it is said, in the same family for thirteen generations.

De-ge State, of recent years cut up by the Chinese into the five magistracies of Teko (De-ge Gönchen), Paiyü (Beyü), Shihch'ü (Seshü), Dengko and T'ungp'u, was in former days divided up into twenty-five *Dzongka* (districts), each ruled by a *Bön* (hereditary headman) under the De-ge King. Of these *Dzongka*, Gaji in the south, and Adu and Seshü in the north, were the largest and most important, their headmen being practically semi-independent chieftains. Other such districts were Mesho, Desho, Dehlung, Racha, Beyü, Horbo, Dzenko, Tzako, Dzogchen, Yilung, Tsando and Barong, all east of the Yangtze, and Polo, Kargung and Nyashi, west of the Yangtze. Wherever one meets with a *Podrang* the same is usually found to be the seat of the official administering one of these *Dzongka*.

We rested to-day at De-ne. Everyone is pleased and relieved at having got through from Batang into peaceful De-ge unharmed. In order to save time and shorten our journey back to Tachienlu, the Chief has arranged for us to travel by a road up the Beyü river and thence straight across to Nyarong, thus avoiding the long détour made by the main road *via* Rongbatsa. This journey should be interesting from a geographical point of view. The *Bön* is making all the necessary preparations, preparing a *lam-yig* (road-bill), and providing *ula* transport for the refugees.

January 25. At BEYÜ.

We left De-ne on January 23, and marched down the valley to a point where the stream turns sharply to the west to join the Yangtze near by. Here we continued north up another valley for a few miles to Gaji Podrang, a big white building conspicuous a long way off. This was the place where a battalion of Chinese troops retreating from Beyü were trapped by the Lhasa Tibetans last summer. This *Podrang* is rightly the seat of the Gaji *Bön*, who was, however, living at De-ne because it had been badly damaged during the time the Chinese were besieged inside. The monastery, the seat of the lama ruler, lies up on the mountain side near by.

From Gaji Podrang we marched up a ravine through pine forests overlooked by gigantic limestone crags for hour after hour. At length reaching the pass, the Me La (14,400 feet), we descended through a similar ravine the other side, and arrived on the following day at a group of farms called Ronged on the Ngü Chu, the river of Beyü.

From here the direct Nyarong trail, which we had proposed following, turns up the Ngü Chu to the east. We were, however, at the last moment deterred from taking it by the discovery that it led for seven days or more across an uninhabited grass plateau called Trungko, the nomads of which region had emigrated to the grass country north of the Yalung owing to their being so constantly harried by raiders from Hsiangch'eng of recent years. As we had our own animals and tents, the passage of this waste, where, in view of the absence of any nomad inhabitants, the pasturage would probably have been very good, presented no particular difficulties for us. But it would have been impossible in the absence of nomads to have provided any transport for our Chinese refugees, who would also have been exposed to great hardship from the cold without tents to sleep in at night-time.

We, therefore, decided to change our plans, and return by the main road *via* Beyü, Dzenko and Kanze.

I was sorry to have to give up the Nyarong trail, as by following it we should probably have been able to get some idea of the unknown upper courses of the Ngü Chu and Dzin Chu, two considerable rivers which are almost entirely unexplored, as well as ascertain the whereabouts of the De-ge-Nyarong boundary, which is said to run across the Trungko plateau, probably along the Yangtze-Yalung watershed. For the benefit of future travellers I give the following particulars of this trail, as reported to me by the headman of Barong, who met us at Ronged.

The first two marches present no difficulty and lie up the valley of the Ngü Chu, which is probably cultivated most of the way, to Tsando and Barong, both seats of small officials under the King of De-ge. From Barong on cultivation and houses apparently cease, and the marches are somewhat as follows: third day to Hlakundo[1], fourth day to an unnamed camp, fifth day to Dorko Gomba, sixth day to Shadundo, seventh day to Tegendo, eighth day to Nawaku. All these are apparently the names of camping grounds or grazing lands without cultivation or houses. Dorko Gomba is said to be the ruins of a big and important monastery which was destroyed by raiders from Hsiangch'eng in 1916 or 1917 and is now uninhabited. Nawaku appears to lie across the Nyarong border, though how far from the cultivated valley of the Yalung, no one seemed to know.

On the next day we left Ronged and marched down the picturesque forested valley of the Ngü Chu to Beyü, where we were met by a Tibetan official, sent down by the *Dabön* commanding at De-ge Gönchen to escort us through Tibetan territory to the Chinese border.

February 20. At TACHIENLU.

From Beyü we returned by the road which we had previously followed over the high Mizo La to Horbo and Dzenko, and for the third time in our journeys crossed the big divide to Rongbatsa. The prosperous Rongbatsa plain

[1] From the name it is evident that this place lies at the confluence of two streams, and it is apparently situated at the junction of the roads from Beyü, Litang, Nyarong and Dzenko.

CROSSING THE YALUNG RIVER BY CORACLE FERRY AT BERI NEAR KANZE

PLATE LVIII

YAK CARRYING CHINESE TEA ASCENDING A PASS ON THE ROAD TO TIBET

IN THE SHE CHU VALLEY NEAR DAWU

seemed strangely quiet and peaceful in comparison with the state of affairs prevailing there during our stay in September and October last, when thousands of Chinese and Tibetan troops were barricaded on opposite sides of the stream within full view of one another, and the people in the villages along the Yalung plain showed us many attentions in demonstration of their gratitude for the change.

At Kanze we received a warm welcome from the Chinese civil and military officials, whose only anxiety was to know whether the Tibetans could be relied upon to observe the terms of the truce. After resting there a day or two we returned to Tachienlu by the main North Road, along which we had originally started on our long journeys through Eastern Tibet. In places the trail was black with yak caravans carrying tea into Tibet. The tea trade, interrupted for the best part of a year owing to the hostilities between Szechuanese and Tibetans, had by now revived with renewed vigour as a result of last autumn's peace negotiations.

We eventually arrived back in Tachienlu in the middle of February, after an absence of nearly a year in Eastern Tibet. Of our original caravan, most of the mules, but very few of the ponies, had survived.

CHAPTER X

GENERAL OBSERVATIONS ON EASTERN TIBET

Physical description of Kam, the eastern portion of the Tibetan plateau—Agricultural valleys and elevated grass country—Geological formation—Mountain ranges—Height limit for corn and trees—Climate—Snow line—Big game, stag, gazelle, antelope, wild sheep, serow, takin, wild goat, wild asses, wild yak, marmots, monkeys, bears, wolves, foxes, leopards, lynx—Small game, the common pheasant, the long-tailed pheasant, the silver or eared pheasant, pheasant grouse, wild fowl, snipe, partridges, hares—Transport animals, mules, ponies, yak—Packing and picketing methods—*Ula*, or forced transport—Ethnography and language—Missionaries and lamas on the borders of Eastern Tibet.

THE portion of Eastern Tibet comprised in the basins of the Salween, Mekong, Yangtze and Yalung rivers, between the latitudes of Jyekundo in the Kokonor in the north and Atuntze in Yunnan in the south, is known to the Tibetans as Kam; which name, like Amdo further north-east, is only a vague geographical term, without political significance. The whole region forms the eastern portion of the great Tibetan plateau, here furrowed by the canyons of the above rivers and their affluents, and slopes and drains from the highlands of the *Jang Tang* (Northern Plains) of Tibet in the north-west towards the lowlands of China in the south-east. All the big rivers flow in their upper courses through broad and open ice-formed valleys in the grass country and in their lower courses through deep and narrow water-eroded gorges. As one proceeds south-east, the valleys become deeper and narrower and on the latitude of Batang, for instance, the rivers are found flowing in tremendous canyons 8000 feet or more in depth. As a result the easiest roads lie in the north, keeping above the deep erosions, while the country becomes more and more difficult to traverse as one proceeds south. Hence arises the contrast between the two highways and their subsidiary branch roads, from Szechuan to Tibet, the North Road from Tachienlu to Jyekundo and the South Road from Tachienlu to Batang and Chamdo. On the former, which might without great difficulty be made passable for cart traffic, one keeps at comparatively high elevations all the way, and, though the passes are big, the gradients are not very steep. On the latter, on the other hand, one is constantly climbing in and out of deep, narrow valleys, which bring one down to 8000 or 9000 feet, and crossing the intervening ranges by steep and difficult passes up to 15,000 and 16,000 feet in height.

Kam is bounded by Yunnan, Burma and Assam on the south, by Central Tibet on the west, by the Kokonor (Chinese Ch'ing Hai) Territory on the north, and by Szechuan on the east. It is a country of snow peaks, rolling grass country, deep narrow valleys, pine forests, and rushing torrents, resembling in some parts Switzerland, in others the downs of England and the moors of Scotland, and in others the pine-clad valleys of British Columbia. The name Tibet conjures up visions of uninhabited desert wastes across which the exhausted traveller wends his way exposed to terrible hardships. This is indeed the nature of the more elevated grass country, such as the great *Jang Tang* (Northern Plains) of Tibet, visited by the early explorers, Welby, Littledale, Bonvalot, De Rhins and others, who entered the country from the north and west. But Kam is a much more agreeable region, consisting largely of *rong* country, that is to say, agricultural valleys from 10,000 to 13,000 feet in elevation, where the people till the fields and live in houses, in contrast to the bleak grass uplands, from 13,000 to 16,000 feet in height, where the inhabitants subsist on their flocks and herds and live in black tents. The line of the main North Road, from Tachienlu *via* Dawu, Kanze and Dzogchen to Jyekundo, marks roughly the northern limit of the more settled agricultural districts of Kam; beyond it lie the elevated grass-lands of the wild nomad tribes, stretching away, without trees or houses, across the Yellow river basin up to the borders of Kansu Province.

The geological formation of Kam consists for the most part of red sandstone with outcroppings in places of the underlying limestone and occasionally of granite. A vast extent of country in Eastern Asia is covered by this red sandstone formation, which extends from Honan, in Eastern China, across Szechuan, Southern Shensi and Kansu, and the Kokonor, to the centre of Tibet.

As regards the mountains of Kam, the country is so universally mountainous and the troughs of the rivers, in which one is so often travelling, are so deep and narrow, that it is difficult to give an accurate description of the trend of the principal ranges. The following observations on the subject are therefore of a very tentative kind, pending the results of further explorations.

The Yu Chu (the river flowing south from the direction of Chamdo between the Mekong and the Salween) flows between two well-marked ranges with high, rocky peaks rising in places far above the line of perpetual snow. These ranges appear to start from the high plateau, which, giving rise to the Yu Chu, lies between Chamdo on the Mekong and Sha-yi Zamka (Chiayü Ch'iao) on the Salween. The more eastern of the two ranges probably runs right down to the huge snow massif which lies west of Atuntze (we only followed it down to the latitude of Yenching).

Another very prominent mountain feature in Kam is the big range which runs parallel to, and on the right-hand side of, the main road from Jyekundo to Tachienlu. It is a huge and imposing barrier wherever seen. South of Jyekundo it forms the divide between the basins of the Yangtze and of the headwater streams of the Mekong and is here crossed by the Shung La, a high pass on one of the roads from Jyekundo to Chamdo. Proceeding south-east, it is pierced by the gorges of the Yangtze below Chunkor Gomba (Dengko) and thence serves as the Yangtze-Yalung divide down to below Kanze. On this stretch of its course it contains some very high peaks and glaciers behind Dzogchen Gomba, below which it is crossed by the Tro La on the main road to De-ge. Further down it appears as the magnificent snow-capped range which stretches along the southern side of the Yalung plain from Rongbatsa to below Kanze; in this neighbourhood it is crossed by the Tsengu La and the Hön La on the road to Beyü and Southern De-ge and by another high pass behind Beri on a road to Nyarong. Below Kanze it is pierced by the gorges of the Yalung, which are overlooked by a giant snow peak, Kawalori, a sacred mountain of Nyarong. From here it continues south-east to Tachienlu, where it serves as a clear-cut racial boundary between Chinese and Tibetan inhabited country; it is here split into two by the valley of the river of Tachienlu, which is overlooked by snows on both sides. From Tachienlu it continues south, containing here

MIDDAY REST ON THE GRASS COUNTRY OF KAM IN THE SUMMER

MIDDAY REST ON THE GRASS COUNTRY OF KAM IN THE WINTER

PLATE LX

FORESTED RIVER VALLEY IN KAM BELOW THE LEVEL OF THE GRASS COUNTRY

YAK CARAVAN WITH BALES OF CHINESE TEA FOR THE TIBETAN MARKET

some very big peaks, towards the Yunnan border. I suspect this great range to be a south-easterly continuation of the Dang La mountains, north of Lhasa, and to be therefore one of the principal features of the mountain system of Tibet.

There are some very high mountains on both sides of the Yangtze between De-ge Gönchen and Batang, including the giants immediately east of the latter; but I have not been able to distinguish the continuity of particular ranges in that neighbourhood.

It is to be hoped that the heights of the principal mountains of Kam will soon be ascertained by scientific measurement, the results of which will probably show the existence of some very high peaks. Amongst the highest will probably prove to be the group of peaks behind Dzogchen Gomba (bearing roughly north from the Mizo La near Beyü); Kawalori on the Yalung below Kanze; some of the peaks on the Mekong-Salween divide between Chamdo and the latitude of Atuntze; the peaks east of Batang; and the peaks north and south of Tachienlu.

At present the heights of even the principal passes, ascertained by various travellers in the past with aneroids and boiling-point thermometers, are open to argument. For instance, the following heights have been assigned at different times by various competent travellers to the Gi La (Chinese Cheto Shan, the first pass out of Tachienlu on the main South Road), which we made 14,000 feet:

Fergusson	12,400 feet	Gill	14,500 feet
Coales	13,500 "	Bower	14,700 "
Hosie	13,900 "	Davies	15,000 "
Rockhill	14,300 "		

Following down one of the valleys of the big rivers from north-west to south-east, cultivation is generally found to begin at 12,000 to 13,000 feet. The usual limit for barley is about 13,500 feet, except on certain favoured slopes, and for wheat 11,000 to 12,000 feet. Trees grow in places up to 14,500 feet. The big pine forests are, however, usually confined to the slopes facing north, as is the case over a vast stretch of North-eastern Asia from Shensi and Kansu in China right across to the Kokonor border and the Himalayas. Again and again the traveller will find himself marching up or down a valley with pine forests on the slope facing north and bare hillsides or juniper woods on the slope facing south. It is difficult to account for this, unless it is due to the young pines being unable to stand the rays of the sun in the rarefied air, or to lack of moisture owing to the snow melting and evaporating sooner on the southern slopes.

The crops of wheat and barley are either winter or spring sown, the former in the lower valleys at an elevation of 8000 to 9000 feet and the latter at higher elevations of 10,000 to 12,000 feet, and are harvested in July and September respectively. The winter-sown crops are usually irrigated, while those sown in the spring rely on the seasonal summer rains.

The wettest seasons of the year are the summer and autumn, when one meets with much rain and snow above 14,000 feet. This season is, however, the best for travel in the grass country, as pasturage is then abundant. After the cessation of the autumn rains and snow a period of extreme dryness sets in. Thus, during the three months November, December and January of the year we spent in Eastern Tibet, snow only fell on two days, the weather being bright and sunny for the rest of the time. These observations apply more particularly to the centre of Eastern Tibet, i.e. the Chamdo neighbourhood. In the spring another snowy season sets in.

The winter cold on the high passes and in the grass country (13,000 to 16,000 feet) is severe and the temperature often falls to zero Fahrenheit; while the cold is felt all the more in these parts, especially when the wind blows, as there are no houses to stop in and one is dependent on yak dung for fuel. In the *rong* country, on the other hand, the winter climate is perfect, bright sunny days alternating with clear, frosty, but not unduly cold, nights. The grass on the plateau country is usually good up to Christmas, by which time it is eaten down and does not reappear until the following June. The intervening period is therefore a very difficult time for travel in parts where one's animals are dependent on pasturage. The best time of the year for travel is the early winter in the *rong* country and the summer on the grass-lands.

As a result of the extreme dryness of November, December and January and the power of the sun's rays in the rarefied air, the snow thaws and evaporates at very high altitudes and the passes are apt to be clearer and the snow line higher in the early winter than at any other time of the year. The worst season for snowed-up passes is the spring. But generally speaking, one can cross any pass at any time of the year, though it may sometimes be necessary to wait a few days.

The true line of perpetual snow in the neighbourhood of Chamdo is probably not far short of 18,000 feet. In the south, on the borders of Burma and Yunnan, however, the precipitation appears to be greater and the snow line lower than in the drier regions further north; thus giving the impression that the mountains are higher.

Though having neither the leisure nor the physical strength to do much big game shooting in the rarefied air of Kam, I always observed with interest the animals we met with on the road and encouraged the men to shoot for the pot. The following species of wild animals came under our notice.

There are probably at least three kinds of stag in Eastern Tibet, the Szechuan Sambar, Thorold's stag and another kind of wapiti. The first-named is the stag of the forests, characterised by large three-tined antlers. The second is the stag of the grass country, carrying large antlers up to five or six points. The third appears to be a wapiti with antlers up to nine points. In the border towns, as elsewhere in China, there is a large trade in deers' horns in velvet for medicinal purposes and in the shed antlers for making glue. We did not shoot any of these stags, but saw them (probably the second of the above-mentioned varieties) on several occasions in the Tzachuka grass country.

The *Gowa*, or Tibetan gazelle, is constantly met with in the grass country all over Eastern Tibet. It carries small horns bent gracefully back and much resembles the Mongolian gazelle (Chinese *Huang Yang*) found on the prairies of Inner Mongolia north of Peking; except that, in the case of the latter, the horns are bent more inwards.

The Tibetan antelope (*Tsura* or *Chiru*) is common in the elevated grass country north of Jyekundo, that is to say, on higher parts of the Tibetan plateau country than are usually met with in Kam. It has long black horns rising nearly straight from the head; these horns are much used as shooting rests by the Tibetans, who affix them to their guns and rifles. It is probably this animal which gave rise to the story of the unicorn in Eastern Tibet, the appearance of the head and horns when seen in profile being exactly that of a unicorn. At Dzogchen, while looking over a heap of old horns, probably collected for export to China, I picked up a single straight black horn, and on asking to what kind of an animal it belonged, was told a unicorn. The horn was, however, undoubtedly that of the ordinary Tibetan antelope.

Huc, whose work is in most respects so very accurate, states that "the unicorn, which has long been regarded as a fabulous creature, really exists in Tibet." He devotes two or three pages to the subject, and first calls it a *serou* and then a *tchirou*, probably mixing up the *serow* with the *chiru*, or Tibetan antelope. His description of the horn is that of the latter animal.

The *Na*, the wild sheep of Eastern Tibet (Blue Sheep or Bharal), are common in the mountains over 13,000 feet. We often met with flocks of them, especially in the country between Jyekundo and Chamdo. They are grey in colour and their wool is more like that of a goat than a sheep; the horns are massive, but not to be compared in size or handsome curvature with those, for instance, of the *argali* sheep found on the Mongolian border, north of Kueihuach'eng.

The *serow* and *takin* are not really Tibetan animals, being found in the precipitous forested country on the Chinese-Tibetan border and not on the real uplands of Tibet. We never met with either, except stuffed specimens hanging in the customary way in the entrances of monasteries and houses.

The wild goat (*Goral*) is common in rocky mountainous country in Eastern Tibet. The range of this animal, or of nearly allied species, must be very great. I have seen them in the hills north of Peking, in the gorges of the Yellow river in Northern Kansu, in the gorges of the Yangtze in Central China and in the heart of Eastern Tibet; apparently they range right across Asia from the Himalayas to Manchuria.

Wild asses (*Chyang* in Tibetan) were met with in large herds on the Tzachuka grass-lands; but we never saw them at very close quarters.

Wild yak are found in Tzachuka, especially north of the Yalung, but we did not meet with them. They are said to be very much larger than the tame variety.

Marmots are very common in the grass country in the

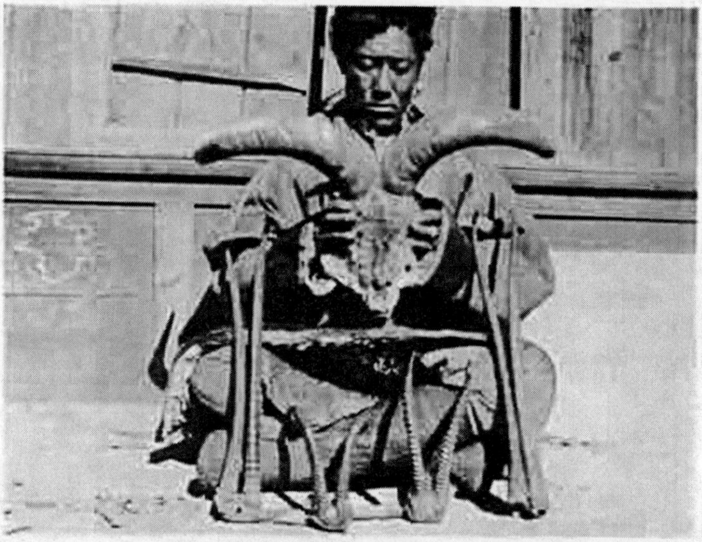

SOME BIG GAME HEADS FROM EASTERN TIBET, WILD SHEEP, ANTELOPE AND GAZELLE

MONKEY OF EASTERN TIBET

PLATE LXII

BIG RIDING MULE FROM GONGBO IN SOUTH-EASTERN TIBET

NOMAD WOMAN OF GONJO AND PACK PONY, ILLUSTRATING TIBETAN PACK SADDLE AND SKIN-COVERED BOXES USED FOR TRAVEL IN KAM

summer months (they hibernate in the winter). The traveller's attention is constantly drawn to their presence because of their habit of sitting up on their hind legs in front of their earths and whistling.

There are probably several varieties of monkeys in Eastern Tibet. We saw them in their wild state on only one occasion, in a pine forest north-west of Chamdo at an elevation of over 13,000 feet. At one time we had a tame monkey, bought for half a rupee on the Chamdo-De-ge border. He became so tame that he followed the caravan on foot like a dog.

Black bears are common in the grass country; we saw one with cubs in the summer. They are perhaps responsible for the common story of the existence of hairy, wild men in Tibet. That remarkable animal, the parti-coloured bear, or giant panda, the skins of which can often be bought in Chengtu in Szechuan, is not really a Tibetan animal, but belongs rather, like the *takin*, to the border country of precipitous mountains and deep wooded valleys between the lowlands of China and the highlands of Tibet.

Wolves and foxes are often met with. Fox skins wound round the head, turban fashion, are the commonest form of head gear amongst the Tibetans in the winter.

Leopard and snow leopard skins are common presents, as well as lynx skins. The latter are perhaps the most useful furs produced in Eastern Tibet.

Amongst the small game of Eastern Tibet the ordinary pheasant (in this case *Phasianus elegans*) provides first-rate sport on the hillsides round Tachienlu, provided one is accompanied by a spaniel (the best sort of dog for this kind of shooting) to rout the birds out of the thick cover. These are small but very handsome birds, with dark green breasts, reddish-yellow sides, and grey-blue-green rumps, and are always to be found where cultivation, cover and water exist side by side, the latter being more particularly a *sine qua non*. They have no vestige of the white ring round the neck. These birds are only found in the lower valleys, from 8,000 to 10,000 feet, and are not really a Tibetan species.

The Amherst pheasant, the most beautiful of all the pheasants, is occasionally met with round Tachienlu when one is out shooting the ordinary variety. They frequent slightly higher and more thickly wooded ground than the ordinary Tachienlu pheasant, and, like the latter, are not found in real Tibetan country, i.e. over, say, 12,000 feet. They are determined runners and have a very deceptive floating kind of flight when in the air. When they get up unexpectedly their appearance is positively dazzling, and one is at first fairly certain to place a charge of shot in their long tails. Their plumage is gorgeous. Immediately behind the head there is a semi-circular white ruff with small black bars and a tuft of scarlet in front; below this ruff a band of brilliant dark green feathers runs round the neck and down the back; below these again on the rump there is a patch of barred yellow and green, with a few bright orange feathers at the base of the tail; then follows the tail itself, three feet long, consisting of nine to ten feathers, spotted white and barred with black; the breast is grey-white and the wings are green, black and brown.

The silver, or eared, pheasants of Tibet (*Crossoptilum Tibetanum*) are very common in the forests from 12,000 to 14,000 feet in Tibetan country west of the border ranges, especially where such forests fringe cultivated fields. When travelling in the early morning one meets with large flocks of them parading the fields on the edge of the forest. They are as large as small turkeys and their appearance is extremely weird. The head is black and red, the body white and covered with hair-like feathers, the wings grey, blue and black, the tail, which is short and square, the same colour, and the legs red. When alarmed they invariably run up hill through the forest at a great pace and can only be shot on the wing if approached from above. Unlike most Chinese pheasants, they are fond of perching in trees. Though they offer such big targets in the air, they must be hit well forward to bring them down. They are rather tough and tasteless eating, but form a useful addition to the pot when nothing else is available. The Chinese call these birds *Ma Chi*. There is another variety of the same bird, a slatey-blue in colour instead of white, which I have seen on the Kansu-Kokonor border; we never met with these latter in Kam.

We came across various kinds of pheasant grouse, or blood pheasants, in the forests at high elevations in the course of our travels, including some sort of snow cock above the tree limit, but I do not know enough about them to distinguish one variety from another. These birds are probably but little known and are perhaps worth studying from an ornithologist's point of view.

Wildfowl, from teal to geese, are common on the rivers of Eastern Tibet in the spring, especially the orange-coloured sheldrake, a handsome bird which, however, is not very good eating. We found them breeding on the Gonjo plateau (14,000 feet) in July.

While out pheasant shooting at Tachienlu I have occasionally come upon solitary snipe, at elevations up to 10,000 and 11,000 feet.

Small partridges, which are delicious eating, are very common all over Eastern Tibet, frequenting bare, stony hillsides at elevations from 10,000 to 13,000 feet. They resemble the *Pallas* partridge (the small partridge of North China) but lack the black patch on the breast which distinguishes the latter. These little birds are very averse to flying and when they do get up, usually pitch again within a hundred yards and start running; consequently they afford but poor sport, but are well worth shooting as a delicacy for the pot.

Hares are very abundant in certain parts of Eastern Tibet, notably in the park-like valleys north-west of Chamdo round about 13,500 feet. When put up they will always, unless pursued by a dog, take cover in bushes not far off, whence they can be easily routed out and shot. They are excellent eating[1].

The traveller in Eastern Tibet will always find it worth his while to carry, if not a rifle, at any rate a shot gun slung on his saddle. On arriving at the end of the day's march, the bag, whatever it may be, hare, partridge, or pheasant, should be put in a pot and well stewed with milk, butter and a pinch of flour or *tsamba*, and a most appetising dish will result.

The transport animals in use in Eastern Tibet are mules, ponies and yak. Camels are used in the Kokonor but are never seen in Kam.

The pack mules of Eastern Tibet are small, but very hardy. In selecting animals for a caravan, care should be taken to choose those of a thickset, short-legged type, preferably too old rather than too young; in the latter case one is sure to have trouble with sore backs. Care should also be taken to avoid purchasing Szechuanese or Yunnanese mules, which

[1] The Tibetans are somewhat averse to eating hares or wild fowl.

can be distinguished by their finer appearance, as they are unable to stand the hardships of life on the Tibetan plateau. Like the Yunnanese mule, the Tibetan mule only carries a load of 80 to 100 Chinese pounds[1], in contrast to the big mules of Shensi and Kansu, which carry twice to three times as much; but he has the great advantage over the latter of being able to do without grain when the pasturage is fairly good. Much larger mules of a different breed, which come from Gongbo in South-eastern Tibet and from the Kansu border, are used for riding, and command big prices (500 to 600 rupees as against 100 to 200 for a pack mule).

The local pony of Kam is useful for riding purposes, but cannot compare with the mule as a pack animal. These ponies are a sturdy breed, not unlike those of Mongolia, but they cannot stand the hardships of poor feeding like the mules, and fall out rapidly when travelling across the grass country in the spring. A better and larger breed of pony comes from the Sining neighbourhood on the Kansu-Kokonor border.

Both ponies and mules are fed on the road, where grain is available, with a couple of handfuls of barley night and morning in a small nose-bag. When grain runs short and a little *tsamba* is available, each animal is given a small ball made of *tsamba* dough and old tea leaves at night-time. Tibetan mules and ponies will eat almost anything at a pinch, including butter and even meat.

Yak are wonderfully surefooted and reliable through deep snow and on bad roads; but as they do not and cannot eat grain, they are no good for a long journey except at a phenomenally slow rate of march, with frequent halts of a week or two to enable them to graze and recuperate. They are often hired by the mule caravans for a few days at a time to rest the mules for a few marches. Unlike ponies and mules, which in Asia always travel in single file, yak charge along in a mob. They are guided by means of whistling and throwing stones. Very few Chinese know how to throw; but nearly every Tibetan can hurl a jagged piece of rock a considerable distance with great accuracy. The effect on the woolly side of the yak is merely to turn him in the required direction.

Chinese and Tibetan packing arrangements are entirely dissimilar. According to the Chinese method a wooden

[1] The Chinese pound equals 1⅓ English pounds.

frame-work, to which the load is tied, rests by balance alone on the pack saddle on the animal's back. The advantages of this method are that the entire load can be taken off the animal at a moment's notice, while the absence of any girth renders girth sores impossible; its disadvantages are that, in the case of a stampeding animal, a blow from a tree or rock will unship the whole load. The Chinese system, for this latter reason, perhaps, is never found in operation west of Tachienlu. According to the Tibetan method the load is tied directly on to a small wooden pack saddle, the latter resting on several felt numnahs on the animal's back and the whole is then tightly girthed up with hide ropes. The disadvantages of this arrangement are that girth sores are a constant source of trouble and that it takes longer to load and unload an animal; on the other hand, however, the load once properly secured is proof against a lot of stampeding and bumping before it falls off.

Owing to the exceptionally rough usage entailed by travel in Eastern Tibet the best kind of load in which to pack one's kit and provisions is the local product, a light wooden box sewn up in a yak skin; the skin is thoroughly soaked in water and sewn on wet with the hair inside; contracting as it dries, it makes a very firm, strong covering. The same principle is applied in a method of execution formerly practised amongst the wilder tribes of Kam, the victim being sewn up in a wet yak skin, which was then left to dry, and contract, in the sun.

In the Chinese-controlled parts of Eastern Tibet robbers and horse thieves are so prevalent that pack animals cannot be allowed to graze at night-time, but have to be picketed near the tents. In the case of mules the Tibetans have a simple and effective method of picketing. A rope is stretched taut between two pegs and each animal is tied up to it by a short cord fastened round his near fore pastern; at the end of the line is tied the Tibetan mastiff (without which no caravan takes the road), or preferably two, one at each end.

The *ula* system of forced transport, under which the local people have to provide animals for travelling officials, is a Tibetan institution. It works, on the whole, smoothly enough in Lhasa-controlled Tibet, where its use is limited to official personages travelling on business. It is, however, much abused in Chinese-controlled Tibet, where it is responsible for much of the unpopularity of Chinese rule. This is due to the frequency of military operations and the chronic scarcity of funds and to its use by officials and soldiers for purposes of trade; every bale of tea, for instance, increases rapidly in value as it goes west, and officials travelling from China into Tibet are therefore tempted to take with them as much tea as they can transport. According to Chao Erh-feng's regulations, all Chinese using *ula* transport were supposed to pay half a rupee per animal per stage; but even this small charge, which is very cheap when compared to the prices paid by merchants hiring animals, is nowadays seldom paid except in the immediate vicinity of Tachienlu. Missionaries and other foreign travellers in Chinese Tibet usually employ *ula*, for unless they possess their own caravans no other means of locomotion are available. This does not tend to increase their popularity with the natives. In Tibet Proper the Tibetans themselves do not usually pay anything for *ula*, which is regarded as a form of taxation levied by the Government. The people, being used to the system from time immemorial, do not appear to object to it as long as it is not abused[1].

Eastern Tibet is a land of great interest and almost a virgin field[2] for the ethnologist in view of the number of racial types met with in this corner of Central Asia. Any non-Tibetan element in the northern part of Kam will probably be found to be of Mongol or Turkish origin, dating from the invasion of Tibet by hordes of Dzungarian Mongols two centuries ago; while any non-Tibetan element in the southern part of Kam will probably be found to belong to

[1] In Tibet Proper monasteries are always exempt from *ula* service, and this is one of the principal sources of friction between the lamas and the Chinese Authorities in Chinese-controlled Tibet.

[2] What has so far been written on the subject of the ethnography of Eastern Tibet is largely taken from the cursory reports of passing travellers, and is not to be relied on. Thus an excellent and invaluable compendium of facts concerning China, *The China Year Book* (1919 edition), devotes a few pages to the races of the Chinese-Tibetan border, basing its information on a well-known geographical work, and gives, *inter alia*, the following names of Mongoloid Tibetan races: *Sokba*, *Horpa*, *Bodpa*, *Drokpa*, *Chakba*, *Kampa*, *Changpa*, and so on. But these are not really the names of races at all, but are Tibetan words meaning Mongols, Turkis, Tibetans, nomads, robbers, men of Kam, men of the North. Thus a passing traveller is told that such and such a region is inhabited by *Chakba* (robbers), or that some horsemen seen in the distance are *Chakba*, and he promptly writes down the word in his note-book as the name of a Tibetan tribe.

PLATE LXIII

Chinese photo

COSTUMES, SWORDS AND HEAD-DRESSES OF EASTERN TIBET: THE MAN IN THE STRIPED TURBAN IS A NYARONG TIBETAN; THE ONE IN THE CENTRE, A CHINESE TIBETAN HALF-CASTE FROM TACHIENLU; AND THE ONE IN THE FOX SKIN TURBAN WITH PRAYER WHEEL, A NORTHERN CHINESE IN TIBETAN DRESS

PLATE LXIV

Chinese photo

A ROPE BRIDGE IN SOUTH-EASTERN TIBET

the Shan, Lolo, or Moso stocks, which constituted perhaps the original inhabitants of the country. As for the Tibetans themselves, I would hazard the guess that, in the same way that the Japanese are apparently a mixture of the Tartars of North-eastern Asia with the Malays of the Southern Seas, the Tibetans are a mixture of Turkis and Mongols from the north and Burmese from the south.

The peoples of Kam speak various dialects of Tibetan, but standard, or Lhasa Tibetan, is everywhere understood by the better educated classes. The Lhasa *ky* and *gy* usually become *ch* and *j* in Kam, thus *chi* instead of *kyi* for *dog*, and *jyelbo* instead of *gyelbo* for *king*. *N* or *m* are always inserted before *d*, *b*, *g*, etc. e.g., Dra(n)go, Dartse(n)do, Cha(m)do, Jyeku(n)do. *Laso* is used instead of *Lalasi* (the much used respectful term for *Yes, Sir*). In some parts the silent prefixes (which in the Lhasa language appear only in the written word) seem to be pronounced, as in Western Tibet.

* * * * *

The Italian Capucins established a mission at Lhasa in the middle of the eighteenth century, but were expelled before the year 1800. In the middle of the nineteenth century the Lazarist fathers, Huc and Gabet, penetrated to Lhasa from Mongolia, but were escorted out by the Chinese through Szechuan after a short stay in the Tibetan capital. At about the same time the Catholic priest, Père Renou, reached Chamdo from the direction of Szechuan but was there turned back. In 1853 Père Krick, attempting to enter South-east Tibet from Assam, was murdered by Mishmis. In 1854 Père Renou founded the mission station of Bonga just across the Tibetan border from North-western Yunnan. In 1861 Bishop Thomine and Pères Renou and Desgodins again reached Chamdo and were again turned back, in spite of the fact that they were provided with Imperial Chinese passports for the journey into Tibet. In 1865, at the time of the Nyarong troubles, when the whole of Eastern Tibet was much disturbed, the Catholic missions on the border were destroyed. The same thing happened in 1873, and again during the disturbances of 1905–6 and 1911–12. It is probable that from the time of the destruction of the Bonga mission no Catholic priest has entered Lhasa-ruled Tibet, though

Catholic missionaries have been courageously working and patiently waiting on the border ever since. By what extraordinary concatenation of circumstances, say the Fathers of the Roman Church, has Tibet, a wretched country of a few million inhabitants, without army or resources, been able, alone of all the nations of the World, to forbid their country to the priests of the Catholic Church and to the nationals of all the Great Powers? But the credit for this feat is due to the skilful diplomacy of the Chinese rather than to the resourcefulness of the Tibetans. The Chinese, by insisting that they were the masters of the country and that no one could deal with the Tibetans except through them, and at the same time permitting and perhaps encouraging the Tibetans to oppose the entry of foreigners into their lands, were able for two generations to maintain a complete *impasse*.

The missions now working on the borders of Eastern Tibet are the Catholic *Mission du Tibet* with headquarters at Tachienlu and stations at Dawu, Sharatong, Batang, Yenching, and at other places in North-western Yunnan, and an American Protestant Mission at Batang. The China Inland Mission engaged for a time in Tibetan work, and had stations for that purpose at Tachienlu, Dawu and Batang, but have now abandoned it, except for one missionary at Tachienlu, apparently for lack of financial support.

The Catholics appear to be too hostile to the Tibetans to make a success of their work, which, although the mission is ostensibly a Tibetan one, is almost entirely confined to the Chinese. For more than two generations the Catholics on this border have been vainly endeavouring to establish their faith amongst, and secure a hold over, the people of the country. But the history of their efforts to do so is one of unceasing conflicts with the lamas, and, as the natives are completely identified with the latter, with the people themselves. This long struggle between the Catholic and Lama Churches has produced a difficult situation, which has not been rendered any easier by the fact that the Catholics have to some extent chosen to shelter themselves behind the Chinese military and identify their interests with those of the Chinese[1]; so that in too many cases the Tibetans have come

[1] China is bound by Treaty to permit Christian missionaries to propagate their doctrines within her territories and to protect them in doing so.

to associate Catholic activities with the punitive measures of undisciplined Chinese soldiery. The Chinese are by nature a kindly and benevolent people. But, owing to an unfortunate combination of circumstances connected with the prolonged civil wars in China Proper, the administration of Western Szechuan and the Tibetan frontier region has of recent years fallen largely into the hands of Chinese military adventurers of the most inferior type, who have cruelly oppressed the natives of the frontier districts under their control (and this misrule has been denounced by no one more forcibly than by some of the Protestant missionaries themselves). As long, therefore, as the missionaries, and more especially the Catholics, choose to identify themselves with Chinese activities, and to propagate their doctrine through the agency of Chinese rifles, they will find it difficult to secure a sympathetic hearing amongst the Tibetans[1].

The Protestant missionaries are in a much better position. Free from the encumbrance of two generations of hostilities with the lamas, they began with a clean sheet a few years ago, and, by standing as much as possible on their own merits and endeavouring to establish friendly relations with the local Tibetans by their own efforts and good works, independent of Chinese official assistance, have been more successful in obtaining a footing in the country. They have perhaps been as unsuccessful as the Catholics in obtaining converts; but a certain much-travelled medical member of the American mission at Batang can probably penetrate without danger into remote parts of the country where a Catholic priest could scarcely venture[2].

[1] The younger Catholic priests appear to realise this (notably the priest in charge at Yenching at the time we visited that place), and to desire to open up friendly relations with the Tibetans rather than to force themselves on the people with the assistance of Chinese bayonets.

[2] The early Protestant missionaries fell in some cases into the same error as the Catholic, that is to say, they were apt to regard the Chinese military as useful instruments for forwarding the cause of Christianity. The following words occur in a Protestant missionary pamphlet, dated 1908, referring to the progress of the work of evangelisation amongst the Tibetans of the border:

"I travelled to Drango in ten days. We found the road still open, though the huge Lamaseries, like sentinels on guard, are a constant obstacle and menace to Christian effort. But our God is a mighty God, and has already shown what he can do by destroying the chief monasteries on the Batang Road."

The writer of these words evidently regarded the Chinese soldiers as divine instruments for the destruction of the monasteries and the subjugation of the Tibetans in the interests of Christianity. Yet eight years later an

The attitude of the majority of Chinese towards missionary work is passive. Perhaps the most materialistic people in the world, with only one really innate religious feeling, that of ancestor worship, they are often ready enough to accept the outward forms of Christianity if there are sufficient material inducements for doing so. The Tibetans, on the other hand, are amongst the most religious people in the world, and their attitude towards an alien religion like Christianity is not passive but actively hostile. The Christian missionary in Tibet to-day is in much the same position as a Buddhist missionary would have been in Italy a century ago; and up to the present the evangelising efforts of both Catholic and Protestant missionaries on the frontiers of Eastern Tibet have failed to make much impression on the Tibetans, the few Christian converts being almost entirely limited to the Chinese living in the country. The power of Tibetan Buddhism thus continues to present an apparently insurmountable obstacle to the spread of any form of Christianity amongst the Tibetans beyond the immediate neighbourhood of a Chinese military centre.

But is it altogether necessary that the Buddhism of the Tibetans should be supplanted by a new religion? The interpretation of Tibetan Buddhism is apt to vary in accordance with the idea of its interpreter. Some missionaries represent it as being the work of the Devil himself; to others its doctrines seem to approach closely to those of Christianity. It is perhaps possible that those adopting the former view are not always very well versed in the subject before attempting to pass judgment upon it. A veteran Protestant mis-

American missionary, a gentleman of long experience of life on the frontier, wrote, in the foreign press of Shanghai, of Chinese rule on the frontier in the following terms:

"There is no method of torture known that is not practised in here on these Tibetans, slicing, skinning, boiling, tearing asunder, and all.... To sum up what China is doing here in Eastern Tibet, the main things are collecting taxes, robbing, oppressing, confiscating, and allowing her representatives to burn and loot and steal."

These are hard words. But lest they should be offensive to Chinese in China Proper, it must be emphasised that the state of affairs they represent is in no way due to any action of the Chinese Government in Peking or the Provincial Authorities in Szechuan, but is merely the result of the internal strife of recent years in China, which has prevented the Chinese Authorities from paying due attention to frontier affairs, and which has discouraged respectable Chinese officials from service in Chinese Tibet. The state of affairs on the frontier, under Chao Erh-feng's rule in the days of the Manchus, was very different.

sionary[1], who, after twenty-odd years of study and original research, may perhaps be considered the greatest living authority on Tibetan Buddhism, has described it as a blind man groping after an open door, the existence of which he senses but cannot find. In spite of its superstitions and other bad excrescences, Tibetan Buddhism is, nevertheless, seeking after the truth; and it should perhaps be the object of the missionary, not to seek to destroy it but rather to attempt to lead it along the right path towards the truth. In other words, the missionary in Tibet should study Tibetan Buddhism, and then endeavour to influence it with Christian principles. It may well be said that this is an impossibility; but direct evangelisation in Tibet and the supplanting of Tibetan Buddhism by the European form of Christianity appear to the writer to present even more insurmountable obstacles.

At a recent West China Missionary Conference a gentleman arose and told his audience that the missionaries were wasting too much of their time over medical and educational activities, and exhorted them not to neglect their real duties, the more important work of evangelisation. But what is needed in Tibet to-day is not evangelisation, but education and an intellectual awakening. Had the lamas of Tibet elected to adopt Christianity instead of Buddhism in the seventh century they would probably by now have overlaid it with the same mass of superstition, taken from the old nature worship of the country, with which they have overlaid the original Buddhism. To evangelise the people in their present state is merely to add to the load of superstition with which their lives are already burdened. The Protestant missionaries at Batang appear to realise this, and educational and medical work stands in the forefront of their programme. To those who object to the temporal powers of the Buddhist Church in Tibet, the writer would suggest that it is not Catholic priests, nor Protestant evangelists, nor Chinese bayonets, but only the diffusion of knowledge, which will ultimately weaken the authority of the lamas of Tibet. Europe awoke as the result of the Reformation and the spread of education amongst the people. Let the missionaries therefore awaken the Tibetans by means of education, while leaving them their Buddhist religion purged of its growth of superstition.

[1] Mr T. Sorensen of Tachienlu.

ITINERARY AND TABLES OF DISTANCES, HEIGHTS, AND TEMPERATURES

Date	Place	Distance of day's march in miles	Temperature at 6 a.m.	Elevation	Weather
Mar.					
1	Dartsendo, or Tachienlu (Chinese border town)	—	30	8,500	Fine, sun.
2–6	Tachienlu	—	*		†
7	Tachienlu, to	8	39	8,500	Fine, sun.
8	Santaochiao (hamlet) to	15	38	9,000	,, ,,
9	Chungku (hamlet), to	12	31	10,400	,, ,,
10	Hsintientzu (camp and huts), *via*	12	25	11,400	,, ,,
	Zhara La (Haitzu Shan), to	—	—	14,000	
11	Camp, to	18	26	12,500	,, ,,
12	Taining (village), and near by	—	—	11,700	,, ,,
	Gata Gomba (Gelugba: 300 monks)				
13	Taining, to	18	15	11,700	,, ,,
14	Nadreheka Dzong (Kuanchai: old Tibetan fort), *via*	15	26	12,400	Snow
	Nadreheka La (Sunglinkou), and	—	—	13,500	
	Mejesumdo (ruined rest-house), to				
15	Chyapa (group of farms), to	12	25	11,200	Fine, sun.
16	Dawu (Taofu: village and official centre), and near by	—	—	10,200	,, ,,
	Nyitso Gomba (Gelugba: 400 monks)				
17	Dawu	—	—	10,200	,, ,,
18	Dawu, to	14	30	10,200	Fine
19	Tromne (Tachai: farms), to	14	37	10,500	Snow
20	Gara (Jentakou: hamlet), to	11	26	10,700	Fine, sun.
21	Sharatong (Chiachilung: Catholic settlement), to	11	33	10,700	,, ,,
22	Hor Drango (Changku or Luho: village and official's house), and near by	—	—	11,400	,, ,,
	Drango Gomba (Gelugba: 1000 monks), and				
	Chokarteng (nunnery)				
23	Hor Drango, to	18	30	11,400	Fine, sun.
24	Dangka (group of farms), *via*	14	25	—	,, ,,
	Chalang (hamlet), and				
	Shochiling (hamlet), to				

Place-names for the most part in Tibetan: where both Tibetan and Chinese names are given the latter are in brackets.

Heights are in feet and approximate only.

As regards temperatures, the thermometer used did not register below 5, so that a reading of 5 means 5 or below.

La = pass. *Gomba* = monastery. The words *Gelugba*, *Nyimaba*, etc. refer to the sect of the monastery named.

* Temp. 6 a.m. 33° to 38°. † Fine and sunny; snow on March 3.

Date	Place	Distance of day's march in miles	Temperature at 6 a.m.	Elevation	Weather
Mar.					
25	Driwo (Chuwo: village and castle of chief), *via*	18	31	11,600	Fine, sun.
	Joro Gomba (Gelugba: 300 monks), and				
	Latse Ka (pass), to	—	—	13,100	
26	Puyulung (hamlet), and near by	8	33	11,400	Fine, sun.
	Tsetso Gomba (Gelugba: 100 monks), to				
27	Kanze (village, monastery, and castles of chiefs)	—	—	11,200	Slight snow
	Kanze Gomba (Gelugba: in reality a combination of two monasteries: 1500 monks), and near by				
	Draga Gomba (Gelugba: 100 monks), and				
	Natso Gomba (Gelugba: 100 monks), and				
	Kangma Gomba (Gelugba: 100 monks)				
28	Kanze	—	—	11,200	Fine, sun.
29	Kanze, *via*	12	27	11,200	" "
	Nyara Gomba (Sajya: 100 monks), and				
	Beri Gomba (Gelugba: 100 monks), and				
	Beri (Paili: village and castle of chief), to				
30	Dumbugo (hamlet), to	10	35	11,200	Snow
31	Shetanda (hamlet and nunnery opposite), to	18	32	11,400	Fine, sun.
April					
1	Deji Podrang (Headman's castle), and	13	29	11,600	" "
	Sangdru Gomba (Gelugba: 100 monks), *via*				
	Jarjo Gomba (Gelugba: 30 monks), and				
	Gesa Gomba (Gelugba: 30 monks), to				
2	Trotsang Podrang (headman's castle), *via*	16½	30	11,800	Fine, sun.
	Dema Podrang (headman's castle), and				
	Denchin Gomba (Bonba: 200 monks), to				
3	Böme Gomba (Bonba: 50 monks), *via*	9	39	12,000	Slight snow
	Bönda (hamlet and coracle ferry), and				
	Nya-ge Gomba (Gelugba: 30 monks), to				
4	Camp, to	12	22	12,000	Fine, sun.
5	Rungu Gomba (Nyimaba: 30 monks), to	16½	27	12,300	Fine, cloudy
6	Nando (hamlet), *via*	17½	25	12,400	Fine, sun.
	She-che Gomba (Nyimaba: 300 monks), to				
7	Dzogchen Gomba (Nyimaba: 1000 monks)	—	—	13,200	Snow
8	Dzogchen Gomba, *via*	26	34	13,200	"
	Latse Kare La, to	—	—	14,100	
9	Camp, *via*	10½	25	13,300	Fine, cloudy
	Jyachi Gomba (Nyimaba: 40 monks), and				
	Dzungo Gomba (Nyimaba: 40 monks), to				
10	Göze Gomba (Sajya: 200 monks), also known as	12	30	12,300	" "
	Lintsung (residence of chief), to				
11	Nojeling Gomba (Garjyuba: 100 monks), to	16½	32	12,800	" "
12	Dengko (cultivated plain along the Yangtze), and	—	—	11,200	" "
	Drölma Hlakang (temple), and				
	Adu Podrang (castle of small Chief), and				
	Chunkor Gomba (Gelugba: 300 monks: on opposite bank of river)				
13	Dengko, to	15	34	11,200	Snow
14	Ngocha (Wohsia: camp and ruined rest-house), *via*	16½	21	13,500	"
	Dzi La, to	—	—	15,800	

Date	Place	Distance of day's march in miles	Temperature at 6 a.m.	Elevation	Weather
April					
15	Camp to	19	10	14,900	Snow
16	Jü Gomba (Gelugba: 40 monks: Chinese Shihch'ü Hsien)	—	—	13,700	Fine, sun.
17	Jü Gomba (Shihch'ü Hsien), to	16½	5	13,700	" "
18	Seshü Gomba (Gelugba: 500 monks), to	18	18	13,300	" "
19	Camp, *via*	19½	5	14,000	" "
	Ngamba La, to	—	—	14,600	
20	Dorgön Gomba (Sajya: 100 monks), and near by	19½	38	12,800	Slight snow
	Shewu (Hsiehwu: hamlet), and				
	Nyidzong Gomba (small), *via*				
	Ba-ge Gomba (Garjyuba: 20 monks), and				
	Dreböndo (Jenta: hamlet and ferry across Yangtze), to				
21	Gala (hamlet), and	12	28	11,800	Fine, sun.
	Gala Gomba, and				
	Bambi Gomba (small monasteries near Gala), *via*				
	Ra La, and	—	—	14,400	
	Manitung (hamlet), to				
22	Jyekundo (Chiehku: village and trading centre), and near by	—	—	11,900	Fine, sun.
	Jyeku Gomba (Sajya: 500 monks)				
23	Jyekundo	—	—	11,900	" "
24	"	—	—	11,900	" "
25	"	—	—	11,900	" "
26	" *via*	16½	28	11,900	Slight snow
	Ashu La, to	—	—	14,400	
27	Camp, *via*	18	32	12,800	Snow
	Shung La, to	—	—	15,800	
28	Yujyesumdo (camp), *via*	18	19	13,500	Fine, sun.
	Rashi (also known as Lungshi) Gomba (Gelugba: 700 monks), to				
29	Luguraka (camp and ford across Dze Chu), to	9	20	12,400	" "
30	Camp, *via*	10½	24	12,800	" "
	Sharu-lagen La, to	—	—	13,700	
May					
1	Camp, to	9	24	12,600	" "
2	Gö-che Gomba (Garjyuba: 100 monks), *via*	16½	36	12,600	Snow
	Ka La, to	—	—	14,000	
3	Kanda (hamlet), *via*	16½	27	12,000	Fine, sun.
	Bangda (hamlet), and				
	Gurde Druka (coracle ferry across Dza Chu), and	—	—	11,800	
	Shungda (hamlet), to				
4	Barmendo (hamlet), and	—	—	12,100	Fine, sun.
	Barme Gomba (Garjyuba: 70 monks)				
5	Barmendo, *via*	15	35	12,100	" "
	Manam La, to	—	—	15,500	
6	Nangchen (Lungchin: hamlet and chief's castle), and	—	—	13,500	Hail storms
	Tsepchu Gomba (Garjyuba: 100 monks: at Nangchen)				
7	Nangchen	—	—	13,500	Fine, sun.
8	Nangchen, *via*	12	24	13,500	" "
	Shigar La, to	—	—	14,300	

Date	Place	Distance of day's march in miles	Temperature at 6 a.m.	Elevation	Weather
May					
9	Camp, to	8	24	12,800	Fine, sun.
10	Camp near Dje Chu ferry, opposite Ne-de Gomba (Nyimaba: 30 monks), *via*	9	25	11,900	" "
	Dungderawa (hamlet), and				
	Dubarawa (hamlet), and				
	Warerawa (hamlet), and				
	Chebarawa (hamlet), to				
11	Guzhi Gomba (also known as Tupde Dorjeling: Gandemba: 150 monks), opposite Chagzamka (hamlet and iron suspension bridge across Dje Chu), *via*	13½	36	11,800	Fine, sun.
	Shambarawa (hamlet), and				
	Dotserawa (hamlet), and				
	Borzo La, to	—	—	14,200	
12	Ngadoraka (camp), *via*	22	36	13,400	Fine, sun.
	Dongma La, and	—	—	15,100	
	Jyola La, to	—	—	14,800	
13	Bangrushi (hamlet), *via*	12	40	11,800	Rain
	Drudu (hamlet), and				
	Zinda (hamlet), and				
	Nendo Gomba (Garjyuba: 40 monks), to				
14	Rangi (hamlet), *via*	13½	37	11,500	Rain
	Monda Gomba (Gandemba: 40 monks), and				
	Benortsoma (hamlet), and				
	Zobarawa (hamlet), and				
	Kalorawa (hamlet), to				
15	Sagang Gomba (Gelugba: 40 monks: bridge across Ngom Chu), *via*	12	40	11,200	Fine, cloudy
	Donuka (hamlet), and				
	Windawa (hamlet), to				
16	Jyoto (hamlet), to	3	37	11,200	Fine, sun.
17	Yongda Gomba (Garjyuba: 70 monks)	—	—	11,200	Rain
18	Yongda Gomba, *via*	13½	42	11,200	"
	Lamda (hamlet and junction with main Lhasa road), to	—	—	11,000	
19	Nguro Zamka (Olo Ch'iao: hamlet and bridge across Ngom Chu), to	9	48	10,700	"
20	Chamdo (village), and	—	—	10,600	"
	Chamdo Gomba (Gelden Jyamba Ling: Gelugba: now in ruins: formerly 1000 monks)				
21	Chamdo	—	—	10,600	Fine, sun.
22	Chamdo, *via*	12	50	10,600	" "
	Sodri La, to	—	—	14,200	
23	Mengpu (hamlet), to	12	40	13,000	" "
24	Bomde (Paotun: hamlet), *via*	18	38	12,800	" "
	Ipi La, to	—	—	15,300	
25	Bagung (hamlet and rest-house), *via*	13½	31	12,300	" "
	Jyane Gomba (Gelugba: 30 monks), to				
26	Wangka (hamlet and rest-house), *via*	15	36	12,100	" "
	Dzo La, and	—	—	14,500	
	Dzondo (hamlet), and				
	Rindzi Gomba (Gelugba: small), and				
	Gamka (hamlet), and				
	Hlahlang Gomba (Gelugba: small), to				
27	Gam (Angti: hamlet), *via*	18	42	13,200	Fine, sun.
	Gam La (Angti Shan), to	—	—	16,000	

Date	Place	Distance of day's march in miles	Temperature at 6 a.m.	Elevation	Weather
May 28	Draya Jyamdun (Chaya: village, official's seat and ruined Gelugba monastery: formerly 1000 monks)	—	—	12,000	Fine, sun.
29	Draya Jyamdun, to	15	42	12,000	Rain
30	Radzi (Lochiatsung: hamlet and rest-house), *via*	18	38	12,700	Fine, sun.
	Puchung La, to	—	—	13,700	
31	Atsur (hamlet and rest-house), *via*	13½	41	12,900	Light rain
	Shepu La, to	—	—	15,500	
June 1	Asenyewango (Shihpankou: hamlet and rest-house), *via* pass, and	21	40	12,700	Fine, sun.
	Aratang (hamlet and small gomba), and pass, to				
2	Rusho (Lishu: hamlet), *via*	18	45	12,400	Rain
	Gangso La, to	—	—	15,200	
3	Camp near rest-house, to	9	42	13,000	Fine, cloudy
4	Markam Gartok (Chiangka or Ningching: village, seat of official, and small gomba)	—	—	12,500	Fine, sun.
5	Markam Gartok, *via*	18	46	12,500	Rain
	Jyarong La, to	—	—	14,700	
6	Gusho (Kushu: hamlet and small gomba), *via*	18	42	12,700	,,
	Lamar La, and	—	—	13,500	
	Hlandun (Nantun: hamlet and small gomba), and	—	—	12,400	
	Bum La (Ningching Shan: old boundary between China and Tibet), to	—	—	13,500	
7	Bum (Pamut'ang: group of farms), *via*	18	48	12,300	Fine, sun.
	Kungtzeding (hamlet), to	—	—	12,000	
8	Gora (Kungla: hamlet), *via*	18	55	8,500	,, ,,
	Drubanang Druka (Chupalung: hamlet and ferry across Yangtze), to				
9	Lewa (Shuimokou: hamlet), *via*	9	55	8,500	,, ,,
	Nyugu (hamlet), to				
10	Ba (Batang: village, castles of former Chiefs, foreign missions, small Gelugba gomba, and ruins of former big monastery)	—	—	9,000	,, ,,
11–29	Batang		*		†
30	Batang, *via*	12	60	9,000	Light rain
	Nyugu (hamlet and ferry across Yangtze), to	—	—	8,500	
July 1	Shisongong (hamlet and small Gelugba gomba), *via*	13	48	12,000	Fine, sun.
	To La, to	—	—	15,200	
2	Rishisumdo (camp), *via*	13	45	12,100	Light rain
	Dru La, to	—	—	15,100	
3	Ukagang (hamlet), *via*	19	47	11,400	Rain
	Jyase Gomba (Nyimaba: 50 monks), and De-ne (hamlet), to				
4	Tara (hamlet and small Nyimaba gomba), *via*	27	47	12,500	Light rain
	Podo Latse Ka (pass), to	—	—	14,000	
5	Camp on Hlato plateau, *via*	12	46	13,700	Rain
	Kado La, to	—	—	14,700	

* Temp. 6 a.m. 50° to 60°; 2 p.m. 70° to 80°.
† Thunderstorms and rain, with fine hot days intervening.

Date	Place	Distance of day's march in miles	Temperature at 6 a.m.	Eleva-tion	Weather
July 6	Dotse (hamlet), opposite	26	47	13,000	Light rain
	Chungsar Gomba (small), *via*				
	Drundre La, and	—	—	13,800	
	Radzi (hamlet and junction with main road), to	—	—	12,700	
7	Draya Jyamdun (village, official's seat, and ruined Gelugba gomba)	—	—	12,000	Light rain
8	Draya Jyamdun	—	—	12,000	Fine, cloudy
9	Draya Jyamdun, *via*	18	50	12,000	,, ,,
	Gam La (Angti Shan), to	—	—	16,000	
10	Gam (Angti: hamlet), *via*	15	50	13,200	Light rain
	Hlahlang Gomba (Gelugba: small), and				
	Gamka (hamlet), and				
	Rindzi Gomba (Gelugba: small), and				
	Dzondo (hamlet), and				
	Dzo La, to	—	—	14,500	
11	Wangka, *via*	13½	50	12,100	Rain
	Jyane Gomba (Gelugba: 30 monks), to				
12	Bagung (hamlet and rest-house), *via*	18	39	12,300	Rain, snow
	Ipi La, to	—	—	15,300	
13	Bomde (Paotun: hamlet), to	12	36	12,800	Light rain
14	Mengpu, *via*	12	37	13,000	Fine, sun.
15	Chamdo (village), and	—	—	10,600	,, ,,
	Chamdo Gomba (Gelden Jyamba Ling: Gelugba: now in ruins: formerly 1000 monks)				
16–31	Chamdo	—	*	10,600	†
Aug. 1–31	Chamdo	—	*	10,600	†
Sept. 1	Chamdo	—	—	10,600	Fine, sun.
2	Chamdo, *via*	15	50	10,600	Light rain
	Tamar La, to	—	—	14,900	
3	Reya (group of farms), *via*	18	46	12,200	,,
	Ja-pe La, to	—	—	15,800	
4	Toba (camp and ruined rest-house), *via*	23	44	13,000	,,
	Lazhi La, to	—	—	14,600	
5	Chorzhung (camp and ruined rest-house), *via*	12½	44	13,400	,,
	Gara La, to	—	—	14,600	
6	Dorka (camp), *via*	12½	41	13,200	Fine, cloudy
	Ge-le La, and	—	—	14,300	
	Tretso Gomba (Sajya: 30 monks), to				
7	Kargung Podrang (Kakung: farms and headman's house), *via*	25	46	12,400	Light rain
	Rando (hamlet), and				
	Jyangda (hamlet), to				
8	Rangsum (T'ungp'u: farms and house of official), *via*	15	52	11,300	,,
	Wara Gomba (Sajya: 50 monks), and				
	Gi (group of farms), and				
	Nge La, to	—	—	14,600	

* Temp. 6 a.m. 45° to 55°; 2 p.m. 60° to 70°.

† In seven weeks there were 23 days without rain, mostly fine and sunny; 15 days with light rain and 10 with heavier rain.

Date	Place	Distance of day's march in miles	Temperature at 6 a.m.	Elevation	Weather
Sept.					
9	Ngenang (Aipa: group of farms), *via*	15	50	11,800	Light rain
	Gangto Druka (hamlet and ferry across Yangtze), and	—	—	10,100	
	Changra Gomba (Sajya: 50 monks), to				
10	Changra Podrang (castle of De-ge Chief), to	8	50	10,500	,,
11	De-ge Gönchen (Teko, Tehua, or Keng-ching: castles of De-ge Chief), and	—	—	10,800	,,
•	De-ge Gomba (or Hlundrubten: Sajya: 500 monks)				
12	De-ge Gönchen, *via*	15	45	10,800	Fine, sun.
	Changra Podrang (see above), and				
	Changra Gomba (see above), to				
13	Shigagarba (group of farms), *via*	10	45	11,600	Rain
	Götse La, to	—	—	14,700	
14	Bagung Gomba (Garjyuba: 200 monks), and near by	15	42	12,200	Fine, sun.
	Dordra Gomba (Nyimaba: 40 monks), *via*				
	Ha La, and	—	—	14,300	
	Dzongsar Gomba (Sajya: 250 monks) to				
15	Mesho (cultivated valley), and	12½	48	11,500	Rain
	Somo Podrang (headman's house), *via*				
	Roda La, and	—	—	13,400	
	Changlung Gomba (Bonba: small), to				
16	Dehlung (cultivated valley), and	15	44	11,800	Light rain
	Dzembum Podrang (headman's house), *via*				
	Kangmar Gomba (Nyimaba: 50 monks), and				
	Baya La, to	—	—	12,900	
17	Dzenko (cultivated valley), *via*	21	44	11,800	Light rain
	Dagmo Gomba (Nyimaba: 100 monks), and				
	Bamdzor Gomba (Sajya: 100 monks), and				
	Darando (group of farms), and				
	Tsengu La, to	—	—	15,800	
18	Camp, to	20	31	14,000	Snow, rain
19	Rongbatsa (village), and near by	—	—	11,600	Rain
	Gesa Gomba (Gelugba: small), and				
	Ripu Gomba (Gelugba: small), and				
	Lona Gomba (Gelugba: small)				
20–30	Rongbatsa	—	*	11,600	†
Oct.					
1–26	Rongbatsa	—	*	11,600	†
27	Rongbatsa, to	20	32	11,600	Fine, sun.
28	Camp, *via*	25	22	14,000	Snow
	Hön La, to	—	—	15,800	
29	Dzenko (cultivated valley), *via*	23	23	11,800	Fine, sun.
	Ranto Gomba (Sajya: small), and				
	Göpa La, and	—	—	14,300	
	Zangsho Gomba (small), and				
	Pass, and	—	—	14,600	
	Racha Hlaba (farms), to				
30	Racha Nachi (group of farms), *via*	11½	28	10,800	Fine, sun.
	Racha Gomba (on opposite cliff), to				
31	Horbo (farms and headman's house), to	6½	29	10,400	,, ,,

* Temp. at 8 a.m. 33° to 47°.

† Rain in the last week of September, some snow about the middle of October, otherwise generally fine.

Date	Place	Distance of day's march in miles	Temperature at 6 a.m.	Elevation	Weather
Nov.					
1	Gato Gomba (Nyimaba: 400 monks), *via*	18	24	13,200	Fine, sun.
	Jyacho La, and	—	—	15,000	
	Mizo La, to	—	—	16,300	
2	Beyü Gomba (Paiyü: Nyimaba: 400 monks)	—	—	10,700	„ „
3	Beyü Gomba	—	—	10,700	„ „
4	Beyü Gomba, *via*	14	30	10,700	„ „
	Lungdri La, to	—	—	15,800	
5	Karnagong (group of farms), *via*	11	28	12,000	„ „
	Rushi Drango Druka (coracle ferry across Yangtze), to	—	—	9,900	
6	Polo Gomba (Sajya: 70 monks), to	5	24	10,000	„ „
7	Shutzashi (group of farms), *via*	14	22	10,400	„ „
	Bomda (group of farms), and				
	Nyingwu La, to	—	—	14,600	
8	Nyashi (farms and headman's house), *via*	15	28	12,400	„ „
	Nadzong La, to	—	—	16,000	
9	Norba (farms), to	10	26	12,400	„ „
10	Ana (farms and headman's house), *via*	23	31	13,000	„ „
	Jinbo Gomba (Nyimaba: 40 monks), and				
	Ramo (hamlet), and				
	Lingchung (hamlet), to				
11	Gonjo Dzong (Kungchueh: seat of official), and	—	—	12,400	Snow
	Drondren Gomba (Gelugba: 30 monks)				
12	Gonjo Dzong, *via*	15	15	12,400	Fine, sun.
	Antsong La, and	—	—	14,600	
	Lamgen La, to	—	—	15,500	
13	Ranjur (group of farms), to	16	14	13,000	„ „
14	Draya Jyamdun (Chaya: village official's seat, and ruined Gelugba monastery, formerly 1000 monks), *via*	15	23	12,000	„ „
	Ge La, and	—	—	14,900	
	Buka Gomba (Gelugba: 10 monks), and				
	Tsotang (hamlet), to				
15	Rangdru (hamlet), *via*	17½	26	11,300	Fine, sun.
	Jyalo (farms), to				
16	Yemdo (ruins of former big Gelugba monastery), *via*	19	26	10,400	„ „
	Dowa (hamlet), and				
	Roporawa (hamlet), to				
17	Jyaragong (group of farms), *via*	16½	18	13,200	„ „
	Ipi La, to	—	—	15,300	
18	Bomde (Paotun: hamlet), *via*	24	19	12,800	„ „
	Mengpu (hamlet), and	—	—	13,000	
	Sodri La, to	—	—	14,200	
19	Chamdo (village), and	—	—	10,600	„ „
	Chamdo Gomba (Gelden Jyamba Ling: now in ruins: formerly 1000 monks or more)				
20–27	Chamdo	—	—	10,600	„ „
28	Chamdo, to	13	20	10,600	„ „
29	Dzo (hamlet), *via*	15	19	10,500	„ „
	Jaka (hamlet), and				
	Bogeka (hamlet), to				
30	Wayo (hamlet), *via*	15	26	10,300	„ „
	Payi (hamlet), and				
	Enang (hamlet), and				
	Bo (hamlet), to				

Date	Place	Distance of day's march in miles	Temperature at 6 a.m.	Elevation	Weather
Dec.					
1	Jyedam (farms and headman's house), to	6½	28	10,800	Fine, sun.
2	Yushi (group of farms), *via*	27	28	12,400	,, ,,
	Pass, and	—	—	14,800	
	Lana (camp), to	—	—	14,300	
3	Chudra (camp), to	19½	9	14,100	,, ,,
4	Bomda Gomba (Gelugba: 70 monks), to	29	5	13,400	,, ,,
5	Tento Gomba (Gelugba: 70 monks), to	12½	7	13,100	,, ,,
6	Tsawa Dzogang (Gelugba monastery of 200 monks: hamlet: residence of official)	—	—	13,000	,, ,,
7	Tsawa Dzogang, *via* Leda (hamlet), to	20	12	13,000	,, ,,
8	Uya (hamlet), *via* Nimaling Gomba (Gelugba: 20 monks), to	12½	7	12,400	,, ,,
9	Moku (hamlet), *via* Doda Gomba (Bonba: 20 monks), to	12	30	12,300	,, ,,
10	Porung (hamlet), to	15	26	12,200	,, ,,
11	Trinder (hamlet), to	10	13	11,700	,, ,,
12	Drayü Gomba (Gelugba: 60 monks), to	12	15	11,300	,, ,,
13	Changmar Gomba (Gelugba: 50 monks: on spur above river), to	12	17	11,500	,, ,,
14	Ba-ge (group of farms), *via*	10	17	11,000	,, ,,
	Do La, to	—	—	14,000	
15	Do (group of farms), to	10	25	11,100	,, ,,
16	Di (group of farms), *via*	15	30	10,500	,, ,,
	Di La, to	—	—	15,000	
17	Trongtse (group of farms), *via*	8	39	9,600	Fine, cloudy
	Lagön (ruined monastery), and	—	—	11,300	
	Jadatira (hamlet and ferry across Mekong), to	—	—	7,900	
18	Tsakalo (Yenching: village and seat of official: salt wells in river valley below)	—	—	9,200	Fine, cloudy
19	Tsakalo, *via* Yakalo (hamlet and Catholic Mission), and Dashoding (hamlet), and Chutsaka (hamlet), to	10	36	9,200	Fine, sun.
20	Lajoshi (hamlet), *via* Tededing (hamlet), and Lupugong (farms), and Tsandogong (farms), and	20	32	7,900	,, ,,
	Hlung La, to	—	—	14,000	
21	Getoding, *via*	15	7	12,100	Fine, sun.
	Pass, and	—	—	13,100	
	Nga-nga (farms), to				
22	Hlandun (Nantun: hamlet and small monastery), *via*	18	12	12,400	,, ,,
	Bum La (Ningching Shan: old boundary between China and Tibet), and	—	—	13,500	
	Bum (Pamut'ang: farms), to	—	—	12,300	
23	Kungtzeding (hamlet), *via* Gora (Kungla: hamlet), to	18	10	12,000	Fine, sun.
24	Drubanang Druka (Chupalung: hamlet and ferry across Yangtze), *via* Lewa (Shuimo-kou: hamlet), and Nyugu (hamlet and ferry), to	18	35	8,500	,, ,,
25	Ba (Batang: village, castles of former chiefs, foreign missions, small Gelugba monastery, and ruins of former big monastery)	—	—	9,000	,, ,,
26–31	Batang	—	—	9,000	,, ,,

Date	Place	Distance of day's march in miles	Temperature at 6 a.m.	Elevation	Weather
Jan.					
1–11	Batang	—	—	9,000	Fine, sun.
12	Batang, to	15	32	9,000	" "
13	Pangchamu (rest-house)	—	16	12,900	" "
14	Pangchamu (rest-house), to	15	14	12,900	" "
15	Batang	—	—	9,000	" "
16	Batang	—	—	9,000	" "
17	Batang, to	10	30	9,000	" "
18	Dam (Tangts'un: hamlet), to	14	28	9,300	" "
19	Sudong (hamlet), *via*	8	21	10,000	" "
	Hlamdo (hamlet), to				
20	Baongshi (Maohsi: farms), *via*	22½	21	10,400	Snow
	Ngupa La, to	—	—	14,000	
21	Sama (group of farms), *via*	19	18	11,400	Fine, sun.
	Dachi (camp and ruined rest-house), to				
22	De-ne (group of farms)	—	—	10,200	" "
23	De-ne, *via*	27	26	10,200	Fine, cloudy
	Gaji Podrang (Kaiyü: official's castle), and				
	Ongtung (camping ground), and				
	Me La, to	—	—	14,400	
24	Sheda (group of farms), to	6	20	12,200	Fine, cloudy
25	Ronged (Jungkai: farms), to	10	25	10,700	Fine, sun.
26	Beyü Gomba (Paiyü: Nyimaba: 400 monks), *via*	18	29	10,700	Fine, cloudy
	Mizo La, and	—	—	16,300	
	Jyacho La, to	—	—	15,000	
27	Gato Gomba (Nyimaba: 400 monks), to	6½	18	13,200	Fine, cloudy
28	Horbo (farms and headman's house), *via*	18½	25	10,400	Fine, sun.
	Racha Nachi (group of farms and monastery on opposite cliff), to				
29	Racha Hlaba (group of farms), *via*	16	27	12,000	" "
	Pass, and	—	—	14,600	
	Zangsho Gomba (small), and				
	Göpa La, and	—	—	14,300	
	Ranto Gomba (Sajya: small), to				
30	Dzenko (cultivated valley), *via*	7½	25	11,800	Fine, sun.
	Dagmo Gomba (Nyimaba: 100 monks), and				
	Bamdzor Gomba (Sajya: 100 monks), to				
31	Darando (group of farms), *via*	13½	28	11,500	" "
	Tsengu La, to	—	—	15,800	
Feb.					
1	Camp, to	20	15	14,000	Snow
2	Rongbatsa (village: several small gomba near by), *via*	20	16	11,600	"
	Darjye Gomba (Gelugba: 500 monks), and				
	Lintso (Lintsung: hamlet), and				
	Beri (Paili: village, castle of chief, and ferry across Yalung), and				
	Beri Gomba (Gelugba: 100 monks), and				
	Nyara Gomba (Sajya: 100 monks), to				
3	Kanze (village and castles of Chiefs)	—	—	11,200	Fine, sun.
	Kanze Gomba (Gelugba: 1500 monks)				
	Draga Gomba, Natso Gomba, and Kangma Gomba (Gelugba monasteries in Kanze plain: 100 monks each)				
4	Kanze, to	8	12	11,200	Fine, sun.
5	Puyulung (hamlet), and	18	7	11,400	" "
	Tsetso Gomba (Gelugba: 100 monks), *via*				

Date	Place	Distance of day's march in miles	Temperature at 6 a.m.	Elevation	Weather
Feb.					
	Latse Ka (pass), and	—	—	13,100	
	Joro Gomba (Gelugba: 300 monks), to				
6	Driwo (Chuwo: village and castle of Chief), *via*	19	7	11,600	Fine, sun.
	Shochiling (hamlet), and				
	Chalang (hamlet), and				
	Dangka (farms), to				
7	Gelo (farms), to	13	27	11,200	Snow
8	Hor Drango (Changku or Luho: village and official's house), and near by	22	12	11,400	Fine, cloudy
	Drango Gomba (Gelugba: 1000 monks), and				
	Chokarteng (nunnery), *via*				
	Sharatong (Chiachilung: Catholic settlement), to				
9	Gara (hamlet), to	14	24	10,700	Fine, cloudy
10	Tromne (Tachai: farms), to	14	8	10,500	Fine, sun.
11	Dawu (Taofu: village and residence of official), and near by	—	—	10,200	„ „
	Nyitso Gomba (Gelugba: 400 monks)				
12	Dawu, *via*	27	15	10,200	Snow
	Chyapa (farms), and				
	Mejesumdo (ruined rest-house), and				
	Nadreheka La (Sunglinkou), to	—	—	13,500	
13	Nadreheka Dzong (Kuanchai: old fort), *via*	25	5	12,400	Fine, sun.
	Taining (village), and	—	—	11,700	
	Gata Gomba (Gelugba: 300 monks), to				
14	Bar-me (hamlet), *via*	28	5	11,200	„ „
	Drungku (Chungku: ruined village), to				
15	Trambadrung (Changpachun: farms), *via*	27	5	12,000	„ „
	Gi La (Cheto Shan), to	—	—	14,000	
16	Cheto (hamlet), to	9	12	10,500	„ „
17	Dartsendo (Tachienlu: Chinese border town)	—	—	8,500	„ „
18–28	Tachienlu	—	*	8,500	†

* Temp. 6 a.m. 25° to 34°.
† Snow on February 21, 22, 23 and slightly on February 28, otherwise fine.

DISTANCES

	Miles
Tachienlu, *via* Haitzu Shan, Taining, and Dawu, to Kanze ...	218
Kanze, *via* Dzogchen and Seshü, to Jyekundo	325
Jyekundo, *via* Nangchen, to Chamdo	256
Chamdo, *via* Draya and Markam Gartok, to Batang	264
Batang, *via* the Ong Chu valley and Draya, to Chamdo	210
Chamdo, *via* De-ge Gönchen and Mesho, to Rongbatsa	252
Rongbatsa, *via* Beyü, Gonjo, Draya, and Yemdo, to Chamdo ...	319
Chamdo, *via* Tsawarong and Yenching, to Batang	373
Batang, *via* Gaji and Beyü, to Kanze	236
Kanze, *via* Dawu, Taining, and Cheto Shan, to Tachienlu ...	224
Total	2677

INDEX